The Scarecrow Author Bibliographies

NATHANIEL HAWTHORNE
AND THE CRITICS

A Checklist of Criticism
1900-1978

by JEANETTA BOSWELL

The Scarecrow Author Bibliographies, No. 57

THE SCARECROW PRESS, INC.
Metuchen, N.J., & London   1982

Library of Congress Cataloging in Publication Data

Boswell, Jeanetta, 1922-
    Nathaniel Hawthorne and the critics.

    (The Scarecrow author bibliographies ; no. 57)
    Includes index.
    1. Hawthorne, Nathaniel, 1804-1864--Criticism and
interpretation--Bibliography. I. Title. II. Series.
Z8393.B67   [PS1888]   813'.3   81-9398
ISBN 0-8108-1471-4   AACR2

Again, to the memory of Fred,
three years later

CONTENTS

A FEW MOSSES ...

"To have known him, to have loved him
        After loneness long;
And then to be estranged in life,
        And neither in the wrong;
And now for death to set his seal--
        Ease me, a little ease, my song!

By wintry hills his hermit-mound
        The sheeted snow drifts drape,
And houseless there the snow-bird flits
        Beneath the fir-trees' crape:
Glazed now with ice the cloistral vine
        That hid the shyest grape."

                    --Herman Melville, "Monody," written
                      in part soon after Hawthorne's death
                      in May, 1864

"Once more--for it is hard to be finite upon an infinite subject, and all subjects are infinite. By some people this en-
tire scrawl of mine may be esteemed altogether unnecessary,
inasmuch 'as years ago' (they may say) 'we found out the rich
and rare stuff in this Hawthorne, whom you now parade forth,
as if only yourself were the discoverer of this Portuguese
diamond in our literature.' But even granting all this--and
adding to it, the assumption that the books of Hawthorne have
sold by the five thousand,--what does it signify? They should
be sold by the hundred thousand; and read by the million; and
admired by every one who is capable of admiration."

                    --Herman Melville, "Hawthorne and His
                      Mosses," in Literary World, August,
                      1850

"In Token
of my admiration for his genius
This book is incribed
to
NATHANIEL HAWTHORNE"

> --Herman Melville, Dedication of
> Moby-Dick, 1850

"Yesterday, May 23, we buried Hawthorne in Sleppy Hollow, in a pomp of sunshine and verdure, and gentle winds ... I thought there was a tragic element in the event, that might be more fully rendered,--in the painful solitude of the man, which, I suppose, could not longer be endured, and he died of it....

"It was easy to talk with him,--there were no barriers,--only, he said so little, that I talked too much, and stopped only because, as he gave no indications, I feared to exceed. He showed no egotism or self-assertion, rather a humility, and, at one time, a fear that he had written himself out. One day, when I found him on the top of his hill, in the woods, he paced back the path to his house, and said 'This path is the only remembrance of me that will remain.'"

> --Ralph Waldo Emerson, Journal,
> May 24, 1864

vii

PREFATORY REMARKS

With the completion of Hawthorne and the Critics, my American Renaissance bibliographical studies come to an end. I am grateful that this series has been brought to a successful conclusion, and at the same time I feel something akin to the regret of leave-taking. As indicated in one of the earlier prefaces, these bibliographies have grown out of a long term of teaching these authors, and all of them--Emerson, Whitman, Melville, Thoreau, and Hawthorne--occupy a very special territory in my reading experiences. My experience in working with their critics is to conclude that some little justice has been done to their works. Much remains to be done, although in each instance the bibliography is rather impressive, in quantity and quality. Perhaps my bibliographies may serve to indicate what has been done, in order that future critics will know what areas need to be studied.

In addition to the many standard bibliographical references--MLA Index, Essay and General Literature Index, American Literature, American Literary Scholarship, etc. --several noteworthy Hawthorne bibliographies have been compiled: A Checklist of Hawthorne Criticism: 1951-1966, annotated with a detailed index, by Buford Jones (Transcendental Books, 1967); "Criticism of Nathaniel Hawthorne: A Selected Checklist," by Maurice Beebe and Jack Hardie, in Studies in the Novel, 2 (1970), pp. 519-587. Theodore L. Gross and Stanley Wertheim published an excellent, although highly selective, bibliography, Hawthorne, Melville, and Stephen Crane (Free Press, 1971), with some 100 pages given to Hawthorne criticism and an equal number to the other two authors. This work is somewhat marred by the compilers' opinionated annotations. Beatrice Ricks, Joseph J. Adams, and Jack O. Hazlerig published a full-scale Hawthorne bibliography covering the twentieth century (G. K. Hall, 1972). This work is now dated, and has long been out of print.

These and many others, of partial and specialized

coverage, are listed in Hawthorne and the Critics and are included in the Subject Index under "Bibliography."

All of these works, plus a good many others, are listed in my checklist and are indexed under "Bibliography." The checklist is based largely on materials of the twentieth century written in English. However, I have included a few nineteenth-century and a few foreign-language items. This seems justifiable on the grounds that these pieces have recently been cited in a critical article or book, or the author has other significant work in the twentieth century or in the English language, and I wanted to make the author's contribution look as complete as possible.

It is now time to say "Thanks" to all who have contributed to making this series possible: my student assistants, Sarah Crouch and Dan Young, who must sometimes feel that they have grown old since the work began; the library staff at the University of Texas at Arlington, who have been courteous and helpful even in the most adverse of circumstances; and to my family, always supportive of my efforts even when it meant their inconveniences and delays. Finally, I would pay tribute to the memory of my dear husband in whose lifetime the series began, and who, had he lived, would have been the coauthor.

Jeanetta Boswell

February, 1981

Arlington, Texas

A NOTE ON USING THIS BOOK

The first 18 numbered entries are of anonymous authorship and are listed chronologically.

Subarrangements under authors' names are chronological.

Abbreviations

DA   Dissertation Abstracts

PMLA   Publications of the Modern Language Association

ESQ   Emerson Society Quarterly; is used in the listing of Cameron citations

ATR   American Transcendental Quarterly; is used in the listing of Cameron citations

THE CHECKLIST

1 ANONYMOUS (listed chronologically). "The Hawthorne
   Statue." Atlantic, 94 (July, 1904), 140-141.

2 "Hawthorne and Thoreau." T. P.'s Weekly, 6 (September
   22, 1905), 369.

3 "Books Read by Hawthorne, 1822-1850: From the 'Charge
   Books' of the Salem Athenaeum." Essex Institute Historical Collections, 68 (January, 1932), 65-87.

4 "Catalogue of Portraits (Nathaniel Hawthorne) in the Essex Institute." Essex Institute Historical Collections,
   71 (April, 1935), 150-151.

5 "Hawthorne Resurrected." Newsweek, 32 (October 11,
   1948), 100.

6 "Puritan Romancer." Times Literary Supplement, November 25, 1949, p. 770.

7 "Centenary of The Scarlet Letter." Publishers' Weekly,
   March 4, and April 8, 1950, pp. 1203 and 1691.

8 "The Literary Artist in America." Times Literary Supplement, August 17, 1956, pp. 20-21.

9 "Nathaniel Hawthorne." Notes and Queries, 8 (June,
   1961), 203.

10 "The Light and the Dark." Times Literary Supplement,
   September 19, 1961, pp. 637-638.

11 "Hawthorne to Samuel M. Cleveland: An Autobiographical

1

Letter. " <u>Nathaniel Hawthorne Journal</u>, 2 (1972), 1-5.

12 "Elizabeth P. Peabody to Mrs. Harriet M. Lathrop: An Unpublished Letter About Hawthorne. " <u>Nathaniel Hawthorne Journal</u>, 2 (1972), 7-8.

13 "Franklin Pierce to Horatio Bridge: An Unpublished Letter from a President. " <u>Nathaniel Hawthorne Journal</u>, 2 (1972), 11-12.

14 "Hawthorne to Joseph B. Boyd: An Unpublished Letter That Mentions Sir Henry Vane. " <u>Nathaniel Hawthorne Journal</u>, 2 (1972), 141-142.

15 "The Funeral of Mr. Hawthorne: As Reported in the <u>Boston Evening Transcript</u>, May 24, 1864, with the Address by Rev. James Freeman Clarke. " <u>Nathaniel Hawthorne Journal</u>, 2 (1972), 257-261.

16 "Katherine Anne Porter, Eudora Welty, and 'Ethan Brand. '" <u>International Fiction Review</u>, 1 (1974), 32-37.

17 "Concord in Winter. " <u>Thoreau Society Bulletin</u>, 136 (1976), 6-8. Originally published in the <u>Springfield Republican</u>, January 20, 1871.

18 "The Sun Has an Ill-Natured Pleasure, I Believe, in Making Me Look as Old as Himself," in Bruccoli, Matthew J. , and C. E. Frazer Clark, Jr. , eds. , <u>Pages: The World of Books, Writers, and Writing</u>, Vol. I. Detroit: Gale, 1976, p. 231. Reproduction of a letter and a photo.

19 AARON, Daniel. <u>The Unwritten War: American Writers and the Civil War</u>. New York: Knopf, 1973. "Hawthorne, the Lonely Dissenter," pp. 41-55.

20 ABCARIAN, Richard. "The Ending of 'Young Goodman Brown. '" <u>Studies in Short Fiction</u>, 3 (Spring, 1966), 343-345.

21 ABEL, Darrel. "The Immortal Pilgrim: An Ethical Interpretation of Nathaniel Hawthorne's Fiction. " Ph. D. diss. , Michigan, 1949.

22 _____. "Hester's Pearl: Symbol and Character."
English Literary History, 18 (March, 1951), 50-66.

23 _____. "The Theme of Isolation in Hawthorne." Personalist, 32 (January and April, 1951), 42-58, 182-
190.

24 _____. "Hawthorne's Hester." College English, 13
(March, 1952), 303-309.

25 _____. "Modes of Ethical Sensibility in Hawthorne."
Modern Language Notes, 68 (February, 1953), 80-86.
Examples from The Scarlet Letter.

26 _____. "Hawthorne's Skepticism about Social Reform
with Especial Reference to The Blithedale Romance."
University of Kansas City Review, 19 (Spring, 1953),
181-193.

27 _____. "Le Sage's Limping Devil and 'Mrs. Bullfrog.'" Notes and Queries, 198 (April, 1953), 165.

28 _____. "A Masque of Love and Death." University
of Toronto Quarterly, 23 (October, 1953), 9-25. Discusses The Marble Faun.

29 _____. "The Devil in Boston." Philological Quarterly, 32 (October, 1953), 366-381. Refers to Roger
Chillingworth.

30 _____. "Hawthorne's House of Tradition." South Atlantic Quarterly, 52 (October, 1953), 561-578. Based
on The House of the Seven Gables.

31 _____. "Immortality or Mortality--Septimius Felton:
Some Possible Sources." American Literature, 27
(January, 1956), 566-570.

32 _____. "Who Wrote Hawthorne's Autobiography?"
American Literature, 28 (March, 1956), 73-77.

33 _____. "Hawthorne's Dimmesdale: Fugitive from
Wrath." Nineteenth-Century Fiction, 11 (September,
1956), 81-105.

34 _____. "Giving Lustre to Gray Shadows: Hawthorne's

Potent Art." _American Literature_, 41 (December, 1969), 373-388.

35   _____. "Black Glove and Pink Ribbon: Hawthorne's Metonymic Symbols." _New England Quarterly_, 42 (1969), 163-180.

36   _____. " 'A More Imaginative Pleasure': Hawthorne on the Play of the Imagination." _Emerson Society Quarterly_, 55 (1969), 63-71.

37   _____. " 'This Troublesome Mortality': Hawthorne's Marbles and Bubbles." _Studies in Romanticism_, 8 (1969), 193-197.

38   _____. " 'A Vast Deal of Human Sympathy': Idea and Device in Hawthorne's 'The Snow Image.' " _Criticism_, 4 (1970), 316-332.

39   _____. "Hawthorne's _The Scarlet Letter_." _Explicator_, 29 (1971), item 62.

40   _____. "Hawthorne and the Strong Division-Lines of Nature." _American Transcendental Quarterly_, 14 (1972), 23-31.

41   _____. "Hawthorne, Ghostland, and the Jurisdiction of Veracity." _American Transcendental Quarterly_, 24 (1974), 30-38.

42   ABERNETHY, P. L. "The Identity of Hawthorne's Major Molineux." _American Transcendental Quarterly_, 31 (1976), 5-8.

43   ABRAHAMSSON, Hans. "The Main Characters of Hawthorne's _The Scarlet Letter_ and Their Interrelationships." _Moderna Sprak_ (Sweden), 68 (1974), 337-348.

44   ADAMS, Charles Siegel. "The Dimensions of Folklore in the Writing of Nathaniel Hawthorne." Ph.D. diss., Indiana, 1973. _DA_, 34 (1974), 5033A.

45   ADAMS, John F. "Hawthorne's Symbolic Gardens." _University of Texas Studies in English_, 5 (Summer, 1963), 242-254.

46 ADAMS, Joseph D. "Initial Ritual in the Early Short
    Fiction of Nathaniel Hawthorne." Ph.D. diss.,
    Lehigh, 1972. DA, 33 (1973), 4397A.

47 _____. "The Societal Initiation and Hawthorne's
    'My Kinsman, Major Molineux': The Night-Journey
    Motif." English Studies Collections (East Meadow,
    New York), 1 (1976), 1-19.

48 ADAMS, Raymond. "Hawthorne and a Glimpse of
    Walden." Essex Institute Historical Collections,
    94 (July, 1958), 191-193.

49 ADAMS, Richard P. "Nathaniel Hawthorne: A Study
    of His Literary Development." Ph.D. diss.,
    Columbia, 1951.

50 _____. "Romanticism and the American Renais-
    sance." American Literature, 23 (January, 1952),
    419-432.

51 _____. "Hawthorne's Provincial Tales." New
    England Quarterly, 30 (March, 1957), 39-57.

52 _____. "Hawthorne: The Old Manse Period."
    Tulane Studies in English, 8 (1958), 115-151.

53 _____. "The Apprenticeship of William Faulkner."
    Tulane Studies in English, 12 (1962), 113-156. Re-
    fers to Faulkner's reading Hawthorne.

54 _____. "American Renaissance: An Epistemological
    Problem." Emerson Society Quarterly, 35 (1964),
    2-7.

55 ADAMS, Robert Martin. "Masks, Screens, Guises:
    Melville and Others," in Nil: Episodes in the Liter-
    ary Conquest of Void During the Nineteenth Century.
    New York: Oxford University Press, 1966, pp.131-
    148.

56 ADAMS, Timothy Dow. "To Prepare a Preface to
    Meet the Faces That You Meet: Autobiographical
    Rhetoric in Hawthorne's Prefaces." Emerson Society
    Quarterly, 23 (1977), 89-98.

57 ADERMAN, Ralph M. "Nathaniel Hawthorne's English
    Reputation." Ph.D. diss., Wisconsin, 1951.

58 _____. "Newly Located Hawthorne Letters." Essex
    Institute Historical Collections, 88 (April, 1952),
    163-165. Dated 1855, in the John Rylands Library.

59 _____. "The Case of James Cook: A Study of Po-
    litical Influence in 1840." Essex Institute Historical
    Collections, 92 (January, 1956), 59-67.

60 ADKINS, Nelson P. "The Early Projected Works of
    Nathaniel Hawthorne." Papers of the Bibliographical
    Society of America, 39 (1945), 119-155.

61 _____. "Hawthorne's Democratic New England Puri-
    tans." Emerson Society Quarterly, 44 (1966), 66-
    72.

62 _____. "Notes on the Hawthorne Canon." Papers
    of the Bibliographical Society of America, 60, (1966),
    364-367.

63 ALBERTINI, Virgil. "Hepzibah and Prayer." American
    Notes and Queries, 12 (1973), 35.

64 ALCOTT, Amos Bronson. Concord Days. Boston:
    Roberts Brothers, 1873. Based on Alcott's Journals.
    Hawthorne, pp.193-197 et passim.

65 ALDEN, John. "Hawthorne and William Henry Smith:
    An Essay in Anglo-American Bibliography." Book
    Collector, 5 (Winter, 1956), 370-374.

66 ALLEN, M.L. "Hawthorne's Art in His Short Stories."
    Studi Americani (Rome), 7 (1961), 9-41.

67 _____. "The Black Veil: Three Versions of a Sym-
    bol." English Studies, 47 (August, 1966), 286-289.

68 ALLEN, John D. "Behind 'The Minister's Black Veil,' "
    in Burton, Thomas G., ed., Essays in Memory of
    Christine Burleson in Language and Literature by
    Former Colleagues and Students. Johnson City:
    Advisory Council of East Tennessee State University,
    1969, pp.3-12.

69 ALLEN, Margaret V. "Imagination and History in Hawthorne's 'Legends of the Province House.'" American Literature, 43 (1971), 432-437.

70 ALLEN, Mary. "Smiles and Laughter in Hawthorne." Philological Quarterly, 52 (1973), 119-128.

71 ALLISON, Alexander W. "The Literary Contents of 'My Kinsman, Major Molineux.'" Nineteenth-Century Fiction, 23 (1968), 304-311.

    ALLISON, Denis see LAPE, Denis A.

72 ALLYN, John. "Hawthorne on Film--Almost." Literature/Film Quarterly, 2 (1974), 124-128.

73 ALSEN, Eberhard. "Hawthorne, a Puritan Tieck: A Comparative Analysis of the Tales of Hawthorne and the Märchen of Tieck." Ph.D. diss., Indiana, 1966. DA, 28 (1967), 2199A.

74 _____. "The Ambitious Experiment of Dr. Rappaccini." American Literature, 43 (November, 1971), 430-431.

75 ALTSCHULER, Glenn C. "The Puritan Dilemma in 'The Minister's Black Veil.'" American Transcendental Quarterly, 24 Supplement 1 (1974), 25-27.

76 AMMIDON, Philip R. "Hawthorne's Last Sketch." New England Magazine, 1 (June, 1886), 516-526.

77 ANDERSON, D.K., Jr. "Hawthorne's Crowds." Nineteenth-Century Fiction, 7 (June, 1952), 39-50.

78 ANDERSON, George K. The Legend of the Wandering Jew. Providence, R.I.: Brown University Press, 1965. "Ethan Brand," pp.212-213.

79 ANDERSON, Norman A. "'Rappaccini's Daughter': A Keatsian Analogue?" PMLA, 83 (1968), 271-283. Refers to Keats's "Lamia."

80 ANDERSON, Quentin. "Hawthorne's Boston," in Anderson, The Imperial Self: An Essay in American Literary and Cultural History. New York: Knopf, 1971, pp.59-87.

81   , ed. with Introduction. Twice-Told Tales and Other Short Stories. New York: Washington Square Press, 1960.

82 ANDERSON, Walter Steve. "The Image of the House in the Works of Nathaniel Hawthorne." Ph.D. diss., Missouri (Columbia), 1974. DA, 36 (1975), 295A.

83 ANDOLA, John A. "Pearl: Symbolic Link Between Two Worlds." Ball State University Forum, 13 (1972), 60-67.

84 ANO, Fumio. "The Mischianza Ball and Hawthorne's 'Howe's Masquerade.'" Nathaniel Hawthorne Journal, 4 (1974), 231-235.

85   . "Hawthorne Studies in Japan." Nathaniel Hawthorne Journal, 5 (1975), 264-269.

86 AOYAMA, Yoshitaka. "'Rappaccini's Daughter': The Garden as a 'Neutral Territory.'" Sophia English Studies, 1 (1976), 37-52.

87 APPLEBAUM, Noah. "Nature's Cunning Alphabet: Multiplicity and Perceptual Ambiguity in Hawthorne and Melville." Ph.D. diss., Washington University, 1974. DA, 36 (1975), 295A-296A.

88 ARAC, Jonathan. "The House and the Railroad: Dombey and Son and The House of the Seven Gables." New England Quarterly, 51 (1978), 3-22.

89 ARADER, Harry F. "American Novelists in Italy: Nathaniel Hawthorne, Howells, James, and F. Marion Crawford." Ph.D., diss., Pennsylvania, 1953.

90 ARCHER, Susan M. "Hawthorne's Use of Spenser." Ph.D. diss, Pennsylvania, 1967. DA, 28 (1968), 1424A.

91 ARDEN, Eugene. "Hawthorne's 'Case of Arthur Dimmesdale.'" American Imago, 18 (Spring, 1961), 45-55.

92 ARNER, Robert D. "Hawthorne and Jones Very: Two Dimensions of Satire in 'Egotism; or, the Bosom Serpent.'" New England Quarterly, 42 (June, 1969),

267-275.

93   _____. "Of Snakes and Those Who Swallow Them: Some Folk Analogues for Hawthorne's 'Egotism; or, the Bosom Serpent.'" Southern Folklore Quarterly, 35 (1971), 336-346.

94   _____. "The Legend of Pygmalion in 'The Birthmark.'" American Transcendental Quarterly, 14 (1972), 168-171.

95   _____. "The Story of Hannah Dustin: Cotton Mather to Thoreau." American Transcendental Quarterly, 18 (1973), 19-23.

96   ARNOLD, Armin. D. H. Lawrence and America. New York: Philological Library, 1959. Hawthorne, pp. 66-74.

97   _____. "The Transcendental Element in American Literature: A Study of Some Unpublished D. H. Lawrence Manuscripts." Modern Philology, 60 (August, 1962), 41-46.

98   _____, ed. The Symbolic Meaning: The Uncollected Versions of "Studies in Classic American Literature." Fontwell, England: Centaur, 1962; New York: Viking, 1964. Hawthorne, pp. 133-172.

99   ARORA, V. N. "The Archetypal Pattern of Individuation in Hawthorne's The Scarlet Letter." Panjab University Research Bulletin in the Arts, 6 (1975), 19-23.

100   ARTHOS, John. "Hawthorne in Florence." Michigan Alumnus Quarterly Review, 59 (Winter, 1953), 118-129. Discusses The Marble Faun.

101   _____. "The Scarlet Letter Once More." Ball State Teachers College Forum (later Ball State University Forum), 5 (Winter, 1964), 31-38.

102   ARVIN, Newton. "The Relevance of Hawthorne." New Student, 7 (1928), 3-5, 18.

103   _____. Hawthorne. Boston: Little, Brown, 1929. Reprinted New York: Russell and Russell, 1960.

104 _____. American Pantheon. Edited by Aaron,
Daniel, and Sylvan Schendler. New York: Delacorte,
1966. Hawthorne, pp. 60-105.

105 _____, ed. The Heart of Hawthorne's Journals.
Boston: Little, Brown, 1929. Reprinted New York:
Barnes and Noble, 1967.

106 _____, ed. with Introduction. Hawthorne's Short
Stories. New York: Knopf, 1946. Contains 29
stories.

107 _____, ed. with Introduction. The Scarlet Letter.
New York: Harper Brothers, 1950. Modern Classics
Series.

108 ASALS, Frederick. "Jeremy Taylor and Hawthorne's
Early Tales." American Transcendental Quarterly,
14 (1972), 15-23.

109 ASKEW, Melvin W. "The Wounded Artist and His
Work." Kansas Magazine, 4 (1961), 73-77.

110 _____. "The Pseudonymic American Hero." Bucknell Review, 10 (March, 1962), 224-231.

111 _____. "Hawthorne, the Fall, and the Psychology
of Maturity." American Literature, 34 (November,
1962), 335-343.

112 ASQUINO, Mark L. "Hawthorne's 'Village Uncle' and
Melville's Moby-Dick." Studies in Short Fiction, 10
(1973), 413-414.

113 ASSELINEAU, Roger. "Hawthorne Abroad," in Pearce,
Roy Harvey, ed., Hawthorne Centenary Essays (1964),
pp. 367-385. Also published in Les Langues Moder-
nes, 59 (March-April, 1965), 156-163.

114 ASTROV, Vladimir. "Hawthorne and Dostoievsky as
Explorers of the Human Conscience." New England
Quarterly, 15 (June, 1942), 296-319.

115 ATKINS, Lois. "Psychological Symbolism of Guilt and
Isolation in Hawthorne." American Imago, 11 (Winter, 1954), 417-425.

116 ATKINSON, Jennifer E. "Recent Hawthorne Scholar-
     ship, 1967-1970: A Checklist." Nathaniel Hawthorne
     Journal, 1 (1971), 295-305.

117 AUBREY, Max. "Hawthorne's Study in Clay." Xavier
     University Studies, 11 (1972), 1-5.

118 AUCHINCLOSS, Louis. "The Blithedale Romance: A
     Study of Form and Point of View." Nathaniel Haw-
     thorne Journal, 2 (1972), 53-58.

119 AUSTIN, Allen. "Distortion in The [Complete] Scarlet
     Letter." College English, 23 (October, 1961), 61-
     62. See article by Sam S. Baskett.

120 _____. "Satire and Theme in The Scarlet Letter."
     Philological Quarterly, 41 (April, 1962), 508-511.

121 _____. "Hester Prynne's Plan of Escape: The
     Moral Problem." University of Kansas City Review,
     28 (June, 1962), 317-318.

122 AUSTIN, Gabriel C. A Descriptive Guide to the Ex-
     hibition Commemorating the Death of Nathaniel Haw-
     thorne, 1804-1864. New York: Grolier Club, 1964.
     17p. pamphlet, containing an unpublished Hawthorne
     letter of 1839.

123 AUSTIN, James C. Fields of the Atlantic Monthly:
     Letters to an Editor. San Marino, Calif.: Hunting-
     ton Library Press, 1953. Hawthorne, pp. 204-244.

124 _____. "The Hawthorne and Browning Acquaintance:
     Including an Unpublished Browning Letter." Vic-
     torian Newsletter, 20 (Fall, 1961), 13-18.

125 AUTREY, Max L. "Hawthorne and the Beautiful Im-
     pulse." American Transcendental Quarterly, 14
     (1972), 48-54.

126 _____. "Flower Imagery in Hawthorne's Post-
     humous Narratives." Studies in the Novel, 7 (1975),
     215-226.

127 _____. "A Source for Roger Chillingworth."
     American Transcendental Quarterly, 26 Supplement

(1975), 24-26. Same name in James M. Rymer,
Varney the Vampire: or the Feast of Blood.

128 AXELSSON, Arne I. "Isolation and Interdependence as
Structure in Hawthorne's Four Major Romances."
Studi Neophilologica (Sweden), 45 (1973), 392-402.

129 _____. The Links in the Chain: Isolation and Interdependence in Nathaniel Hawthorne's Fictional Characters. Uppsala, Sweden: Universitets Biblioteket,
1974.

130 AYO, Nicholas. "The Labyrinthine Ways of 'Rappaccini's Daughter.'" Research Studies, 42 (1974), 56-
69.

131 BAAR, Stephen R. "From Novel to Film: The Adap-
tation of American Renaissance Symbolic Fiction."
Ph.D. diss., Utah, 1973. DA, 34 (1974), 4186A.
Includes The Scarlet Letter, The House of the Seven
Gables, and Moby-Dick.

132 BABIIHA, Thaddeo Kitasimbwa. "James' Washington
Square: More on the Hawthorne Relation." Nathaniel
Hawthorne Journal, 4 (1974), 270-272.

133 _____. "A Review of Research and Criticism on
the James-Hawthorne Relation, 1918-1973." Ph.D.
diss., Brown, 1976. DA, 38 (1977), 3493A.

134 BACON, Delia Salter. The Philosophy of the Plays of
Shakespeare Unfolded. Preface by Nathaniel Hawthorne. London: Groombridge and Sons, 1857.

135 BADER, A.L. "Those Mesmeric Victorians." Colophon, 3 (Summer, 1938), 335-353.

136 BALAKIAN, Anna. " ' . . . and the pursuit of happi-
ness': The Scarlet Letter and A Spy in the House of
Love." Mosaic, 11 (1978), 163-170.

137 BALDENSPERGER, Fernand. "A Propos de 'Nathaniel
Hawthorne en France.'" Modern Language Notes,
56 (May, 1941), 343-345. In French.

138 BALES, Allen. "A Study of Point of View in the

Novels of Nathaniel Hawthorne." Ph.D. diss., North-western, 1959. <u>DA</u>, 20 (1960), 3724.

139 BALES, Kent Roslyn. "Nathaniel Hawthorne's Use of the Sublime." Ph.D. diss., California (Berkeley), 1967. <u>DA</u>, 28 (1968), 4162A-4163A.

140 _____. "The Blithedale Romance: Coverdale's Mean and Subversive Egotism." <u>Bucknell Review</u>, 21 (1973), 60-82.

141 _____. "The Allegory and the Radical Romantic Ethic of <u>The Blithedale Romance</u>." <u>American Liter-ature</u>, 46 (1974), 41-53.

142 _____. "Hawthorne's Prefaces and Romantic Per-spectivism." <u>Emerson Society Quarterly</u>, 23 (1977), 69-88.

143 _____. "Sexual Exploitation and the Fall from Natural Virtue in Rappaccini's Garden." <u>Emerson Society Quarterly</u>, 24 (1978), 133-144.

144 BANGS, Richard F. "The American Criticism of Hawthorne: 1949-1964." Ph.D., diss., St. John's (New York), 1965.

145 BANK, Stanley. "Nathaniel Hawthorne's <u>Blithedale Romance</u>: A Pivotal Work for Studying American Literature." Ph.D. diss., Columbia, 1966. <u>DA</u>, 28 (1967), 663A-664A.

146 _____, ed. with Introduction. <u>American Romanticism: A Shape for Fiction</u>. New York: Capricorn, 1969. "Hawthorne: The Truth of the Human Heart," pp. 244-288; includes selections by Hawthorne and an article by Henry T. Tuckerman, "The Prose-Poet: Nathaniel Hawthorne," from <u>Mental Portraits</u> (1853).

147 BARKAU, Jane A. "Rome and Monte Beni Revisited: A New Reading of Hawthorne's <u>The Marble Faun</u>." Ph.D. diss., Vanderbilt, 1972. <u>DA</u>, 34 (1973), 2547A.

148 BARNES, Daniel R. " 'Physical Fact' and Folklore: Hawthorne's 'Egotism; or, the Bosom Serpent.' " <u>American Literature</u>, 43 (1971), 117-121.

149 _____. "Faulkner's Miss Emily and Hawthorne's
Old Maid." Studies in Short Fiction, 9 (1972), 373-
378. Refers to Hawthorne's "The White Old Maid"
(1838).

150 _____. "The Bosom Serpent: A Legend in American
Literature and Culture." Journal of American Folklore, 85 (1972), 111-122.

151 _____. "Orestes Brownson and Hawthorne's Holgrave." American Literature, 45 (1973), 271-278.

152 _____, ed. "Two Reviews of The Scarlet Letter in
Holden's Dollar Magazine." American Literature,
44 (1973), 648-652. Reprint material.

153 BARNETT, Gene Austin. "Hawthorne's Use of Setting
in His Major Novels." Ph. D. diss., Wisconsin,
1960. DA, 22 (1961), 1991-1992.

154 _____. "Hawthorne's Italian Towers." Studies in
Romanticism, 3 (1964), 252-256.

155 _____. "Art as Setting in The Marble Faun."
Transactions of the Wisconsin Academy of Sciences,
Arts, and Letters, 54 (1965), 231-247.

156 _____. "Hawthorne's Italian Calendar." Emerson
Society Quarterly, 43 (1966), 68-70. Discusses The
Marble Faun.

157 BARNETT, Louise K. Ignoble Savage: American
Literary Racism, 1790-1890. Westport, Conn.:
Greenwood, 1975. Hawthorne, pp. 143-190 et passim.

158 BARNEY, Stephen A. Allegories of History, Allegories of Love. Hamden, Conn.: Shoe String, 1979.
Discusses "Rappaccini's Daughter."

159 BARRET, C. Waller. Italian Influence on American
Literature. New York: Grolier Club, 1962. Hawthorne, passim.

160 BARTH, J. Robert. "Faulkner and the Calvinist Tradition." Thought, 39 (Spring, 1964), 100-120.

161 BARTLETT, I. H. "The Democratic Imagination," in

Bartlett, The American Mind in Mid-Nineteenth Century. New York: Crowell, 1967, pp. 94-113.

162 BASHORE, James Robert, Jr. "The Villains in the Major Works of Nathaniel Hawthorne and Henry James." Ph.D. diss., Wisconsin, 1958. DA, 19 (1959), 2939.

163 BASKETT, Sam S. "The [Complete] Scarlet Letter." College English, 22 (February, 1961), 321-329. See article by Allen Austin (1961).

164 BASS, Eben. "The Sculptor of the Beautiful." Colby Library Quarterly, 14 (1978), 28-35.

165 BASSAN, Maurice. "A New Account of Hawthorne's Last Days, Death, and Funeral." American Literature, 27 (January, 1956), 561-565.

166 _____. "Julian Hawthorne Edits Aunt Ebe." Essex Institute Historical Collections, 100 (1964), 274-278.

167 _____. "The Literary Career of Julian Hawthorne: A Selected Checklist." Bulletin of Bibliography, 24 (1965), 157-162.

168 _____. Hawthorne's Son: The Life and Literary Career of Julian Hawthorne. Columbus: Ohio State University Press, 1970.

169 _____. "Bay Area Hawthorniana." Nathaniel Hawthorne Journal, 6 (1976), 69-79.

170 BATES, Katharine Lee, ed. The Marble Faun. New York: Crowell, 1901.

171 BATTAGLIA, Francis Joseph. "The House of the Seven Gables: New Light on Old Problems." PMLA, 82 (1967), 579-590.

172 _____. "The (Unmeretricious) House of the Seven Gables." Studies in the Novel, 2 (1970), 468-473.

173 BAUGHMAN, Ernest W. "Public Confession and The Scarlet Letter." New England Quarterly, 40 (1967), 532-550.

174 BAUMGARTNER, Alex M., and Michael J. Hoffman.

"Illusion and Role in The Scarlet Letter." Papers on Language and Literature, 7 (1971), 168-184.

175 BAXTER, Annette K. "Independence vs Isolation: Hawthorne and James on the Problem of the Artist." Nineteenth-Century Fiction, 10 (December, 1955), 225-231.

176 BAXTER, David J. " 'The Birthmark' in Perspective." Nathaniel Hawthorne Journal, 5 (1975), 232-240.

177 BAYM, Nina Z. "The Head, the Heart, and the Unpardonable Sin." New England Quarterly, 40 (March, 1967), 31-47.

178 _____. "The Blithedale Romance: A Radical Reading." Journal of English and Germanic Philology, 67 (1968), 545-569.

179 _____. "Passion and Authority in The Scarlet Letter." New England Quarterly, 43 (1970), 209-230.

180 _____. "Hawthorne's Holgrave: The Failure of the Artist-Hero." Journal of English and Germanic Philology, 69 (1970), 584-598.

181 _____. "Hawthorne." Review of Current Scholarship in American Literary Scholarship, 1970, 1971, 1972, 1973, and 1974, pp.18-32, 24-40, 18-39, 15-31, 15-27.

182 _____. "Hawthorne's Women: The Tyranny of Social Myths." Centennial Review, 15 (1971), 250-272.

183 _____. "The Marble Faun: Hawthorne's Elegy for Art." New England Quarterly, 44 (1971), 355-376.

184 _____. "Hawthorne's Myths for Children: The Author Versus His Audience." Studies in Short Fiction, 10 (1973), 35-46. Wonder-Book and Tanglewood Tales.

185 _____. "The Romantic Malgré Lui: Hawthorne in the Custom House." Emerson Society Quarterly, 19 (1973), 14-25.

17   Baym

186 _____. "Hawthorne's Gothic Discards: Fanshawe
and 'Alice Doane.'" Nathaniel Hawthorne Journal, 4
(1974), 105-115.

187 _____. The Shape of Hawthorne's Career. Ithaca,
N. Y.: Cornell University Press, 1976.

188 BEARD, James F., ed. with Introduction. The House
of the Seven Gables. Barre, Mass.: Imprint Society,
1969.

189 BEATTY, Lillian. "Typee and Blithedale: Rejected
Ideal Communities." Personalist, 37 (Autumn, 1956),
367-378.

190 BEAVER, Harold Lowther. "The Writer as Mesmerist."
Times Literary Supplement, December 1, 1978,
p. 1386.

191 BEBB, Bruce, and Hershel Parker. "Freehafer on
Greg and the CEAA: Secure Footing and 'Substantial
Shortfalls.'" Studies in the Novel, 7 (1975), 391-
394. See articles by John Freehafer, 1970, and
1975.

192 BECKER, Isadore H. "Tragic Irony in 'Rappaccini's
Daughter.'" Hudson Review, 4 (1971), 89-93.

193 _____. The Ironic Dimension in Hawthorne's Short
Fiction. New York: Carlton, 1971.

194 BECKER, John E., S.J. "Hawthorne's Historical
Allegory." Ph.D. diss., Yale, 1968. DA, 30 (1969),
715A.

195 _____. Hawthorne's Historical Allegory: An Examination of the American Conscience. Port Washington, N. Y.: Kennikat, 1971.

196 BEEBE, Maurice. "The Fall of the House of Pyncheon."
Nineteenth-Century Fiction, 11 (June, 1956), 1-17.

197 _____. Ivory Towers and Sacred Founts: The
Artist as Hero in Fiction from Goethe to Joyce. New
York: New York University Press, 1964. "The
Blithedale Romance," pp. 206-215.

198   _____, and Jack Hardie. "A Checklist of Hawthorne
       Criticism." Studies in the Novel, 2 (1970), 519-587.

199   BEERS, Henry Augustin. Four Americans: Roosevelt,
       Hawthorne, Emerson, Whitman. New Haven: Yale
       University Press, 1919. "Fifty Years of Hawthorne,"
       pp. 33-57. Reprinted Freeport, N. Y.: Books for
       Libraries, 1968. Printed earlier in Yale Review,
       4 (January, 1915), 300-315.

200   BEIDLER, Peter G. "The Theme of the Fortunate
       Fall in The Marble Faun." Emerson Society Quarterly,
       47 (1967), 56-62.

201   BELDEN, Henry M. "Poe's Criticism of Hawthorne."
       Anglia, 23 (1901), 376-404.

202   BELL, John M. "Hawthorne's The Scarlet Letter:
       An Artist's Intuitive Understanding of Plague, Ar-
       mor, and Health." Journal of Orgonomy, 3 (1969),
       102-115.

203   BELL, Michael Davitt. Hawthorne and the Historical
       Romance of New England. Princeton, N. J.: Prince-
       ton University Press, 1971.

204   BELL, Millicent. "Melville and Hawthorne at the
       Grave of St. John (A Debt to Pierre Bayle)." Modern
       Language Notes, 67 (February, 1952), 116-118.

205   _____. "Hawthorne's 'Fire Worship': Interpreta-
       tion and Source." American Literature, 24 (March,
       1952), 31-39.

206   _____. Hawthorne's View of the Artist. Albany:
       State University of New York Press, 1962.

207   BELLMAN, Samuel I. " 'The Joke's on You!': Sud-
       den Revelation in Hawthorne." Nathaniel Hawthorne
       Journal, 5 (1975), 192-199.

208   _____. "Outward Bound from Hawthorne." College
       English, 37 (1975), 3-7. How Hawthorne would
       write on contemporary problems.

209   BENNETT, James O'Donnell. "Hawthorne's The
       Scarlet Letter," in Much Loved Books. New York:

Liveright, 1927, pp. 103-108. Reprinted in a shorter
form New York: Fawcett World Library, 1959.
"Hawthorne's The Scarlet Letter, " pp. 58-63.

210 BENOIT, Raymond. "Hawthorne's Psychology of Death:
'The Minister's Black Veil. '" Studies in Short Fiction, 8 (1971), 553-560.

211 _____. "Hawthorne's Ape Man: 'My Kinsman,
Major Molineux. '" American Transcendental Quarterly, 14 (1972), 8-9.

212 _____. "Theology and Literature: The Scarlet
Letter." Bucknell Review, 20 (1972), 83-92.

213 _____. "A Letter--the Letter A: Nathaniel Haw-
thorne," in Benoit, Single Nature's Double Name.
Atlantic Highlands, N. J.: Humanities; The Hague:
Mouton, 1973.

214 BENSON, Adolph B. "Hawthorne's Sketch of Queen
Christina: A Note." Scandinavian Studies, 31
(November, 1959), 166-167.

215 BENSON, Eugene. "Poe and Hawthorne." The Galaxy,
6 (December, 1868), 742-748. Reprinted in Cameron,
ed. , Hawthorne Among His Contemporaries (1968),
pp. 120-123.

216 BERCOVITCH, Sacvan. "Hawthorne's 'Seven-Branched
Allegory': An Echo from Cotton Mather in The
Marble Faun." Early American Literature News-
letter, 1 (Summer, 1966), 5-6.

217 _____. "The Frontier Fable of Hawthorne's The
Marble Faun." South Dakota Review, 4 (Summer,
1966), 44-50.

218 _____. "Endicott's Breastplate: Symbolism and
Typology in 'Endicott and the Red Cross. '" Studies
in Short Fiction, 4 (1967), 289-299.

219 _____. "Of Wise and Foolish Virgins: Hilda Versus Miriam in Hawthorne's Marble Faun. " New
England Quarterly, 41 (1968), 281-286.

220 _____. "Miriam as Shylock: An Echo from Shakes-

peare in Hawthorne's Marble Faun." Forum for
Modern Language Studies (Scotland), 5 (1969), 385-
387.

221 _____. "Diabolus in Salem." English Language
Notes, 6 (1969), 280-285. Influence of Bunyan's
The Holy War (1682), on Hawthorne's portrait of
John Endicott.

222 BEREK, Peter. The Transformation of Allegory from
Spenser to Hawthorne. Amherst, Mass.: Amherst
College Press, 1962.

223 BERGER, Peter, and Thomas Luckmann. The Social
Construction of Reality. New York: Doubleday,
1966. Hawthorne, passim.

224 BERGERON, David M. "Arthur Miller's The Crucible
and Nathaniel Hawthorne: Some Parallels." English
Journal, 58 (January, 1969), 47-55.

225 BERGMAN, Herbert. " 'The Interior of a Heart': The
Crucible and The Scarlet Letter." University College
Quarterly, 15 (1970), 27-32.

226 BERTHOLD, Dennis A. "Hawthorne's Aesthetics of
Imperfection." Ph.D. diss., Wisconsin, 1971. DA,
33 (1972), 2885A.

227 _____. "Hawthorne, Ruskin, and the Gothic Revival: Transcendent Gothic in The Marble Faun."
Emerson Society Quarterly, 20 (1974), 15-32.

228 _____. "From Freud to Marx: Recent Directions
in Hawthorne Criticism." Emerson Society Quarterly,
22 (1976), 107-119. Review article.

229 BEWLEY, Marius. Introduction by F.R. Leavis.
The Complex Fate: Hawthorne, Henry James, and
Some Other Writers. London: Chatto and Windus,
1952. Contains the following essays: "Hawthorne,
Henry James, and the American Novel," pp.1-10;
"The Blithedale Romance and The Bostonians," pp.
11-30; "The Marble Faun and The Wings of the Dove,"
pp.31-54; "The American Problem," pp.55-78.

230 _____. "Hawthorne and 'The Deeper Psychology.' "

Mandrake, 2 (Winter, 1955-56), 366-373.

231 _____. "Hawthorne: A New Evaluation." Sewanee
Review, 64 (Winter, 1956), 152-161. Essay-review
of Hyatt H. Waggoner's Hawthorne: A Critical Study
(1955).

232 _____. The Eccentric Design: Form in the Classic
American Novel. New York: Columbia University
Press, 1959. "Hawthorne's Short Stories," pp. 113-
146; "Hawthorne's Novels," pp. 147-186.

233 _____. "Solitude and Society: Nathaniel Hawthorne."
Excerpt from The Eccentric Design (1959), in Strout,
Cushing, ed., Intellectual History in America, 2
vols. New York: Harper, 1968. Vol. I, pp. 179-
191.

234 BEZANSON, Walter E. "The Hawthorne Game: 'Graves
and Goblins.'" Emerson Society Quarterly, 54 (1969),
73-77.

235 BICKFORD, Gail H. "Lovewell's Fight, 1725-1958."
American Quarterly, 10 (Fall, 1958), 358-366. Relates to "Roger Malvin's Burial."

236 BICKLEY, Robert Bruce, Jr. "The Minor Fiction of
Hawthorne and Melville." American Transcendental
Quarterly, 14 (1972), 149-152.

237 BICKNELL, John W. "The Marble Faun Reconsidered."
University of Kansas City Review, 10 (Spring, 1954),
193-199.

238 BIER, Jesse. "Hawthorne on the Romance: His Prefaces Related and Examined." Modern Philology,
53 (August, 1955), 17-24.

239 BILLY, Ted. "Time and Transformation in 'The
Artist of the Beautiful.'" American Transcendental
Quarterly, 29 (1976), 33-35.

240 BIRDSALL, Richard D. "Berkshire's Golden Age."
American Quarterly, 8 (Winter, 1956), 328-355.

241 _____. Berkshire County: A Cultural History.
New Haven: Yale University Press, 1959. Haw-

thorne, pp. 353-365.

242 BIRDSALL, Virginia Ogden. "Hawthorne's Fair-Haired
     Maidens: The Fading Light." PMLA, 75 (June,
     1960), 250-256.

243 _____. "Hawthorne's Oak Tree Image." Nineteenth-
     Century Fiction, 15 (September, 1960), 181-185. Re-
     lates to "Roger Malvin's Burial."

244 BIRRELL, Augustine. "Nathaniel Hawthorne," in
     Birrell, Et Cetera. New York: Musson, 1930, pp.
     199-222.

245 _____. "Nathaniel Hawthorne." Life and Letters,
     1 (June-December, 1928), 102-119.

246 BLACK, Stephen Ames. "The Scarlet Letter: Death
     by Symbols." Paunch, 24 (October, 1965), 51-74.

247 BLACKMUR, Richard P. "American Literary Ex-
     patriate," in Blackmur, The Lion and the Honey-
     comb. New York: Harcourt, Brace, 1955, pp. 61-78.

248 _____, ed. with an Afterword. The Celestial Rail-
     road and Other Stories. New York: New American
     Library, 1963, pp. 289-297.

249 BLACKSTOCK, Walter. "Hawthorne's Cool, Switched-
     on Media of Communication in The Marble Faun."
     Language Quarterly, 7 (1969), 41-42.

250 BLAIR, Walter. "Color, Light, and Shadow in Haw-
     thorne's Fiction." New England Quarterly, 15
     (March, 1942), 74-94.

251 _____. "Hawthorne," in Stovall, Floyd, ed., Eight
     American Authors. New York: Modern Language
     Association, 1956, pp. 100-152. Reprinted with Sup-
     plement by J. Chesley Mathews. New York: Nor-
     ton, 1963. Revised with additional material and
     edited by James Woodress. New York: Norton,
     1971. "Hawthorne," by Walter Blair, pp. 85-128.

252 _____, and Hamlin Hill. America's Humor: From
     Poor Richard to Doonesbury. New York: Oxford
     University Press, 1978. Includes discussion of

Hawthorne.

253 BLAIR, William T. " 'Dr. Heidegger's Experiment':
     An Allegory of Sin. " Nathaniel Hawthorne Journal,
     6 (1977), 286-291.

254 BLANCK, Jacob. Bibliography of American Literature,
     6 vols. New Haven: Yale University Press, 1955-
     1963. Hawthorne, Vol. IV, pp. 1-36.

255 BLAND, Robert Lamar. "The Role of Folklore in
     Hawthorne's Literary Nationalism. " Ph. D. diss.,
     North Carolina (Greensboro), 1976. DA, 37 (1976),
     2868A.

256 BLISSERT, Albert Duryea. "The Function of Play and
     Possession in the Works of Nathaniel Hawthorne. "
     Ph. D. diss., Johns Hopkins, 1976. DA, 37 (1976),
     2177A.

257 BLODGETT, Harold. "Hawthorne as Poetry Critic:
     Six Unpublished Letters to Lewis Mansfield. "
     American Literature, 12 (May, 1940), 173-184.

258 BLOEMKER, Vernon L. "Allegiance as a Recurring
     Theme in the Writings of Nathaniel Hawthorne. "
     Ph. D. diss., Nebraska, 1966. DA, 27 (1967),
     3419A-3420A.

259 BLOOM, Edward A. The Order of Fiction. New
     York: Odyssey, 1964. "Wakefield, " pp. 227-231.

260 BLOW, Suzanne. "Pre-Raphaelite Allegory in The
     Marble Faun. " American Literature, 44 (1972), 122-
     127.

261 BLUESTEIN, Gene. "The Brotherhood of Sinners:
     Literary Calvinism. " New England Quarterly, 50
     (1977), 195-213.

262 BLYTH, Marion Dalrymple. "The Paganism of
     Nathaniel Hawthorne. " Ph. D. diss., Southern
     California, 1961. DA, 23 (1962), 1015-1016.

263 BOCHNER, Jay. "Life in a Picture Gallery: Things
     in The Portrait of a Lady and The Marble Faun. "
     Texas Studies in Literature and Language, 11 (1969),
     761-777.

264   BODE, Carl. "Hawthorne's Fanshawe: The Promising
      of Greatness." New England Quarterly, 23 (June,
      1950), 235-242. Reprinted in Bode, The Half-World
      of American Culture." Carbondale: Southern Illinois
      University Press, 1965, p. 85-94.

265   BODFREY, Sondra. "The Changing Vision of Evil in
      Hawthorne's Fiction." Ph. D. diss., City University
      of New York, 1976. DA, 36 (1976), 7421A.

266   BOEWE, Charles Ernest. "Heredity in the Writings of
      Nathaniel Hawthorne, Holmes, and Howells." Ph. D.
      diss., Wisconsin, 1955.

267   _____. "Rappaccini's Garden." American Literature,
      30 (March, 1958), 37-49.

268   _____. "Romanticism Bracketed." Emerson So-
      ciety Quarterly, 35 (1964), 7-10.

269   _____, and Murray G. Murphey. "Hester Prynne
      in History." American Literature, 32 (1960), 202-
      204.

270   BOHNER, Lina. "Brook Farm und Nathaniel Hawthornes
      Blithedale Romance." Ph. D. diss., Berlin, 1936.
      In German.

271   BONHAM, Sister M. Hilda. "Hawthorne's Symbols
      Sotto Voce." College English, 20 (January, 1959),
      184-186.

272   _____. "John Erskine's 'Hester of Troy.'" Papers
      of the Michigan Academy of Science, Arts, and Let-
      ters, 48 (1963), 665-674.

273   BOOTH, Edward Townsend. God Made the Country.
      New York: Knopf, 1946. "The New Adam and Eve
      in the Old Manse," pp. 202-219.

274   BORDEN, Caroline. "Bourgeois Social Relations in
      Nathaniel Hawthorne." Literature and Ideas, 10
      (1971), 21-28.

275   BORGES, Jorge Luis. "Nathaniel Hawthorne," in Bor-
      ges, Other Inquisitions, 1937-1952. Austin: Uni-
      versity of Texas Press, 1964, p. 47-65. Translated

by Ruth L. C. Simms.

276 _____. "Hawthorne." Les Lettres Nouvelles
(September-October, 1970), 69-90.

277 BOSWELL, Jackson Campbell. "Bosom Serpents Before
Hawthorne: Origin of a Symbol." English Language
Notes, 12 (1975), 279-287.

278 _____. "Another Generation of Vipers." English
Language Notes, 14 (1976), 124-131. Continuation of
1975 article.

279 BOUDREAU, Gordon V. "The Summons of Young
Goodman Brown." Greyfriar, 13 (1972), 15-24.

280 BOWDEN, Edwin T. The Dungeon of the Heart: Human Isolation and the American Novel. New York:
Macmillan, 1961. Hawthorne's The Scarlet Letter,
pp. 73-89.

281 BOWEN, James K. "More on Hawthorne and Keats."
American Transcendental Quarterly, 2 (1969), 12.

282 BOWERS, Fredson T. "Some Principles for Scholarly
Editions of Nineteenth-Century American Authors."
Studies in Bibliography (University of Virginia), 17
(1963), 223-228.

283 _____. "Hawthorne's Text," in Pearce, Roy Harvey, ed., Hawthorne's Centenary Essays (1964), pp.
401-425.

284 _____. "Practical Texts and Definitive Editing,"
in Charles Hinman and Fredson Bowers, Two Lec-
tures on Editing: Shakespeare and Hawthorne. Columbus: Ohio State University Press, 1969, pp. 21-
70.

285 _____. "Old Wine in New Bottles: Problems of
Machine Printing," in Bowers, Essays in Bibliography,
Text and Editing. Charlottesville: Published for
the Bibliographical Society of the University of Virginia by the University Press of Virginia, 1976, pp.
392-411.

286 _____, Introduction. The Scarlet Letter. Columbus:

Ohio State University Press, 1962. Centenary edition.

287 _____, textual ed. The Blithedale Romance and Fanshawe. General Introduction by Roy Harvey Pearce.
Columbus: Ohio State University Press, 1964.

288 _____, textual ed. The House of the Seven Gables.
General Introduction by William Charvat. Columbus:
Ohio State University Press, 1965.

289 _____, textual ed. True Stories from History and
Biography. Historical Introduction by Roy Harvey
Pearce. Columbus: Ohio State University Press,
1972.

290 _____, textual ed. A Wonder Book and Tanglewood
Tales. General Introduction by Roy Harvey Pearce.
Columbus: Ohio State University Press, 1972.

291 _____, textual ed. Twice-Told Tales. Historical
Introduction by J. Donald Crowley. Bibliographical
information by John Manning. Columbus: Ohio
State University Press, 1974.

292 _____, textual ed. Mosses from an Old Manse.
Historical Introduction by J. Donald Crowley. Columbus: Ohio State University Press, 1974.

293 _____, textual ed. The Snow-Image and Uncollected
Tales. Historical Introduction by J. Donald Crowley.
Textual commentary by L. Neal Smith; bibliographical
information by John Manning. Columbus: Ohio State
University Press, 1974.

294 BOWMAN, George William. "Hawthorne and Religion."
Ph.D. diss., Indiana, 1953. DA, 14 (1954), 2063-
2064.

295 BOYERS, Robert. Excursions: Selected Literary Essays. Port Washington, N.Y.: Kennikat, 1977.
Emerson, Melville, and Hawthorne, passim.

296 BOYET, Aggie. "Characterizing Phrases Used in Hawthorne's Fiction," in Tarpley, Fred, and Ann Moseley,
eds., Of Edsels and Marauders. Commerce, Tex.:
Names Institution Press, 1971, pp. 82-88.

297 BOYNTON, Percy H. Contemporary Americans. Chi-
     cago: University of Chicago Press, 1924. Haw-
     thorne, passim.

298 _____. More Contemporary Americans. Chicago:
     University of Chicago Press, 1927. Revised and re-
     printed as Literature and American Life. Chicago:
     University of Chicago Press, 1936. Hawthorne, pp.
     518-537.

299 BRACK, O. M., Jr. "The Centenary of Hawthorne
     Eight Years Later: A Review Article." Proof, 1
     (1971), 358-367.

300 BRADLEY, Sculley; R. C. Beatty; and E. H. Long; eds.
     The Scarlet Letter: An Annotated Text, Backgrounds
     and Sources, and Essays in Criticism. New York:
     Norton, 1962. Norton Critical Edition.

301 BRANCACCIO, Patrick. "The Ramble and the Pilgrim-
     age: A Critical Reading of Hawthorne's The Marble
     Faun." Ph. D. diss., Rutgers, 1967. DA, 28 (1968),
     4165A.

302 _____. "Hawthorne and the English Working Class."
     Nathaniel Hawthorne Journal, 4 (1974), 135-149.

303 BRAND, Howard. "Hawthorne on the Therapeutic Role."
     Journal of Abnormal and Social Psychology, 47
     (October, 1952), 856.

304 BRANT, Robert Louis. "Hawthorne and Marvell."
     American Literature, 30 (November, 1958), 366.

305 _____. "Nathaniel Hawthorne's Unfortunate Lovers."
     Ph. D. diss., University of Washington, 1960. DA,
     21 (1961), 3778-3779.

306 BRENNAN, Joseph X., and Seymour L. Gross. "The
     Origin of Hawthorne's Unpardonable Sin." Boston
     University Studies in English, 3 (Summer, 1957),
     123-129.

307 BRENZO, Richard. "Beatrice Rappaccini: A Victim
     of Male Love and Horror." American Literature,
     48 (1976), 152-164.

308 BRETZ, Joan Helene, O.S.U. "The Tragicomic _Eiron_ in Hawthorne and Poe: Dimensions of Irony Within Their Fiction." Ph.D. diss., St. Louis, 1975. _DA_, 37 (1976), 2178A.

309 BRICKELL, Herschel. "What Happened to the Short Story?" _Atlantic_, 178 (September, 1951), 74-76. Relates the contemporary short story to much in Hawthorne.

310 BRIDGE, Horatio. _Journal of an African Cruiser_, edited by Nathaniel Hawthorne. New York: Putnam's, 1853. Reprinted Detroit: Negro History, 1968.

311 _____. _Personal Recollections of Nathaniel Hawthorne._ New York: Harper and Brothers, 1893.

312 BRIDGEMAN, Richard. "As Hester Prynne Lay Dying." _English Language Notes_, 2 (June, 1965), 294-296. Refers to Faulkner's novel _As I Lay Dying._

313 BRIGGS, Thomas H., ed. _American Literature._ Boston: Houghton Mifflin, 1940. Hawthorne, p. 312 et passim.

314 BRILL, Lesley W. "Conflict and Accommodation in Hawthorne's 'The Artist of the Beautiful.'" _Studies in Short Fiction_, 12 (1975), 381-386.

315 BRODERICK, John C. "The Concord Club." _Notes and Queries_, 2 (February, 1955), 83.

316 BRODHEAD, Richard H. "Polysensum: Hawthorne, Melville, and the Form of the Novel." Ph.D. diss., Yale, 1972. _DA_, 33 (1973), 6863A.

317 _____. _Hawthorne, Melville, and the Novel._ Chicago: University of Chicago Press, 1976.

318 BRODSKY, Patricia P. "Fertile Fields and Poisoned Gardens: Sologub's Debt to Hoffmann, Pushkin, and Hawthorne." _Essays in Literature_ (Western Illinois University), 1 (1974), 96-108. Refers to Fedor Sologub, Russian author, 1863-1927.

319 BRODTKORB, Paul Jr. "Art Allegory in _The Marble Faun._" _PMLA_, 77 (June, 1962), 254-267.

320 _____. Ishmael's White World. New Haven: Yale
University Press, 1965. Hawthorne, passim.

321 BRODWIN, Stanley. "Hawthorne and the Function of
History: A Reading of 'Alice Doane's Appeal.' "
Nathaniel Hawthorne Journal, 4 (1974), 116-128.

322 BROES, Arthur T. "Journey into Moral Darkness:
'My Kinsman, Major Molineux' as Allegory." Nineteenth-Century Fiction, 19 (September, 1964), 171-
184.

323 BROMFIELD, Louis. "Hawthorne," in Macy, John A.,
ed., American Writers on American Literature.
New York: Liveright, 1931, pp. 97-104.

324 BROOKS, Cleanth, and Robert Penn Warren. Under-
standing Fiction. New York: Appleton-Century-
Crofts, 1943. "The Birthmark," pp. 103-106.

325 _____; John T. Purser; and Robert Penn Warren;
eds. An Approach to Literature. Revised edition,
New York: Appleton-Century-Crofts, 1947. The
Scarlet Letter, pp. 213-217.

326 BROOKS, Van Wyck. "Retreat from Utopia." Saturday Review of Literature, 13 (February 22, 1936),
3-4 et passim. Hawthorne and Brook Farm.

327 _____. "Hawthorne in Salem," in Brooks, The
Flowering of New England, 1815-1865. New York:
Dutton, 1937, pp. 217-235. Reprinted in Brooks,
Chilmark Miscellany. New York: Dutton, 1948.

328 _____. "Concord: 1840-1844," in Brooks, Flowering (1937), pp. 268-285.

329 _____. "West of Boston," in Brooks, Flowering
(1937), pp. 385-398.

330 _____. "Romantic Exiles," in Brooks, Flowering
(1937), pp. 471-489.

331 _____. "Nathaniel Hawthorne," in Brooks, Our
Literary Heritage: A Pictorial History of the Writer
in America. New York: Dutton, 1956, pp. 77-83.

332 _____. "Rome: Hawthorne," in Brooks, The Dream
of Arcadia: American Writers and Artists in Italy,
1760-1915. New York: Dutton, 1958, pp.135-144.

333/4 _____, ed. with Introduction. The House of the
Seven Gables. New York: Random House, 1950.
Modern Library Edition.

BROTHER, Joseph see JOSEPH, Brother

335 BROWN, Clarence A., ed., with a Foreword by Harry
Hayden Clark. The Achievement of American Criticism: Representative Selections from Three Hundred Years of American Criticism. New York:
Ronald, 1954. "The Aesthetics of Romanticism,"
pp.163-167.

336 BROWN, Dennis. "Literature and Existential Psycho-
analysis: 'My Kinsman, Major Molineux' and 'Young
Goodman Brown.' " Canadian Review of American
Studies, 4 (1973), 65-73. Discusses R.D. Laing and
Hawthorne.

337 BROWN, E. K. "Hawthorne, Melville, and 'Ethan
Brand.' " American Literature, 3 (March, 1931),
72-75.

338 BROWN, Merle Elliott. "The Structure and Significance
of The Marble Faun." Ph.D. diss., Michigan, 1953.
DA, 14 (1954), 1074-1075.

339 _____. "The Structure of The Marble Faun."
American Literature, 28 (November, 1956), 302-313.

340 BROWNE, Matthew (pseudonym of William Brightly
Rands). "Nathaniel Hawthorne." St. Paul's Magazine, 8 (May, 1871), 150-161. Reprinted in part in
Cohen, Benjamin Bernard, ed., Recognition (1969),
pp.119-120.

341 BROWNE, Nina Elizabeth. A Bibliography of Nathaniel
Hawthorne. Boston: Houghton Mifflin, 1905. Includes primary and secondary materials.

342 BROWNE, Ray Broadus. "The Oft-Told Twice-Told
Tales: Their Folklore Motifs." Southern Folklore
Quarterly, 22 (June, 1958), 69-85.

31   Brownell

343 BROWNELL, William C. "Hawthorne." Scribner's
     Magazine, 43 (January, 1908), 69-84.

344 _____. "Hawthorne," in American Prose Masters.
     New York: Scribner, 1909, pp. 63-130. New edition,
     1923. Reprinted Cambridge, Mass.: Belknap, 1963,
     pp. 45-89.

345 BROWNING, Preston M., Jr. "Hester Prynne as a
     Secular Saint." Midwest Quarterly, 13 (1972), 351-
     362.

346 BRUBAKER, B. R. "Hawthorne's Experiment in Popular
     Form: 'Mr. Higginbotham's Catastrophe.'" Southern
     Humanities Review, 7 (1973), 155-166.

347 BRUCCOLI, Matthew J. "Concealed Printings in Haw-
     thorne." Papers of the Bibliographical Society of
     America, 57 (1963), 42-49.

348 _____. "Negative Evidence About 'The Celestial
     Railroad.'" Papers of the Bibliographical Society
     of America, 58 (1964), 290-292.

349 _____. "Hawthorne as a Collector's Item, 1885-
     1924," in Pearce, Roy Harvey, ed., Centenary
     Essays (1964), pp. 387-400.

350 _____. "A Sophisticated Copy of The House of the
     Seven Gables." Papers of the Bibliographical Society
     of America, 59 (1965), 438-439.

351 _____. "Notes on the Destruction of The Scarlet
     Letter Manuscript." Studies in Bibliography, 20
     (1967), 257-259.

352 _____, ed. The Chief Glory of Every People:
     Essays on Classic American Writers. Carbondale:
     Southern Illinois University Press, 1973. "Con-
     sistency in the Mind and Work of Hawthorne," by
     Arlin Turner, pp. 97-116.

353 _____, and C.E. Frazer Clark, Jr., eds. Pages:
     The World of Books, Writers, and Writing, Vol. I.
     Detroit: Gale, 1976. Contains the first publication
     of a letter by Hawthorne and a photograph, p. 231.

354 _____; C. E. Frazer Clark, Jr.; Richard Layman;
and Benjamin Franklin V.; eds. First Printings of
American Authors: Contributions Toward Descriptive
Checklists, Vol. I. Detroit: Gale, 1977. Pro-
jected 4-volume set: Vols. II, III, in 1978; Vol.
IV in 1979.

355 BRUMBAUGH, Thomas B. "Concerning Nathaniel Hawthorne and Art as Magic." American Imago, 11
(1954), 399-405.

356 _____. "On Horatio and Richard Greenough: A
Defense of Neo-Classicism in America." American
Quarterly, 12 (Fall, 1960), 414-417. Hawthorne,
passim.

357 BRUMM, Ursula. American Thought and Religious
Typology. Translated by John Hoaglund. New
Brunswick, N.J.: Rutgers University Press, 1970.
"Nathaniel Hawthorne: The Problem of Allegory,"
pp. 111-128; and "Nathaniel Hawthorne: The Cyclical
View of History," pp. 128-161.

358 _____. "Hawthorne's 'The Custom House' and the
Problem of Point of View in Historical Fiction."
Anglia (West Germany), 93 (1975), 391-412.

359 BUCKINGHAM, Leroy H. "Hawthorne and the British
Income Tax." American Literature, 11 (January,
1940), 451-453.

360 BUDZ, Judith Kaufman. "Nathaniel Hawthorne and the
Visual Arts." Ph. D. diss., Northwestern, 1973.
DA, 34 (1974), 4245A-4246A.

361 _____. "Cherubs and Humblebees: Nathaniel Hawthorne and the Visual Arts." Criticism, 17 (1975),
168-181.

362 BUITENHUIS, Peter. "Henry James on Hawthorne."
New England Quarterly, 32 (June, 1959), 207-225.

363 BUNGE, Nancy Liddell. "A Thematic Analysis of
Forty Short Stories by Hawthorne." Ph. D. diss.,
Wisconsin, 1970. DA, 31 (1971), 4707A.

364 _____. "Unreliable Artist-Narrators in Hawthorne's

Short Stories." Studies in Short Fiction, 14 (1977),
145-150.

365 BURBANK, R., and J.B. Moore, eds. The Literature
of the American Renaissance. Columbus: Ohio
State University Press, 1969.

366 BURDETT, Osbert. "Nathaniel Hawthorne," in Burdett,
Critical Essays. London: Faber and Gwyer, 1925,
pp. 7-22.

367 BURHANS, Clinton S., Jr. "Hawthorne's Mind and Art
in 'The Hollow of the Three Hills.'" Journal of
English and Germanic Philology, 60 (April, 1961),
286-295.

368 BURKE, Christine. "Hawthorne's Vision of the Wilderness." Graduate English Papers (Arizona), 6 (1974),
8-16.

369 BURKE, Kenneth. " 'Ethan Brand': A Preparatory Investigation." Hopkins Review, 5 (Winter, 1952), 45-
65.

370 BURNHAM, Philip E. "Hawthorne's Fanshawe and
Bowdoin College." Essex Institute Historical Collections, 80 (April, 1944), 131-138.

371 BURNS, Rex S. "Hawthorne's Romance of Traditional
Success." Texas Studies in Literature and Language,
12 (1970), 443-454. Refers to The House of the
Seven Gables.

372 _____. Success in America: The Yeoman Dream
and the Industrial Revolution. Amherst: University
of Massachusetts Press, 1976. Hawthorne, passim.

373 BURNS, Thomas S. " 'A More Life-Like Warmth':
Reality in Hawthorne's Tales." Ph.D. diss., Ohio,
1973. DA, 35 (1974), 2932A.

374 BURRESS, Lee A., Jr. "Hawthorne's Alternate Choice
as a Fictional Device." Wisconsin Studies in Literature (Oshkosh), 4 (1967), 1-17.

375 BURTON, K. "Rose of All Hawthorne's." Catholic
World, 142 (February, 1936), 562-566.

376 BURTON, Richard. "Hawthorne," in Literary Leaders of
    America. New York: Scribner, 1904; reissued
    1909, pp. 99-134.

377 _____. "American Contribution," in Masters of the
    English Novel. New York: Holt, 1909, pp. 313-331.

378 BUSCAROLI, Piero. "Hawthorne's Italy." L'Italia
    (Rome), 205 (English edition, 1965), 26-39.

379 BUSH, Sargent, Jr. "The Relevance of Puritanism to
    Major Themes in Hawthorne's Fiction." Ph.D. diss.,
    State University of Iowa, 1967. DA, 28 (1968),
    2677A.

380 _____. "Bosom Serpents before Hawthorne: The
    Origins of a Symbol." American Literature, 43
    (1971), 181-199.

381 _____. " 'Peter Goldthwaite's Treasure' and The
    House of the Seven Gables." Emerson Society Quar-
    terly 62 (1971), 35-38.

382 BUTLER, John F. Exercises in Literary Understand-
    ing. Chicago: Scott, Foresman, 1956. The Scarlet
    Letter, pp. 18-22.

383 BYERS, John R., Jr. "The House of the Seven Gables
    and 'The Daughters of Dr. Byles': A Probable
    Source." PMLA, 89 (1974), 174-177.

384 _____. "The Geography and Framework of Haw-
    thorne's 'Roger Malvin's Burial.'" Tennessee Studies
    in Literature, 21 (1976), 11-20.

385 CABLE, L.L. "Old Salem and the Scarlet Letter."
    Bookman, 26 (December, 1907), 398-403.

386 CADY, Edwin Harrison. "The Wizard Hand: Hawthorne,
    1864-1900," in Pearce, Roy Harvey, ed., Centenary
    Essays (1964), pp. 317-334. Reprinted in Cady, The
    Light of Common Day: Realism in American Fiction.
    Bloomington: Indiana University Press, 1971, pp.
    120-137.

387 _____. "Three Sensibilities: Romancer, Realist,

Naturalist," in Cady, The Light of Common Day
(1971), pp. 23-52.

388 _____, ed. with Introduction. The Scarlet Letter.
Columbus, Ohio: Merrill, 1969. Merrill Edition.

389 _____; Frederick J. Hoffman; and Roy Harvey
Pearce; eds. The Growth of American Literature:
A Critical and Historical Survey, 2 vols. New York:
American Book, 1956. The Scarlet Letter, Vol. I,
pp. 459-466.

390 CAHN, Edmund. "Hawthorne's Set of the State Trials."
Times Literary Supplement (London), 7 (October,
1955), 589.

391 CAHOON, Herbert. "Some Manuscripts of Concord
Authors." Thoreau Society Bulletin, 92 (Summer,
1965), 2-3.

392 _____; Thomas V. Lange; and Charles Ryskamp.
American Literary Autographs: From Washington
Irving to Henry James. New York: Dover, 1977.
Hawthorne, pp. 26-28.

393 CAIRNS, William B. A History of American Literature.
New York and London: Oxford University Press,
1912. Hawthorne, pp. 298-320.

394 CALDWELL, Wayne Troy. "The Emblem Tradition
and the Symbolic Mode: Clothing Imagery in The
House of the Seven Gables." Emerson Society
Quarterly, 19 (1973), 32-42.

395 CALHOUN, Thomas O. "Hawthorne's Gothic: An
Approach to the Four Last Fragments: 'The Ancestral Footstep,' Dr. Grimshawe's Secret, The
Dolliver Romance, and Septimius Felton." Genre,
3 (1970), 229-241.

396 CALLOW, James T., and Robert J. Reilly. Guide to
American Literature from Its Beginnings Through
Walt Whitman. New York: Barnes and Noble, 1976.
Contains long bibliography.

397 CAMERON, Kenneth Walter. "Genesis of Hawthorne's
'The Ambitious Guest.'" Historiographer of the

Episcopal Diocese of Connecticut, 14 (December, 1955), 2-36. Also published as book, Hartford, Conn.: Thistle, 1955.

398 _____. "Privileges at the Boston Athenaeum: Hawthorne, Miss Peabody, and Sampson Reed." Emerson Society Quarterly, 6 (1957), 21. Hereafter referred to as ESQ in Cameron listing.

399 _____. "Background of Hawthorne's 'The Canterbury Pilgrims.'" ESQ 13 (1958), 41-45-

400 _____. "Hawthorne in Early Newspapers." ESQ, 13 (1958), 45.

401 _____. "Arthur Cleveland Coxe on Hawthorne: An Anglican Estimate in 1851." ESQ, 13 (1958), 51-64.

402 _____. "New Light on Hawthorne's Removal from the Customs House." ESQ, 23 (1961), 2-5.

403 _____. "Notes on Hawthorne's Manuscripts." ESQ, 25 (1961), 35-36.

404 _____. "Prints of American Authors." ESQ, 28 (1962), 77-106. Includes Hawthorne.

405 _____. "Inventory of Hawthorne's Manuscripts, Part I." ESQ, 29 (1962), 5-20.

406 _____. "Twenty Pictures of Hawthorne." ESQ, 39 (1965), 2-12.

407 _____. Hawthorne Index to Themes, Motifs, Topics, etc. in recent Criticism. Hartford, Conn.: Transcendental, 1968. Based on Buford Jones, Checklist of Hawthorne Criticism, 1951-1966.

408 _____. "Literary News in American Renaissance Newspapers." American Transcendental Quarterly, 20 Supplement (1973), 13-36. Referred to as ATQ in Cameron listings.

409 _____. "An Early Lending Library in Hawthorne's Salem." ATQ, 20 Supplement (1973), 37-50.

410 _____. "Hawthorne Memorabilia in the National

Records. " ATQ, 20 Supplement (1973), 144-153.

411 _____. "Thoreau's Schoolmate, Alfred Munroe,
Remembers Concord. " ATQ, 36 (1977), 10-38.
Hawthorne, passim.

412 _____, ed. Hawthorne Among His Contemporaries.
Hartford, Conn.: Transcendental, 1968. Reprinted
material.

413 _____, ed. The Massachusetts Lyceum During the
American Renaissance: Materials for the Study of
the Oral Tradition in American Letters: Emerson,
Thoreau, Hawthorne, and Other New England Lec-
turers. Hartford, Conn.: Transcendental, 1969.
Reprinted as Emerson and Thoreau Speak: Lecturing
in Concord and Lincoln During the American Renaissance. Hartford, Conn.: Transcendental, 1972.

414 CAMPBELL, Donald Allen. "A Critical Analysis of
Nathaniel Hawthorne's The Blithedale Romance. "
Ph.D. diss., Yale, 1960.

415 _____. A Critical Analysis of Nathaniel Hawthorne's
The Blithedale Romance. New Haven: Yale University Press, 1960.

416 CAMPBELL, Harry Modean. "Freudianism, American
Romanticism, and 'Young Goodman Brown.'" CEA
Critic, 33 (1971), 3-6.

417 CANADAY, Nicholas, Jr. "Ironic Humor as Defense
in The Scarlet Letter. " South Central Bulletin, 21
(Winter, 1961), 17-18.

418 _____. "Hawthorne's Minister and the Veiling Deception of Self. " Studies in Short Fiction, 4 (1967),
135-142.

419 _____. " 'Some Sweet Moral Blossom': A Note on
Hawthorne's Rose. " Papers on Language and Liter-
ature, 3 (1967), 186-187. Canto 29 of Dante's
Purgatorio as source for Chapter 1, The Scarlet
Letter.

420 _____. "Hawthorne's The Scarlet Letter. " Explicator, 28 (1969), item 39.

Canaday   38

421 _____. "Community and Identity at Blithedale."
    South Atlantic Quarterly, 71 (1972), 30-39.

422 CANBY, Henry Seidel. "Hawthorne and Melville," in
    Classic Americans: Eminent American Writers from
    Irving to Whitman. New York: Harcourt, Brace,
    1931. Reprinted New York: Russell and Russell,
    1959, pp. 226-262.

423 CANTWELL, Robert. Nathaniel Hawthorne: The
    American Years. New York: Rinehart, 1948.
    Life to 1850.

424 _____. "Hawthorne and Delia Bacon." American
    Quarterly, 1 (Winter, 1949), 343-360.

425 CARGAS, Harry J. "The Arc of Rebirth in 'Young
    Goodman Brown.'" New Laurel Review, 4 (1975),
    5-7. Compares story with Coleridge, "The Ancient
    Mariner."

426 CARGILL, Oscar. "Nemesis and Nathaniel Hawthorne."
    PMLA, 52 (September, 1937), 848-862. Hawthorne's
    dislike for Margaret Fuller.

427 _____. Intellectual America: Ideas on the March.
    New York: Macmillan, 1941. Hawthorne, passim.

428 CARLETON, William G. "Hawthorne Discovers the
    English." Yale Review, 53 (Spring, 1964), 395-414.
    Reprinted in Carleton, Technology and Humanism.
    Nashville, Tenn.: Vanderbilt University Press, 1970,
    pp. 191-209.

429 CARLISLE, Kathryn. "Wit and Humor in Nathaniel
    Hawthorne." Bardic Review, 3 (April, 1949), 86-93.

430 CARLSON, Constance H. "Wit and Irony in Hawthorne's
    The House of the Seven Gables," in Sprague, Richard
    S., ed., A Handful of Spice: A Miscellany of Maine
    Literature and History. Orono: University of Maine
    Press, 1968, pp. 159-168.

431 CARLSON, Patricia Ann. "Hawthorne's Functional
    Settings: A Study of Artistic Method." Ph.D. diss.,
    Duke, 1973. DA, 34 (1974), 7183A.

432 _____. "National Typology and Hawthorne's Historical Allegory." CEA Critic, 37 (1974), 11-13.

433 _____. "The Function of the Lamp in Hawthorne's
'The Wives of the Dead.'" South Atlantic Bulletin,
40 (1975), 62-64.

434 _____. "Image and Structure in Hawthorne's 'Roger
Malvin's Burial.'" South Atlantic Bulletin, 41
(1976), 3-9.

435 _____. Hawthorne's Functional Settings: A Study
of Artistic Method. Amsterdam: Editions Rodolphi;
Atlantic Highlands, N.J.: Humanities, 1977.

436 CARLTON, W.N.C. "Hawthorne's First Book--
Fanshawe: A Tale." American Collector, 4 (June,
1927), 82-86.

437 CARMAN, Bliss. Nathaniel Hawthorne. Palo Alto,
Calif.: N. Van Patten, 1929.

438 CARNOCHAN, W.B. "'The Minister's Black Veil':
Symbol, Meaning, and the Context of Hawthorne's
Art." Nineteenth-Century Fiction, 24 (1969), 182-
192.

439 CARPENTER, Frederic I. "Puritans Preferred
Blondes: The Heroines of Melville and Hawthorne."
New England Quarterly, 9 (June, 1936), 253-272.

440 _____. "Scarlet A Minus." College English, 5
(January, 1944), 173-180. Reprinted in Carpenter,
American Literature and the Dream. New York:
Philosophical Library, 1956, pp.63-72.

441 _____. "Hester, the Heretic." College English,
13 (May, 1952), 457-458. Response to Darrell Abel,
March, 1952.

442 _____. "'The American Myth': Paradise (To Be)
Regained." PMLA, 74 (December, 1959), 599-606.

443 CARPENTER, Nan Cooke. "Louisa May Alcott and
'Thoreau's Flute': Two Letters." Huntington Library Quarterly, 24 (1960), 71-74.

444 CARPENTER, Richard C. "Hawthorne's Scarlet Bean Flowers." University of Kansas City Review, 30 (October, 1963), 65-71. Discusses The House of the Seven Gables.

445 _____. "Hawthorne's Polar Explorations." Nineteenth-Century Fiction, 24 (1969), 45-56. Discusses "Young Goodman Brown" and "My Kinsman, Major Molineux."

446 CARTER, Everett. The American Idea: The Literary Response to American Optimism. Chapel Hill: University of North Carolina Press, 1977. Hawthorne, pp. 134-160 et passim.

447 CARUTHERS, Clifford M. "The 'Povera Picciola' and The Scarlet Letter." Papers on Language and Literature, 7 (Winter, 1971), 90-94. Refers to a novel by Joseph Xavier Boniface Saintine, published 1836.

448 CARY, Elizabeth Luther. "Hawthorne and Emerson." Critic, 45 (July, 1904), 25-27.

449 CASSERES, Benjamin de. "Hawthorne: Emperor of Shadows." Critic, 45 (July, 1904), 37-45. Reprinted in Casseres, Forty Immortals. New York: Lawren, 1926, pp. 303-310.

450 CASSILL, R. V. "That Blue-Eyed Darling Nathaniel." Horizon, 8 (Summer, 1966), 32-39.

451 CASSON, Allan. "The Scarlet Letter and Adam Bede." Victorian Newsletter, 20 (Fall, 1961), 18-19.

452 CATE, Herma R. "Shakers in American Fiction." Tennessee Folklore Society Bulletin, 41 (1975), 19-24.

453 CATHCART, Wallace Hugh. Bibliography of the Works of Nathaniel Hawthorne. Cleveland: World, for the Rowfant Club, 1905.

454 CATHER, Willa. "The Novel Démeublé," in Cather, On Writing. New York: Knopf, 1949. The Scarlet Letter, pp. 35-43.

455 CAVANAUGH, Miriam Katherine. "The Romantic Hero

in Byron, Hawthorne, and Melville." Ph.D. diss.,
Massachusetts, 1978. <u>DA</u>, 39 (1978), 1563A.

456   CECIL, L. Moffitt. "Hawthorne's Optical Device."
<u>American Quarterly</u>, 15 (Spring, 1963), 76-84.

457   _____. "Symbolic Patterns in <u>The Yemassee</u>."
<u>American Literature</u>, 35 (January, 1964), 510-514.
Relates novel by Simms to Hawthorne.

458   _____. "<u>The Scarlet Letter</u>: A Puritan Love
Story," in Walker, W.E., and R.L. Walker, eds.,
<u>Reality and Myth: Essays in American Literature
in Memory of Richard Croom Beatty.</u> Nashville,
Tenn.: Vanderbilt University Press, 1964, pp. 52-59.

459   CERVO, Nathan A. "The Gargouille Anti-Hero: Victim of Christian Satire." <u>Renascence</u>, 22 (1970),
69-77. Discusses "My Kinsman, Major Molineux."

460   CHAMBERLAIN, Joseph Chester. <u>First Editions of
the Works of Nathaniel Hawthorne.</u> New York:
Anderson, 1905.

461   _____. <u>First Editions of the Works of American
Authors.</u> New York: Anderson, 1909.

462   CHAMBERS, Jane. "Two Legends of Temperance:
Spenser's and Hawthorne's." <u>Emerson Society
Quarterly</u>, 20 (1974), 275-279. Discusses "The
Birthmark."

463   CHANDLER, Elizabeth Lathrop. "A Study of the
Sources of the Tales and Romances Written by
Nathaniel Hawthorne Before 1853." <u>Smith College
Studies in Modern Languages</u> (Northampton, Mass.),
7 (July, 1926), 1-64.

464   _____, ed. "Hawthorne's <u>Spectator</u>." <u>New England
Quarterly</u>, 4 (April, 1931), 288-330. Reprint of a
manuscript weekly of verse and prose in 1820.

465   CHARNEY, Maurice. "Hawthorne and Sidney's <u>Ar-
cadia</u>." <u>Notes and Queries</u>, 7 (July, 1960), 264-265.

466   _____. "Hawthorne and the Gothic Style." <u>New
England Quarterly</u>, 34 (March, 1961), 36-49.

467 CHARVAT, William, ed. with Introduction. The Scarlet
     Letter. Boston: Houghton Mifflin, 1963. River-
     side Edition.

468 _____; Roy Harvey Pearce; Claude M. Simpson;
     Matthew J. Bruccoli; J. Donald Crowley; Fredson
     Bowers; Edward H. Davidson; and L. Neal Smith;
     eds.; with bibliography by John Manning. The
     Centenary Edition of the Works of Nathaniel Haw-
     thorne. Columbus: Ohio State University Press,
     1962-1977, 13 vols. to date, as follows:
        Vol. I, The Scarlet Letter (1962)
        Vol. II, The House of the Seven Gables (1965)
        Vol. III, The Blithedale Romance and Fanshawe
           (1964)
        Vol. IV, The Marble Faun (1968)
        Vol. V, Our Old Home: A Series of English
           Sketches (1970)
        Vol. VI, True Stories from History and Biography
           (1972)
        Vol. VII, The Wonder Book and Tanglewood Tales
           (1972)
        Vol. VIII, The American Notebooks (1972)
        Vol. IX, Twice-Told Tales (1974)
        Vol. X, Mosses from an Old Manse (1974)
        Vol. XI, The Snow Image and Uncollected Tales
           (1974)
        Vol. XII, The American Claimant Manuscripts
           (1977)
        Vol. XIII, The Elixir of Life Manuscripts (1977)

     These volumes are listed elsewhere, under the
     names of the individual editors.

469 CHASE, Richard. "The Progressive Hawthorne."
     Partisan Review, 16 (January, 1949), 96-100.

470 _____. The American Novel and Its Tradition.
     Garden City, N.Y.: Doubleday/Anchor, 1957.
     "Hawthorne and the Twilight of Romance," pp.67-87.

471 CHAUDHRY, Ghulam Ali. "Dickens and Hawthorne."
     Essex Institute Historical Collections, 100 (October,
     1964), 256-273.

472 CHERRY, Fannye N. "The Sources of Hawthorne's
     'Young Goodman Brown.'" American Literature, 5

(January, 1934), 342-348. Cervantes and Bacon.

473 _____. "A Note on the Source of Hawthorne's 'Lady Eleanore's Mantle.' " American Literature, 6 (January, 1935), 437-439.

474 CHISHOLM, Richard M. "The Use of Gothic Materials in Hawthorne's Mature Romances." Ph.D. diss., Columbia, 1969. DA, 31 (1970), 382A.

475 CHISLETT, W.A. "A Henry James Paragraph on Hawthorne," in Chislett, Moderns and Near Moderns. New York: Grafton, 1928, pp. 107-108.

476 CHRISTOPHER, J.R. "The Marble Faun: A Whydunit." The Armchair Dectective, 11 (1978), 78.

477 CHRISTY, Wallace McVay. "The Shock of Recognition: A Psycho-Literary Study of Hawthorne's Influence on Melville's Short Fiction." Ph.D. diss., Brown, 1970. DA, 31 (1971), 6543A-6544A.

478 CHUBB, E.W. "Curtis and Hawthorne at the Brook Farm," in Chubb, Stories of Authors. New York: McClurg, 1914, pp. 266-269.

479 _____. "Hawthorne and The Scarlet Letter," in Chubb, Stories of Authors (1914), pp. 270-278.

480 CIFELLI, Edward. "Hawthorne and the Italian." Studi Americani, 14 (1968), 87-96.

481 _____. "Hawthorne as Humorist: A Look at Fanshawe." CEA Critic, 38 (1976), 11-17.

482 CLARK, C.E. Frazer, Jr. "Posthumous Papers of a Decapitated Surveyer: The Scarlet Letter in the Salem Press." Studies in the Novel, 2 (1970), 395-419.

483 _____. "Hawthorne's First Appearance in England." Certified Editions of American Authors Newsletter, 3 (1970), 10-11.

484 _____. Checklist of Hawthorne Criticism. Columbus, Ohio: Merrill, 1970. Merrill Checklist Series.

485   . " 'The Interrupted Nuptials': A Question of
Attribution." Nathaniel Hawthorne Journal, 1 (1971),
49-66. Article and reprint of 1827 story.

486   . "Census of Nathaniel Hawthorne Letters,
Part I, 1813-1849." Nathaniel Hawthorne Journal,
1 (1971), 257-282.

487   . "Hawthorne and the Pirates." Proof, 1
(1971), 90-121. The Blithedale Romance; includes
17 plates and appendix.

488   . Nathaniel Hawthorne, Consul of the United
States of America, Liverpool, England, 1853-1857:
An Exhibition. Liverpool: Nathaniel Hawthorne
Journal, 1971. 16p. pamphlet.

489   . Hawthorne at Auction: 1894-1971. Appendix by Matthew J. Bruccoli. Detroit: Gale, 1972.
419pp.

490   . "Unexplored Areas of Hawthorne Bibliography." Nathaniel Hawthorne Journal, 2 (1972),
47-51. Hawthorne in American newspapers; Hawthorne in American periodicals; Hawthorne in the
English mass media.

491   . "New Light on the Editing of the 1842
Edition of Twice-Told Tales: Discovery of a Family
Copy of the 1833 Token Annotated by Hawthorne."
Nathaniel Hawthorne Journal, 2 (1972), 91-103.

492   . "An Exhibition Commemorating Nathaniel
Hawthorne in England: Liverpool, England, July
15-20, 1971." Nathaniel Hawthorne Journal, 2
(1972), 203-218.

493   . "House-Hunting with Hawthorne: Hawthorne
to William B. Pike." Nathaniel Hawthorne Journal,
3 (1973), 3-7.

494   . "First and Second Printings of The Blithedale Romance Distinguished." Nathaniel Hawthorne
Journal, 3 (1973), 172-176.

495   . "Census of Nathaniel Hawthorne Letters,
Part II, 1850-1864." Nathaniel Hawthorne Journal,

3 (1973), 202-252.   407 letters in Part I; 233 letters
in Part II.

496 _____. "The Scarlet Letter: A 'Fourteen-Mile
Long Story.'" Nathaniel Hawthorne Journal, 5 (1975),
2-4. A previously unpublished Hawthorne letter to
Miss L. Jewett.

497 _____. "Primary Bibliography [of Hawthorne]. "
Hawthorne Society Newsletter, 1 (1975), 1.

498 _____. "Hawthorne to John Appleton: An Unpublished Letter. " Nathaniel Hawthorne Journal, 6
(1976), 14-16.

499 _____. "A Lost Miniature of Hawthorne. " Nathaniel
Hawthorne Journal, 6 (1976), 80-85.

500 _____. "Origins of the American Renaissance:
A Front-Page Story, " in Myerson, ed., Studies:
1977 (1978), pp. 155-164.

501 _____. Nathaniel Hawthorne: A Descriptive Bibliography. Pittsburgh: University of Pittsburgh Press,
1978. Studies primary source material.

502 _____, ed. Longfellow, Hawthorne, and "Evangeline"; A Letter from Henry Wadsworth Longfellow,
November 29, 1847, to Nathaniel Hawthorne. Brunswick, Maine: Bowdoin College Press, 1966. Pamphlet.

503 _____, ed. and publisher; Matthew J. Bruccoli, con-
sulting editor. The Nathaniel Hawthorne Journal, an
annual volume, 1971 to present. Published by NCR
Microcard Editions, Washington, D. C.

504 _____, ed. The Love Letters of Nathaniel Hawthorne. Reprinted in one volume from a 2-volume
set printed in 1907. Washington, D. C.: NCR Microcard Editions, 1972. See listing under Field, Roswell, editor.

505 _____, ed. Letters of Hawthorne to William D.
Ticknor. Reprinted in one volume from a private
2-volume issue in 1910. Washington, D. C.: NCR
Microcard Editions, 1972. See listing under Ticknor,
William D., editor.

506   CLARK, Harry Hayden. "Early American Criticism,"
      in Stovall, Floyd. ed., The Development of American
      Literary Criticism. Chapel Hill: University of
      North Carolina Press, 1955. Hawthorne, passim.

507   _____. "Hawthorne's Literary and Aesthetic Doc-
      trines as Embodied in His Tales." Transactions
      of the Wisconsin Academy of Sciences, Arts, and
      Letters, 50 (1961), 251-275.

508   _____. "Hawthorne: Tradition versus Innovation,"
      in La France, Marston, ed., Patterns of Commit-
      ment in American Literature. Toronto: University
      of Toronto Press, 1967, pp. 19-37.

509   CLARK, James W., Jr. "Hawthorne's Use of Evidence
      in 'Young Goodman Brown.'" Essex Institute His-
      torical Collections, 111 (1975), 12-34.

510   CLARK, Marsden J. "The Wages of Sin in Hawthorne."
      Brigham Young University Studies, 1 (Winter, 1959),
      21-36.

511   CLARK, Sylvia. "The Hens in The House of the Seven
      Gables." Journal of Education, 32 (August 14, 1890),
      101-102.

512   CLARKE, Austin. "The Impuritans: A Play in One
      Act Freely Adapted from the Short Story 'Young
      Goodman Brown' by Nathaniel Hawthorne." Irish
      University Review (Dublin), 1 (1970), 131-148.

513   CLARKE, Helen Archibald. Hawthorne's Country.
      New York: Baker and Taylor, 1910.

514   CLAY, Edward Miller. "Nathaniel Hawthorne's Symbol-
      ism as a Synthesis of Permanence and Change."
      Ph.D. diss., Missouri, 1965. DA, 27 (1966),
      1815A-1816A.

515   _____. "The 'Dominating Symbol' in Hawthorne's
      Last Phase." American Literature, 39 (1968), 506-
      516.

516   CLAYTON, Lawrence. "'Lady Eleanore's Mantle':
      A Metaphysical Key to Hawthorne's 'Legends of the
      Province House.'" English Language Notes, 9 (1971),

47   Clayton

49-51.

517 CLEARY, Barbara Ann Rathman. "The Scarlet Amulet:
     The Woman's Limitations as Redeemer in Hawthorne's
     Major Fiction." Ph.D. diss., Nebraska (Lincoln),
     1975. DA, 36 (1976), 5293A-5294A.

518 CLINE, John. "Nathaniel Hawthorne and the Bible."
     Ph.D. diss., Duke, 1948.

519 CLIVE, Geoffrey. "The Teleological Suspension of the
     Ethical in Nineteenth-Century Literature." Journal
     of Religion, 34 (April, 1954), 75-87. Hawthorne,
     passim.

520 COALE, Samuel. "Frederic and Hawthorne: The
     Romantic Roots of Naturalism." American Literature,
     48 (1976), 29-45.

521 _____. "Hawthorne's American Notebooks: Con-
     tours of a Haunted Mind." Nathaniel Hawthorne
     Journal, 6 (1976), 257-268.

522 COANDA, Richard Joseph. "Hawthorne on the Imagi-
     nation." Ph.D. diss., Wisconsin, 1959. DA, 21
     (1960), 1563.

523 _____. "Hawthorne's Scarlet Alphabet." Renascence,
     19 (Spring, 1967), 161-166. Hester, Arthur, Roger,
     and Pearl.

524 COBB, Robert Paul. "Society versus Solitude: Studies
     in Ralph Waldo Emerson, Thoreau, Hawthorne, and
     Whitman." Ph.D. diss., Michigan, 1955. DA, 15
     (1955), 1396.

525 COCHRAN, Robert W. "Hawthorne's Choice: The
     Veil or the Jaundiced Eye." College English, 23
     (February, 1962), 342-346. "Young Goodman Brown"
     and "The Minister's Black Veil."

526 COFFEE, Jessie A. "Margaret Fuller as Zenobia in
     The Blithedale Romance," in Kobler, J.F., ed.,
     Proceedings of the Conference of College Teachers
     of English of Texas. Denton: Conference of College
     Teachers of English Publication, 1973, pp. 23-27.

527 COFFEY, Dennis Graham. "The Paradigm of Dis-
     solving Form in Hawthorne's Short Stories." Ph. D.
     diss., State University of New York (Binghamton),
     1975. DA, 36 (1975), 1500A-1501A.

528 _____. "Hawthorne's 'Alice Doane's Appeal': The
     Artist Absolved." Emerson Society Quarterly, 21
     (1975).

529 COHEN, Benjamin Bernard. "The Gray Champion."
     Indiana University Folio, 13 (February, 1948), 11-
     12.

530 _____. "The Composition of Hawthorne's 'The
     Duston Family.'" New England Quarterly, 21 (June
     1948), 236-242.

531 _____. "Hawthorne and Legends." Hoosier Folk-
     lore, 7 (September, 1948), 94-95.

532 _____. "Eternal Truth: A Study of Nathaniel Haw-
     thorne's Philosophy." Ph. D. diss., Indiana, 1950.

533 _____. "A New Critical Approach to the Works of
     Hawthorne." Wayne English Remembrancer, 4
     (June, 1950), 43-47.

534 _____. "The Sources of 'The Ambitious Guest.'"
     Boston Public Library Quarterly, 4 (October, 1952),
     221-224.

535 _____. "Hawthorne's 'Mrs. Bullfrog' and The Ram-
     bler." Philological Quarterly, 32 (October, 1953),
     382-387. Hawthorne's debt to Johnson.

536 _____. "Hawthorne and Parley's Universal History."
     Papers of the Bibliographical Society of America,
     48 (1954), 77-90.

537 _____. "Emerson's 'The Young American' and
     Hawthorne's 'The Intelligence Office.'" American
     Literature, 26 (March, 1954), 32-43.

538 _____. "Edward Everett and Hawthorne's Removal
     from the Salem Custom House." American Litera-
     ture, 27 (May, 1955), 245-249.

539 _____. "Henry James and the Hawthorne Centennial."
      Essex Institute Historical Collections, 92 (July, 1956),
      279-283.

540 _____. "Emerson and Hawthorne on England."
      Boston Public Library Quarterly, 9 (April, 1957),
      73-85.

541 _____. "Paradise Lost and 'Young Goodman Brown.'"
      Essex Institute Historical Collections, 94 (July, 1958),
      282-296.

542 _____. " 'The Ambitious Guest': From Fact to
      Fiction," in Writing About Literature. Chicago:
      Scott, Foresman, 1963, pp. 104-109. Revised version
      of 1952 article.

543 _____. "Deodat Lawson's Christ's Fidelity and Haw-
      thorne's 'Young Goodman Brown.' " Essex Institute
      Historical Collections, 104 (1968), 349-370.

544 _____. Guide to Nathaniel Hawthorne. Columbus,
      Ohio: Merrill, 1970.

545 _____. "Hawthorne's Library: An Approach to the
      Man and His Mind." Nathaniel Hawthorne Journal,
      1 (1971), 125-139.

546 _____, ed. with Preface. The Recognition of
      Nathaniel Hawthorne: Selected Criticism Since 1828.
      Ann Arbor: University of Michigan Press, 1969.

547 COHEN, Hennig. " 'Heterogeny'--A Word Hawthorne
      Made." American Notes and Queries, 10 (1972),
      117.

548 _____. "A Comic Mode of the Romantic Imagination:
      Poe, Hawthorne, Melville," in Rubin, Louis, ed.,
      The Comic Imagination in American Literature. New
      Brunswick, N.J.: Rutgers University Press, 1973.

549 _____. "Hawthorne's Israel Potter." Extracts, 14
      (1973), 9-10.

550 _____, ed. The American Culture: Approaches to
      the Study of the United States. Boston: Houghton

Mifflin, 1968.

551 _____, ed. Landmarks of American Writing. New York and London: Basic Books, 1969; Washington, D.C.: U.S. Information Agency, 1970. "Nathaniel Hawthorne: The House of the Seven Gables," by Richard Fogle, pp. 111-120.

552 COHEN, Hubert I. "The Grotesque in the Fiction of Nathaniel Hawthorne." Ph.D. diss., Michigan, 1970. DA, 31 (1971), 4153A.

553 _____. "Hoffmann's 'The Sandman': A Possible Source for 'Rappaccini's Daughter.'" Emerson Society Quarterly, 18 (1972), 148-153.

554 COLACURCIO, Michael Joseph, Jr. "The Progress of Piety: Hawthorne's Critique of the Puritan Spirit." Ph.D. diss., Illinois, 1963. DA, 24 (1964), 5405-5406.

554a _____. "Footsteps of Ann Hutchinson: The Context of The Scarlet Letter." English Literary History, 39 (1972), 459-494.

555 _____. "Visible Sanctity and Specter Evidence: The Moral World of 'Young Goodman Brown.'" Essex Institute Historical Collections, 110 (1974), 259-299.

556 COLERIDGE, M.E. "Questionable Shapes of Nathaniel Hawthorne." Littell's Living Age, 242 (August 6, 1904), 348-353.

557 COLLINS, Helen. "The Nature and Power of Hawthorne's Women as Seen Through A Wonder Book and Tanglewood-Tales." Nassau Review, 3 (1976),

558 COLSON, Theodore Lewis. "The Characters of Hawthorne and Faulkner: A Typology of Sinners." Ph.D. diss., Michigan, 1967. DA, 28 (1967), 2204A-2205A.

559 _____. "Analogues of Faulkner's The Wild Palms and Hawthorne's 'The Birthmark.'" Dalhousie Review, 56 (1976), 510-518.

560 COMMAGER, Henry Steele. "Hawthorne as Editor."

American Historical Review, 47 (January, 1942),
358-359.

561 CONDON, Richard A. "The Broken Conduit: A Study
     of Alienation in American Literature." Pacific
     Spectator, 8 (Autumn, 1954), 326-332.

562 CONLEY, Brian Patrick. "A Formal and Structural
     Study of Hawthorne's Tales." Ph.D. diss., Ohio
     State, 1975. DA, 36 (1975), 3709A-3710A.

563 CONNOLLY, Thomas E. "Hawthorne's 'Young Good-
     man Brown': An Attack on Puritanic Calvinism."
     American Literature, 28 (November, 1956), 370-375.

564 _____. "How Young Goodman Brown Became Old
     Badman Brown." College English, 24 (November,
     1962), 153. Reply to Cochran article; also Cochran's
     reply to Connolly.

565 _____, ed. with Introduction. Nathaniel Hawthorne:
     "Young Goodman Brown." Columbus, Ohio: Merrill,
     1968. Merrill Casebook Series.

566 _____, ed. with Introduction. The Scarlet Letter
     and Selected Tales. Baltimore: Penguin, 1970.

567 CONNORS, Thomas E. " 'My Kinsman, Major
     Molineux': A Reading." Modern Language Notes,
     74 (April, 1959), 299-302.

568 CONWAY, Moncure Daniel. Life of Hawthorne. New
     York: Scribner and Welford; London: W. Scott,
     1890.

569 _____. "The Secret of Hawthorne." Nation, 88
     (June 30, 1904), 509-510.

570 _____. "My Hawthorne Experience." Critic, 45
     (July, 1904), 21-25.

571 COOK, Larry W. "Narrators in the Works of Nathaniel
     Hawthorne." Ph.D. diss., Duke, 1968. DA, 30
     (1969), 2478A.

572 COOK, Reginald L. "The Forest of Goodman Brown's
     Night: A Reading of Hawthorne's 'Young Goodman

Cook 52

Brown.'" New England Quarterly, 43 (1970), 473-481.

573 _____, ed. Themes, Tones, and Motifs in the American Renaissance: A Symposium. Hartford, Conn.: Transcendental, 1968. Later published as Emerson Society Quarterly, 54 (1969). "The Extraordinary Man as Idealist in the Novels by Hawthorne and Melville," by Paul McCarthy, pp. 43-51.

574 COOK, William Alfred. "Hawthorne's Artistic Theory and Practice." Ph.D. diss., Lehigh, 1971. DA, 32 (1971), 2634A-2635A.

575 COOKE, Mrs. Alice Lovelace. "Some Evidences of Hawthorne's Indebtedness to Swift." University of Texas Studies in English, 18 (July, 1938), 140-162.

576 _____. "The Shadow of Martinus Scriblerus in Hawthorne's 'The Prophetic Pictures.'" New England Quarterly, 17 (December, 1944), 597-604.

577 COPELAND, C.T. "Hawthorne's Use of His Materials." Critic, 45 (July, 1904), 56-60.

578 CORTISSOZ, Paul C. "The Political Life of Nathaniel Hawthorne." Ph.D. diss., New York University, 1955. DA, 18 (1958), 764.

579 COUSER, G. Thomas. "'The Old Manse,' Walden, and the Hawthorne-Thoreau Relationship." Emerson Society Quarterly, 21 (1975), 11-20.

580 COWEN, Wilson Walker. "Melville's Marginalia: Hawthorne," in Myerson, ed., Studies: 1978 (1978), pp. 279-302.

581 COWIE, Alexander. The Rise of the American Novel. New York: American Book, 1948. Hawthorne, pp. 327-362.

582 COWLEY, Malcolm. "Hawthorne in the Looking Glass." Sewanee Review, 56 (August, 1948), 545-563.

583 _____. "Hawthorne in Solitude." New Republic, 119 (August 2, 1948), 29-33.

584 _____. "100 Years Ago: Hawthorne Set a Great
New Pattern." New York Herald Tribune Book Review, August 6, 1950, pp. 1, 13. Refers to publication of The Scarlet Letter.

585 _____. "Five Acts of The Scarlet Letter." College
English, 19 (October, 1957), 11-16. Reprinted in revised and expanded form in Shapiro, Charles, ed.,
Twelve Original Essays on Great American Novels.
Detroit: Wayne State University Press, 1958, pp.
23-44. Original essay reprinted in Bradley, et al.,
eds., The Scarlet Letter (1961), pp. 323-330.

586 _____. "The Hawthornes in Paradise." American
Heritage, 10 (December, 1958), 30-35, 112-115.

587 _____. "Hawthorne in Solitude," in Cowley, A
Many-Windowed House, ed. by Henry Dan Piper.
Carbondale: Southern Illinois University Press, 1970,
pp. 3-34. Based on 2 articles (1948) listed above.

588 _____, ed. with Introduction. The Portable Hawthorne. New York: Viking, 1948.

589 COX, James M. "Emerson and Hawthorne: Trust
and Doubt." Virginia Quarterly Review, 45 (1969),
88-107.

590 _____. "The Scarlet Letter: Through the Old
Manse and the Custom House." Virginia Quarterly
Review, 51 (1975), 432-447.

591 COX, James T.; Margaret Putnam; and Marvin Williams;
eds. "Textual Studies in the Novel: A Selected
Checklist, 1950-1974." Studies in the Novel, 7
(1975), 445-471. Includes Hawthorne.

592 COXE, Arthur Cleveland. "The Writings of Hawthorne."
Church Review, 3 (January, 1851), 489-511. Reprinted as "The Scarlet Letter by Nathaniel Hawthorne," in Mordell, Albert, ed., Notorious Literary
Attacks. New York: Boni and Liveright, 1926,
pp. 122-137. Reprinted as "The Writings. . ." in
Cameron, ed., Hawthorne Among His Contemporaries
(1968), pp. 13-20; and in Cohen, Benjamin Bernard,
ed., Recognition (1969), pp. 49-54.

593   CRACROFT, Richard H. "Liverpool 1856: Nathaniel
       Hawthorne Meets Oson Pratt." Brigham Young
       University Studies, 8 (1968), 270-272.

594   CRANE, Maurice Aaron. "A Textual and Critical
       Edition of Hawthorne's The Blithedale Romance."
       Ph.D. diss., Illinois, 1953. DA, 14 (1954), 355.

595   _____. "The Blithedale Romance as Theatre."
       Notes and Queries, 5 (February, 1958), 84-86.

596   CRAVER, Donald Henry. "Hawthorne's Short Fiction."
       Ph. D. diss., George Washington, 1971. DA, 33
       (1972), 1677A.

597   CRETIEN, L. E. "La Pensée morale de Nathaniel
       Hawthorne (1804-1864), symboliste Néo-puritain."
       Ph.D. diss., Paris, 1932. In French.

598   CREWS, Frederick C. "A New Reading of The
       Blithedale Romance." American Literature, 29
       (May, 1957), 147-170.

599   _____. "The Logic of Compulsion in 'Roger Mal-
       vin's Burial.'" PMLA, 79 (September, 1964), 457-
       465. Reprinted in Kaul, ed., Hawthorne (1966),
       pp. 111-122.

600   _____. "Giovanni's Garden." American Quarterly,
       16 (Fall, 1964), 402-418.

601   _____. "The Ruined Wall: Unconscious Motivation
       in The Scarlet Letter." New England Quarterly, 38
       (September, 1965), 312-330.

602   _____. The Sins of the Fathers: Hawthorne's
       Psychological Themes. Edited by William Charvat.
       New York: Oxford University Press, 1966.

603   _____, ed. with Introduction. Great Short Works of
       Nathaniel Hawthorne. New York: Harper and Row,
       1967.

604   CRIE, Robert D. "'The Minister's Black Veil': Mr.
       Hooper's Symbolic Fig Leaf." Literature and Psy-
       chology, 17 (1967), 211-218.

605   CRONIN, Morton. "Hawthorne on Romantic Love and
      the Status of Women." PMLA, 69 (March, 1954),
      89-98.

606   CRONKHITE, George Ferris. "The Transcendental
      Railroad." New England Quarterly, 24 (September,
      1951), 306-328. Railroad as image in Emerson,
      Hawthorne, and Thoreau.

607   CROTHERS, Samuel McChord. "Man Under Enchant-
      ment," in Crothers, Pardoner's Wallet. Boston:
      Houghton Mifflin, 1905, pp. 249-266.

608   CROWLEY, Joseph Donald. "Nathaniel Hawthorne's
      Twice-Told Tales: A Textual Study Based on An
      Analysis of the Tales in the Three Major Collections."
      Ph. D. diss., Ohio State, 1964. DA, 25 (1965), 7242.

609   _____. "A False Edition of Hawthorne's Twice-Told
      Tales." Papers of the Bibliographical Society of
      America, 59 (1965), 182-188.

610   _____. "The Artist as Mediator: The Rationale of
      Hawthorne's Large-Scale Revisions in His Collected
      Tales and Sketches," in Vincent, Howard P., ed.,
      Melville and Hawthorne in the Berkshires (1968),
      pp. 79-88.

611   _____. Nathaniel Hawthorne. London: Routledge
      and Kegan Paul; New York: Humanities, 1971.

612   _____. "The Unity of Hawthorne's Twice-Told
      Tales." Studies in American Fiction, 1 (1973), 35-
      61.

613   _____. "Hawthorne Criticism and the Return to
      History." Studies in the Novel, 6 (1974), 98-105.
      Review-essay.

614   _____. "Hawthorne and Frost: The Making of a
      Poem," in Tharpe, Jac, ed., Frost Centennial
      Essays. Jackson: University Press of Mississippi,
      1974, pp. 288-309.

615   _____. "Historical Commentary," in Bowers et al.,
      eds., Twice-Told Tales (1974).

616 _____. "Historical Commentary," in Bowers et al.,
eds., Mosses from an Old Manse (1974).

617 _____. "Historical Commentary," in Bowers et al.,
eds., The Snow-Image and Uncollected Tales (1974).

618 _____. "Hawthorne," Review of Current Scholarship
in American Literary Scholarship, 1975, 1976, 1977,
pp. 17-34, 15-32, 17-33.

619 _____, ed. Hawthorne: The Critical Heritage.
New York: Barnes and Noble, 1970. Lists over
140 items, early reviews, essays, etc.

620 _____, ed. with Introduction. Hawthorne: A Collection of Criticism. New York: McGraw-Hill,
1975. Contemporary Studies in Literature Series.

621 CUDDY, Lois A. "Symbolic Identification of Whitman
with Hawthorne." American Notes and Queries, 15
(1977), 71-72.

622 CUFF, Roger Penn. "A Study of Classical Mythology
in Nathaniel Hawthorne's Writings." Ph. D. diss.,
George Peabody, 1936.

623 CUMMINGS, Abbott Lowell. "Nathaniel Hawthorne's
Birthplace: An Architectural Study." Essex Institute Historical Collections, 94 (July, 1958), 196-204.

624 CUNLIFFE, Marcus. The Literature of the United
States. Baltimore and London: Penguin, 1961.
"New England's Day: Emerson, Thoreau, Haw-
thorne," pp. 75-104.

625 _____. "On The House of the Seven Gables," in
Pearce, Roy Harvey, ed., Centenary Essays (1964),
pp. 79-101.

626 CURET, Peggy J. "The Coverdale Cop-out: A Study
of Hawthorne's Ironic View of Women in The Blithedale Romance." Publications of the Arkansas Philological Association, 1 (1976), 19-25.

627 CURL, Vega. Pasteboard Masks: Fact as Spiritual
Symbol in the Novels of Hawthorne and Melville.
Cambridge: Harvard University Press, 1931. Based

on Honors thesis, Radcliffe, 1931.

628 CURLE, Richard. Collecting American First Editions:
     Its Pitfalls and Its Pleasures. Indianapolis: Bobbs-
     Merrill, 1930. Hawthorne, pp. 45-49, 185-187, et
     passim.

629 CURRAN, Ronald T. "Irony: Another Thematic Ap-
     proach to 'The Artist of the Beautiful.'" Studies in
     Romanticism, 6 (August, 1966), 34-45.

630 _____. "Hawthorne as Gothicist." Ph.D. diss.,
     Pennsylvania, 1969. DA, 30 (1970), 4404A-4405A.

631 _____. "The Reluctant Yankee in Hawthorne's
     Abortive Gothic Romances." Nathaniel Hawthorne
     Journal, 4 (1974), 179-194.

632 _____. "'Yankee Gothic': Hawthorne's 'Castle of
     Pyncheon.'" Studies in the Novel, 8 (1976), 69-79.

633 CURRIE, William J. "Against the Dragon: Approaches
     to Nature in Hawthorne and Poe." English Literature
     and Language Studies (Tokyo), 11 (1974), 77-82.

634 CURTI, Merle. "Human Nature in American Thought:
     The Age of Reason and Morality, 1750-1860." Po-
     litical Science Quarterly, 68 (Summer, 1953), 354-
     375. Hawthorne, passim.

635 CURTIS, Edith Roelker. A Season in Utopia. New
     York: Nelson, 1961. Hawthorne, passim.

636 CURTIS, George William. "Hawthorne," in Curtis,
     Homes of American Authors. New York: Harper
     Brothers, 1853, pp. 291-313.

637 _____. "Hawthorne and Brook Farm," in Curtis,
     From the Easy Chair: Third Series. New York:
     Harper Brothers, 1894, pp. 1-19.

638 _____. "The Works of Nathaniel Hawthorne."
     North American Review, 99 (1864), 539-557. Re-
     printed in Curtis, Literary and Social Essays. New
     York: Harper Brothers, 1894, pp. 61-93.

639 CURTIS, Jessie Kingsley. "The Marble Faun: An

Interpretation." <u>Andover Review,</u> 18 (August, 1892), 139-147.

640 CURTSINGER, Eugene C., Jr. "The Byronic Hero and Hawthorne's Seekers: A Comparative Study." Ph. D. diss., Notre Dame, 1955. <u>DA,</u> 15 (1955), 2203.

641 CUSHMAN, Bigelow Paine. "Nathaniel Hawthorne's Moral Ambiguity and Bi-polarity." Ph. D. diss., Wisconsin, 1965. <u>DA,</u> 26 (1965), 3298.

642 DAHL, Curtis. "The Devil Is a Wise One." <u>Cithara,</u> 6 (1967), 52-58.

643 _____. "When the Deity Returns: <u>The Marble Faun</u> and <u>Romola,</u>" in Partlow, Robert, ed., <u>Studies in American Literature.</u> Edwardsville: Southern Illinois University Press, 1969. Also published in <u>Papers on Language and Literature,</u> 5 (1969), 82-99.

644 DALY, Robert J. "Fideism and Allusive Mode in 'Rappaccini's Daughter.'" <u>Nineteenth-Century Fiction,</u> 28 (June, 1973), 25-37.

645 _____. "History and Chivalric Myth in 'Roger Malvin's Burial.'" <u>Essex Institute Historical Collections,</u> 109 (1973), 99-115.

646 DAMERON, J. Lasley. "Hawthorne's <u>The House of the Seven Gables:</u> A Serpent Image." <u>Notes and Queries,</u> 6 (July-August, 1959), 289-290.

647 _____. "Hawthorne and <u>Blackwood's</u> Review of Goethe's <u>Faust.</u>" <u>Emerson Society Quarterly,</u> 19 (1960), 25.

648 _____. "Hawthorne and the <u>Edinburgh Review</u> on the Prose Romance." <u>Nathaniel Hawthorne Journal,</u> 5 (1975), 170-176.

649 DANA, Henry W. L., and Manning Hawthorne. "'The Maiden Aunt of the Whole Human Race': Fredrika Bremer's Friendship with Longfellow and Hawthorne." <u>American-Scandinavian Review,</u> 37 (September, 1949), 217-229.

650 DARBY, Michael H. "An Analysis of the Major Causes of Social Isolation in Selected Tales by Nathaniel Hawthorne." Ph.D. diss., George Peabody, 1973. DA, 34 (1974), 4193A.

651 DARNELL, Donald Gene. "Hawthorne's Emblematic Method." Ph. D. diss., Texas (Austin), 1964. DA, 25 (1965), 5903.

652 _____. "'Doctrine by Ensample': The Emblem and The Marble Faun." Texas Studies in Literature and Language, 15 (1973), 301-310.

653 _____. "'Visions of Hereditary Rank': The Loyalist in the Fiction of Hawthorne, Cooper, and Frederic." South Atlantic Bulletin, 42 (1977), 45-54.

654 DAUBER, Kenneth M. "Hawthorne's Purpose: A Theory of Literary Meaning." Ph. D. diss., Princeton, 1973. DA, 34 (1974), 7226A.

655 _____. Re-discovering Hawthorne. Princeton, N. J.: Princeton University Press, 1977.

656 DAUNER, Louise. "The 'Case' of Tobias Pearson: Hawthorne and the Ambiguities." American Literature, 21 (January, 1950), 464-472. Relates to "The Gentle Boy" and Melville's Pierre.

657 DAUPHIN, V. A. "Religious Content in Hawthorne's Works." Southern University Bulletin, 46 (September, 1959), 115-123.

658 D'AVANZO, Mario L. "The Literary Sources of 'My Kinsman, Major Molineux': Shakespeare, Coleridge Milton." Studies in Short Fiction, 10 (1973), 121-136.

659 _____. "The Ambitious Guest in the Hands of an Angry God." English Language Notes, 14 (1976), 38-42.

660 DAVENPORT, Basil, ed. with Foreword. The Scarlet Letter. New York: Dodd, Mead, 1948.

661 DAVIDSON, Edward Hutchins. "The Last Phase of Nathaniel Hawthorne's Art." Ph.D. diss., Yale, 1940.

662 _____. Hawthorne's Last Phase. New Haven:
Yale University Press, 1949. Reprinted Hamden,
Conn.: Shoe String, 1967.

663 _____. "Hawthorne and the Pathetic Fallacy."
Journal of English and Germanic Philology, 54
(October, 1955), 486-497. Reprinted in Studies by
Members of the English Department in Memory of
John Jay Parry. Urbana: University of Illinois
Press, 1955, pp. 26-37.

664 _____. "The Question of History in The Scarlet
Letter." Emerson Society Quarterly, 25 (1961),
2-3.

665 _____. "Dimmesdale's Fall." New England
Quarterly, 36 (September, 1963), 358-370.

666 _____. "The Unfinished Romances," in Pearce,
Roy Harvey, ed., Centenary Essays (1964), pp. 141-
163.

667 _____, ed. with Introduction and Notes. Doctor
Grimshawe's Secret. Cambridge: Harvard University Press, 1954.

668 _____; Claude M. Simpson; and L. Neal Smith;
eds. The American Claimant Manuscripts: The Ancestral Footstep, Etherege, and Grimshawe. Columbus: Ohio State University Press, 1977.

669 _____; Claude M. Simpson; and L. Neal Smith;
eds. The Elixir of Life Manuscripts: Septimius
Felton, Septimius Norton, and The Dolliver Romance.
Columbus: Ohio State University Press, 1977.

670 DAVIDSON, Frank. "Hawthorne's Hive of Honey."
Modern Language Notes, 61 (January, 1946), 14-21.

671 _____. "Thoreau's Contribution to Hawthorne's
Mosses." New England Quarterly, 20 (December,
1947), 535-542.

672 _____. "Hawthorne's Use of Pattern from The
Rambler." Modern Language Notes, 63 (January,
1949), 545-548.

673 _____. "Voltaire and Hawthorne's 'The Christmas
      Banquet.'" Boston Public Library Quarterly, 3
      (July, 1951), 244-246.

674 _____. "Toward a Re-Evaluation of The Blithedale
      Romance." New England Quarterly, 25 (September,
      1952), 374-383.

675 _____. "'Young Goodman Brown': Hawthorne's In-
      tention." Emerson Society Quarterly, 31 (1963),
      68-71.

676 DAVIES, Horton. "Preachers and Evangelists," in
      Davies, A Mirror of the Ministry in Modern Novels.
      New York: Oxford University Press, 1959, pp. 21-47.

677 DAVIS, Elizabeth A. "The Spirit of the Letter: Ri-
      chardson and the Early American Novel: A Study
      of the Evolution of the Form." Ph. D. diss.,
      Yale, 1973. DA, 34 (1974), 7185A-7186A.

678 DAVIS, Joe. "The Myth of the Garden: Nathaniel
      Hawthorne's 'Rappaccini's Daughter.'" Studies in the
      Literary Imagination, 2 (April, 1969), 3-12.

679 DAVIS, Joseph A. "The Oldest Puritan: A Study of
      the Angel of Hadley Legend in Hawthorne's 'The
      Gray Champion.'" Regional Language Studies, 4
      (1973), 25-43.

680 DAVIS, Richard Beale. "Hawthorne, Fanny Kemble,
      and 'The Artist of the Beautiful.'" Modern Language
      Notes, 70 (December, 1955), 89-92.

681 _____. "The America of American Literature:
      Folk and Historical Themes and Materials in Formal
      Writing." Literary Criterion (India), 3 (Summer,
      1959), 10-22.

682 DAVIS, William V. "Hawthorne's 'Young Goodman
      Brown.'" Nathaniel Hawthorne Journal, 3 (1973),
      198-199.

683 DAVISON, Richard Allan. "The Villagers and 'Ethan
      Brand,'" Studies in Short Fiction, 4 (Spring, 1967),
      260-262.

684 _____. "Redburn, Pierre, and Robin: Melville's
Debt to Hawthorne?" Emerson Society Quarterly,
47 (1967), 32-34.

685 DAWSON, Edward B. "Nathaniel Hawthorne's Knowledge
and Use of New England History: A Study of Sources."
Ph. D. diss., Vanderbilt, 1938.

686 _____. Hawthorne's Knowledge and Use of New
England History. Nashville, Tenn.: Privately
printed, 1939.

687 DEAN, Sharon W. "Lost Ladies: The Isolated Heroine
in the Fiction of Hawthorne, James, Fitzgerald,
Hemingway, and Faulkner." Ph. D. diss., New
Hampshire, 1973. DA, 34 (1973), 2616A.

688 DE CARO, Rosan Jordon. "A Note About Folklore and
Literature ('The Bosom Serpent' Revisited)," Journal of
American Folklore, 86 (January-March, 1973), 62-65.

689 DE HAYES, R. "Charting Hawthorne's Invisible World."
CEA Critic, 27 (May, 1965), 5-6.

690 DEISS, Joseph J. The Roman Years of Margaret
Fuller: A Biography. New York: Crowell, 1969.

691 DEJOVINE, Jane Feldmeier. "Classical Myths and
Moral Growth in the Four Major Romances of
Nathaniel Hawthorne." Ph. D. diss., Northern
Illinois (De Kalb), 1977. DA, 39 (1978), 883A.

692 DELAUNE, Henry M. "The Beautiful of 'The Artist
of the Beautiful.'" Xavier University Studies, 1
(December, 1961), 94-99.

693 DEMING, Robert H. "The Use of the Past: Herrick
and Hawthorne." Journal of Popular Culture, 2
(February, 1968), 278-291.

694 DENHAM, William Paul. "Nathaniel Hawthorne's Use
of Europe and the Past: A Study of Nathaniel Hawthorne's Notebooks, 1853-1860." Ph. D. diss.,
Toronto, 1973. DA, 34 (1974), 5163A-5164A.

695 DENNIS, Carl Edward. "How to Live in Hell: The
Bleak Vision of Hawthorne's 'My Kinsman, Major
Molineux.'" University Review, 37 (1971), 250-258.

696 _____. "The Blithedale Romance and the Problem
         of Self-Integration." Texas Studies in Literature
         and Language, 15 (1973), 93-110.

697 DENNY, Margaret, and William H. Gilman, eds. The
         American Writer and the European Tradition. Min-
         neapolis: University of Minnesota Press, 1952.
         "American Writers as Critics of Nineteenth-Century
         Society," by Willard Thorp, pp. 90-105. Hawthorne,
         passim.

698 DESMAND, M. E. "Association of Hawthorne." Catho-
         lic World, 74 (January, 1902), 455-465.

699 DETLAFF, Shirley M. "The Concept of Beauty in
         'The Artist of the Beautiful' and Hugh Blair's
         Rhetoric." Studies in Short Fiction, 13 (1976),
         512, 515. Blair (1718-1800), influenced by Edmund
         Burke, in Lectures on Rhetoric and Belles Lettres,
         believed to have influenced Hawthorne's story.

700 DEUSEN, Marshall Jan. "Narrative Tone in 'The
         Custom House' and The Scarlet Letter." Nineteenth-
         Century Fiction, 21 (1966), 61-71.

701 DEUTSCH, Raymond H. "Nathaniel Hawthorne Peri-
         odical Criticism, 1940-1963: An Annotated Biblio-
         graphy." Ph. D. diss., Loyola (Chicago), 1964.

702 DEVLIN, James E. "A German Analogue for 'The
         Ambitious Guest.'" American Transcendental
         Quarterly, 17 (1973), 171-174.

703 DHALEINE, L. "Nathaniel Hawthorne: Sa vie et son
         oeuvre." Ph. D. diss., Paris, 1905. Published in
         French, Paris: Hachette, 1905.

704 DICEY, Edward. "Three Great Authors," excerpt
         from Dicey, Six Months in the Federal States.
         London: Macmillan, 1863. Reprinted in Nevins,
         Allan, ed., America Through British Eyes. New
         York: Oxford University Press, 1948, pp. 285-287.

705 _____. "Nathaniel Hawthorne." Macmillan's
         Magazine, 10 (July, 1864), 241-246.

706 DICHMANN, Mary E. "Hawthorne's 'Prophetic Pictures.'"
         American Literature, 23 (May, 1951), 188-202.

707 DICKSON, Wayne. "Hawthorne's 'Young Goodman
     Brown.'" Explicator, 29 (1971), item 44.

708 DILLINGHAM, William B. "Structure and Theme in
     The House of the Seven Gables." Nineteenth-Century
     Fiction, 14 (June, 1959), 59-70.

709 _____. "Arthur Dimmesdale's Confession." Studies
     in the Literary Imagination, 2 (1969), 21-26.

710 DOBBS, Jeannine. "Hawthorne's Dr. Rappaccini and
     Father George Rapp." American Literature, 43
     (1971), 427-430.

711 DOHERTY, Joseph F. "Hawthorne's Communal Para-
     digm: The American Novel Reconsidered." Genre,
     7 (1974), 30-53.

712 DOLON, Paul J. "Hawthorne: The Politics of Puberty,"
     in Dolon, ed., Of War and War's Alarms: Fiction
     and Politics in the Modern World. New York: Free
     Press/Macmillan; London: Collier/Macmillan, 1976,
     pp. 16-35. Discusses "My Kinsman, Major Molineux."

713 DOLEZAL, Richard P. "The Individual and Society in
     Selected Novels and Tales of Nathaniel Hawthorne:
     A Study of Hawthorne's Use of the Crowd." Ph. D.
     diss., Loyola (Chicago), 1966.

714 DOLIS, John J., Jr. "Hawthorne's Ontological Models:
     Daguerreotype and Diorama." Ph. D. diss., Loyola
     (Chicago), 1978. DA, 38 (1978), 6713A-6714A.

715 DONOHUE, Agnes McNeill. "'From Whose Bourn No
     Traveller Returns': A Reading of 'Roger Malvin's
     Burial.'" Nineteenth-Century Fiction, 18 (June, 1963),
     1-19.

716 _____ "'The Fruit of That Forbidden Tree': A
     Reading of 'The Gentle Boy,'" in Donohue, The
     Hawthorne Question (1963), pp. 158-170.

717 _____. "The Endless Journey to No End: Journey
     and Eden Symbolism in Hawthorne and Steinbeck,"
     in The Grapes of Wrath (1968), pp. 257-266.

718 _____, ed. A Casebook on the Hawthorne Question.
     New York: Crowell, 1963.

719 _____, ed. A Casebook on The Grapes of Wrath.
New York: Crowell, 1968.

720 DONY, Françoise. "Romantisme et Puritanisme chez
Hawthorne, à propos de la 'Lettre Pourpre.'" Etudes
Anglaises, 4 (January-March, 1940), 15-30. Studies
The Scarlet Letter; in French.

721 DORSON, Richard M. "Five Directions in American
Folklore." Midwest Folklore, 1 (Fall, 1951), 149-
165. Hawthorne, passim.

722 DOUBLEDAY, Neal Frank. "Nathaniel Hawthorne's
Appraisal of New England Life and Thought." Ph. D.
diss., Wisconsin, 1938.

723 _____. "The Theme of Hawthorne's 'Fancy's Show
Box.'" American Literature, 10 (November, 1938),
341-343.

724 _____. "Hawthorne's Hester and Feminism."
PMLA, 54 (September, 1939), 825-828.

725 _____. "Hawthorne's Inferno." College English,
1 (May, 1940), 658-670.

726 _____. "Hawthorne and Literary Nationalism."
American Literature, 12 (January, 1941), 447, 453.

727 _____. "Hawthorne's Criticism of New England
Life." College English, 2 (April, 1941), 639-653.

728 _____. "Hawthorne's Satirical Allegory." College
English, 3 (January, 1942), 325-337.

729 _____. "Hawthorne's Use of Three Gothic Patterns."
College English, 7 (February, 1946), 250-262.

730 _____. "Classroom Considerations of Hawthorne's
Tales." Emerson Society Quarterly, 25 (1961), 4-6.

731 _____. "Hawthorne's Estimate of His Early Work."
American Literature, 37 (January, 1966), 403-409.

732 _____. Hawthorne's Early Tales: A Critical Study.
Durham, N. C.: Duke University Press, 1972.

733 _____. Variety of Attempt: A Collection of Essays.

Lincoln: University of Nebraska Press, 1977. "Hawthorne's Showman and His Audience, " pp. 176-188; "Hawthorne and the Immunities of Romance, " pp. 189-202.

734 _____, ed. Hawthorne: Tales of His Native Land. Boston: Heath, 1962. Contains tales and selected source materials for college research papers.

735 DOUGLAS, Harold J. , and Robert Daniel. "Faulkner and the Puritanism of the South. " Tennessee Studies in Literature, 2 (1957), 1-13. Hawthorne, passim.

736 DRYDEN, Edgar A. "Hawthorne's Castle in the Air: Form and Theme in The House of the Seven Gables. " English Literary History, 38 (1971), 294-317.

737 _____. "The Limits of Romance: A Reading of The Marble Faun, " in Baldwin, K. H. , and D. K. Kirby, eds. , Individual and Community. Durham, N. C. : Duke University Press, 1975, pp. 17-48.

738 _____. Nathaniel Hawthorne: The Poetics of Enchantment. Ithaca, N. Y. : Cornell University Press, 1977.

739 DUBAN, James. "The Skeptical Context of Hawthorne's 'Mr. Higginbotham's Catastrophe.'" American Literature, 48 (1976), 292-301.

740 _____. "Hawthorne's Debt to Edmund Spenser and Charles Chauncy in 'The Gentle Boy.'" Nathaniel Hawthorne Journal, 6 (1976), 189-195.

741 DUERKSEN, Roland A. "The Double Image of Beatrice Cenci in The Marble Faun. " Michigan Academician, 1 (1969), 47-55.

742 DUFFEY, Bernard. "Hawthorne Seen in a Steeple. " Christian Scholar, 38 (June, 1955), 134-141.

743 DUGGAN, Francis X. "Paul Elmer More and the New England Tradition. " American Literature, 34 (January, 1963), 542-561.

744 DUNLAP, Leslie W. , ed. "The Letters of Willis Gaylord Clark and Lewis Gaylord Clark." Bulletin of the New York Public Library, 42 (1938), 455-476, 523-548, 613-636, 753-779, 857-881.

745 _____, ed. with Introduction. The Letters of Willis
     Gaylord Clark and Lewis Gaylord Clark. New York:
     New York Public Library, 1940. Refers to twin
     brothers, editors of The Knickerbocker Magazine,
     1834-1861. Published many authors of the day, in-
     cluding Hawthorne.

746 DUNNE, Michael F. "Order and Excess in Hawthorne's
     Fiction." Ph. D. diss., Louisiana State, 1969. DA,
     30 (1970), 3003A-3004A.

747 _____. "Hawthorne, the Reader, and Hester Prynne."
     Interpretations, 10 (1978), 34-40.

748 DURHAM, Frank. "Hawthorne and Goldsmith: A
     Note." Journal of American Speech, 4 (1970), 103-
     105.

749 DURR, Robert Allen. "Feathertop's Unlikely Love
     Affair." Modern Language Notes, 72 (November,
     1957), 492-493.

750 _____. "Hawthorne's Ironic Mode." New England
     Quarterly, 30 (December, 1957), 486-495.

751 DURSTON, J. H. "Fourteen Unknown Hawthorne Works
     Reported Found by Collector." New York Herald
     Tribune, September 12, 1948, p. 15.

752 DUSENBERG, Robert. "Hawthorne's Merry Company:
     The Anatomy of Laughter in the Tales and Short
     Stories." PMLA, 82 (May, 1967), 285-288.

753 DUSSINGER, Gloria R. "The Romantic Concept of the
     Self Applied to the Works of Emerson, Whitman,
     Hawthorne, and Melville." Ph. D. diss., Lehigh,
     1973. DA, 34 (1974), 5963A.

754 DWIGHT, Sheila. "Hawthorne and the Unpardonable
     Sin." Studies in the Novel, 2 (1970), 449-458.

755 EAGLE, Nancy L. "An Unpublished Hawthorne Letter."
     American Literature, 23 (November, 1951), 360-362.

756 EAKIN, Paul John. "Hawthorne's Imagination and the
     Structure of 'The Custom-House.'" American
     Literature, 43 (November, 1971), 346-358.

757 _____. "Margaret Fuller, Hawthorne, James, and
Sexual Politics." South Atlantic Quarterly, 75 (1976),
323-338.

758 _____. "Self-Culture: Margaret Fuller and Hawthorne's Heroines," in Eakin, The New England Girl:
Cultural Ideals in Hawthorne, Stowe, Howells, and
James. Athens: University of Georgia Press, 1976,
pp. 49-79.

759 EARNEST, Ernest. "The Ambivalent Puritan: Nathaniel
Hawthorne," in Expatriates and Patriots: American
Artists, Scholars, and Writers in Europe. Durham,
N.C.: Duke University Press, 1968, pp. 152-181.

760 EBERWEIN, Jane Donahue. "Temporal Perspective in
'The Legends of the Province House.'" American
Transcendental Quarterly, 14 (1972), 41-45.

761 EDEL, Leon. "Hawthorne's Symbolism and Psycho-
Analysis," in Manheim, L. F., and E. B. Manheim,
eds., Hidden Patterns. New York: Macmillan,
1966, pp. 93-111.

762 EDGAR, Pelham. "Nathaniel Hawthorne and The
Scarlet Letter," in The Art of the Novel from 1700
to the Present Time. New York: Macmillan, 1933,
pp. 125-129.

763 EDGREN, C. Hobart. "Hawthorne's 'The Ambitious
Guest': An Interpretation." Nineteenth-Century
Fiction, 10 (September, 1955), 151-156.

764 EDWIN, John, Jr. "Hawthorne and the English Romantic Poets." Ph.D. diss., Duke, 1976. DA,
37 (1976), 3624A.

765 EHRENPREIS, Ann Henry. "Elizabeth Gaskell and
Nathaniel Hawthorne." Nathaniel Hawthorne Journal,
3 (1973), 89 119.

766 _____, ed. with Introduction. Happy Country This
America: The Travel Diary of Henry Arthur Bright.
Columbus: Ohio State University Press, 1978.
British traveler, toured the United States in 1852;
related to Hawthorne's English Notebooks.

767 EIGNER, Edwin M. "Hawthorne: The House of the
     Seven Gables, " in Lang, Hans-Joachim, ed. , The
     American Novel. Dusseldorf, Germany: August
     Bagel, 1972, pp. 51-68.

768 _____. The Metaphysical Novel in England and
     America: Dickens, Bulwer-Lytton, Hawthorne, and
     Melville. Berkeley: University of California Press,
     1978.

769 EISIMINGER, Sterling. "The Legend of Shelley's Heart
     and Hawthorne's 'Ethan Brand. '" Hawthorne Society
     Newsletter, 2 (1976), 3-4.

770 EISINGER, Chester E. "Pearl and the Puritan Herit-
     age. " College English, 12 (March, 1951), 323-329.

771 _____. "Hawthorne as Champion of the Middle
     Way. " New England Quarterly, 27 (March, 1954),
     27-52.

772 ELDER, Marjorie J. "Transcendental Symbolists:
     Nathaniel Hawthorne and Melville. " Ph. D. diss. ,
     Chicago, 1964.

773 _____. Nathaniel Hawthorne: Transcendental
     Symbolist. Athens: Ohio University Press, 1969.

774 _____. "Hawthorne's The Marble Faun: A Gothic
     Structure. " Costerus, 1 (1972), 81-88.

775 ELIAS, Helen L. "Alice Doane's Innocence: The
     Wizard Absolved. " Emerson Society Quarterly, 62
     (1971), 28-32.

776 ELIOT, T. S. "The Hawthorne Aspect. " The Little
     Review, 5 (August, 1918), 47-53. Reprinted in
     Cohen, Benjamin Bernard, ed. , Recognition (1969),
     pp. 157-163.

777 ELLIOTT, Robert C. "The Blithedale Romance, " in
     Pearce, Roy Harvey, ed. , Centenary Essays (1964),
     pp. 103-117.

778 _____. The Shape of Utopia: Studies in a Literary
     Genre. Chicago: University of Chicago Press, 1970.

"Hawthorne and Utopia: The Blithedale Romance, "
pp. 68-83. Similar to 1964 article.

779 ELLIS, James. "Frost's 'Desert Places' and Hawthorne. "
English Record, 15 (April, 1965), 15-17.

780 EMERICK, Ronald Rine. "Romance, Allegory, Vision:
The Influence of Hawthorne on Flannery O'Connor. "
Ph. D. diss., Pittsburgh, 1975. DA, 36 (1976),
4485A-4486A.

781 EMERSON, Edward W. "Nathaniel Hawthorne, " in
Early Years of the Saturday Club: 1855-1870.
Boston: Houghton Mifflin, 1918, pp. 207-216.

782 EMERSON, Everett H. "Hawthorne in General Education. " CEA Journal, 25 (June, 1963), 1, 6.

783 EMERSON SOCIETY QUARTERLY, 47 (1967), in two
parts. Special Hawthorne Issue.

784 EMRY, Hazel Thornberg. "Two Houses of Pride:
Spenser's and Hawthorne's. " Philological Quarterly,
33 (January, 1954), 91-94.

785 ENGLAND, A.B. "Robin Molineux and the Young Ben
Franklin: A Reconsideration. " Journal of American
Studies, 6 (1972), 181-188.

786 ENSCOE, Gerald E., and Robert Russell, eds., with
Introductions. The Disciplined Imagination: An
Approach to the Reading of Fiction. Reading, Mass.:
Addison-Wesley, 1969. "Young Goodman Brown, "
text and discussion, pp. 63-93.

787 ENSOR, Allison R. "'Whispers of the Bad Angel':
A Scarlet Letter Passage as a Commentary on
Hawthorne's 'Young Goodman Brown.'" Studies in
Short Fiction, 7 (1970), 467-469.

788 _____. "The Downfall of Poor Richard: Benjamin
Franklin as Seen by Hawthorne, Melville, and Mark
Twain. " Mark Twain Journal, 17 (1975), 14-18.

789 ERISMAN, Fred. "'Young Goodman Brown': Warning
to Idealists. " American Transcendental Quarterly,
14 (1972), 156-158.

71 Erlich

790 ERLICH, Gloria Chasson. "Deadly Innocence: Hawthorne's Dark Women." New England Quarterly,
41 (June, 1968), 163-179.

791 _____. "Guilt and Expiation in 'Roger Malvin's
Burial.'" Nineteenth-Century Fiction, 26 (1971),
377-389.

792 _____. "The Paradox of Benevolence: Hawthorne
and the Mannings." Ph.D. diss., Princeton, 1977.
DA, 38 (1978), 5474A-5475A.

793 ERSKINE, John. Leading American Novelists. New
York: Holt, 1910. Reprinted Freeport, N.Y.:
Books for Libraries, 1966. Hawthorne, pp.179-275,
et passim.

794 _____. "Hawthorne," in Trent, William P., et
al., eds., Cambridge History (1917-1921), Vol. II,
pp.16-31.

795 ESSEX INSTITUTE HISTORICAL COLLECTIONS. "Books
Read by Hawthorne, 1822-1850: From the 'Charge
Books' of the Salem Athenaeum." 68 (January, 1932),
65-87. Also listed as "Anonymous" (1932).

796 _____. Special Hawthorne Issue. Edited by Walter
M. Merrill. 94 (July, 1958), 170-308.

797 _____. Special Hawthorne Issue. 100 (October,
1964), 235-305.

798 ESTRIN, Mark W. "Dramatizations of American
Fiction: Hawthorne and Melville on Stage and
Screen." Ph.D. diss., New York University, 1969.
DA, 30 (1970), 3428A.

799 _____. "'Triumphant Ignominy': The Scarlet
Letter on Screen." Literature/Film Quarterly, 2
(1974), 110-122. Reprinted with revisions in Peary,
Gerald, and Roger Shatzin, eds., The Classic
American Novel in the Movies. New York: Ungar,
1977, pp.20-29.

800 _____. "Narrative Ambivalence in Hawthorne's
'Feathertop.'" Journal of Narrative Technique,
5 (1975), 164-173.

801 EVANOFF, Alexander. "Some Principal Themes in The Scarlet Letter." Discourse, 5 (Summer, 1962), 270-277.

802 EVANS, Oliver. "The Cavern and the Fountain: Paradox and Double Paradox in 'Rappaccini's Daughter.'" College English, 24 (March, 1963), 461-463.

803 _____. "Allegory and Incest in 'Rappaccini's Daughter.'" Nineteenth-Century Fiction, 19 (September, 1964), 185-195.

804 EVANS, Walter. "Poe's Revisions in His Reviews of Hawthorne's Twice-Told Tales." Papers of the Bibliographical Society of America, 66 (1972), 407-419.

805 _____. "Poe's 'The Masque of the Red Death' and Hawthorne's 'The Wedding Knell.'" Poe Studies, 10 (1977), 42-43.

806 EVERETT, L.B. "How the Great Ones Did It." Overland, 88 (March, 1930), 88. Relates indirectly to Hawthorne.

807 FAIRBANKS, Henry G. "Nathaniel Hawthorne's 'Catholic Critique.'" Ph.D. diss., Notre Dame, 1954. DA, 15 (1955), 265-266.

808 _____. "Hawthorne and the Catholic Church." Boston University Studies in English, 1 (August, 1955), 148-165.

809 _____. "Hawthorne Amid the Alien Corn." College English, 17 (February, 1956), 263-268. Hawthorne's treatment of the artist in America.

810 _____. "Hawthorne and the Machine Age." American Literature, 38 (May, 1956), 155-163.

811 _____. "Sin, Free Will, and 'Pessimism' in Hawthorne." PMLA, 71 (December, 1956), 975-989.

812 _____. "Hawthorne and the Vanishing Venus." University of Texas Studies in English, 36 (1957), 52-70.

813 _____. "Hawthorne and Confession." Catholic
    Historical Review, 43 (April, 1957), 38-45.

814 _____. "Hawthorne and the Nature of Man: Chang-
    ing Personality Concepts in the Nineteenth-Century."
    Revue de l'Université d'Ottawa, 28 (July-September,
    1958), 309-322.

815 _____. "Citizen Hawthorne and the Perennial Prob-
    lems of American Society." Revue de l'Université
    d'Ottawa, 29 (January-March, 1959), 26-38.

816 _____. "Man's Separation from Nature: Hawthorne's
    Philosophy of Suffering and Death." Christian
    Scholar, 42 (March, 1959), 51-63.

817 _____. "Hawthorne and the Atomic Age." Revue
    de l'Université d'Ottawa, 31 (July-September, 1961),
    436-451.

818 _____. The Lasting Loneliness of Hawthorne: A
    Study of the Sources of Alienation in Modern Man.
    Albany, N. Y.: Magi, 1965.

819 _____. "Theocracy to Transcendentalism in Ameri-
    ca." Emerson Society Quarterly, 44 (1966), 45-59.

820 FAIRCHILD, B. H., Jr. "A Technique of Discovery:
    The Dream Vision in Hawthorne's Fiction." Essays
    in Literature (University of Denver), 1 (1973), 17-
    28.

821 FALES, Dean A. "Note on Special Hawthorne Edition
    of EIHC." Essex Institute Historical Collections,
    100 (October, 1964), 233-234. Serves as Introduc-
    tion.

822 FARMER, Norman J., Jr. "Maule's Curse and the
    Rev. Nicholas Noyes: A Note on Hawthorne's
    Source." Notes and Queries, 11 (June, 1964), 224-
    225.

823 FARNHAM, Anne. "Uncle Venner's Farm: Refuge or
    Workhouse for Salem's Poor?" Essex Institute
    Historical Collections, 109 (January, 1973), 60-86.
    Refers to The House of the Seven Gables.

824 FASS, Barbara. "Rejection of Paternalism: Hawthorne's 'My Kinsman, Major Molineux,' and Ellison's
Invisible Man." College Language Association Journal, 14 (1971), 317-323.

825 FAUST, Bertha B. "Nathaniel Hawthorne's Contempo-
rary Reputation: A Study of Literary Opinion in
England and America, 1828-1864." Ph.D. diss.,
Pennsylvania, 1937.

826 _____. Hawthorne's Contemporaneous Reputation:
A Study of Literary Opinion in America and England,
1828-1864. Philadelphia: University of Pennsylvania
Press, 1939. Reprinted New York: Octagon, 1968.

827 FEENEY, Joseph J., S.J. "The Structure of Ambiguity in Hawthorne's 'The Maypole of Merry Mount.'"
Studies in American Fiction, 3 (1975), 211-216.

828 FEIDELSON, Charles Jr. "The Idea of Symbolism in
American Writing, with Particular Reference to
Emerson and Melville." Ph.D. diss., Yale, 1948.

829 _____. Symbolism and American Literature.
Chicago: University of Chicago Press, 1953. Hawthorne, pp.6-16 et passim.

830 _____. "Moral Meanings in The Scarlet Letter,"
in Pearce, Roy Harvey, ed., Centenary Essays
(1964), pp.31-77. Excerpted from Symbolism (1953).

831 _____. "Hawthorne as Symbolist," in Kaul, ed.,
Hawthorne: A Collection (1966), pp.64-71. Excerpt
from Symbolism (1953).

832 _____, and Paul Brodtkorb, Jr., eds. Interpreta-
tions of American Literature. New York: Oxford
University Press, 1959. "Hawthorne as Poet," by
Q.D. Leavis, pp.30-50.

833 FENSON, Harry, and Hildreth Kritzer, eds. Writing
About the Short Story. New York: Free Press, 1966.
"Rappaccini's Daughter," pp.61-62.

834 FERGUSON, J.D. "Earliest Translation of Hawthorne."
Nation, 100 (January 7, 1915), 14-15.

835 FERGUSON, J.M., Jr. "Hawthorne's 'Young Goodman
     Brown.'" Explicator, 28 (1969), item 32.

836 FERRELL, Margaret Jean C. "Dissolving the Gross
     Actuality of Fact: Hawthorne's Attack on Matter."
     Ph.D. diss., Oklahoma, 1967. DA, 28 (1968),
     1432A.

837 _____. "Imbalance in Hawthorne's Characters."
     South Dakota Review, 10 (1972), 45-59.

838 FETTERLY, Judith. The Resisting Reader: A Femi-
     nist Approach to American Fiction. Bloomington:
     Indiana University Press, 1978. "Palpable Designs:
     Women Beware Science: 'The Birthmark,'" pp.
     22-33.

839 FICK, Rev. Leonard J. "The Theology of Nathaniel
     Hawthorne." Ph.D. diss., Ohio State, 1951.

840 _____. The Light Beyond: A Study of Hawthorne's
     Theology. Westminster, Md.: Newman, 1955.

841 FIEDLER, Leslie A. "Boys Will Be Boys." New
     Leader, 41 (April 28, 1958), 23-26.

842 _____. Love and Death in the American Novel.
     New York: Criterion, 1960. Reprinted New York:
     Meridian, 1962. "The Scarlet Letter: Woman as
     Faust," pp. 485-519. Revised edition New York:
     Stein and Day, 1966. "Clarissa in America: To-
     ward Marjorie Moringstar," pp. 217-258; and "The
     Power of Blackness: Faustian Man and the Cult of
     Violence," pp. 430-505.

843 _____. "Le Viol des Temple: de Richardson à
     Faulkner." Preuves, 138 (August, 1962), 75-81.
     In French.

844 _____, ed. The Art of the Essay. New York:
     Crowell, 1958. "The Custom House--Introductory,"
     pp. 99-122.

845 FIELD, Roswell, ed. with Preface. Love Letters of
     Nathaniel Hawthorne: 1839-1841 and 1841-1863, to
     Sophia Peabody, 2 vols. Chicago: Privately printed

for the Society of the Dofobs, 1907. Reprinted in one-volume edition, edited by C. E. Frazer Clark, Jr. Washington, D. C.: NCR Microcard Editions, 1972.

846 FIELDS, Annie Adams. Hawthorne. Boston: Small and Maynard, 1899.

847 FIELDS, James T. "Hawthorne," in Yesterdays with Authors. Boston: Osgood, 1871, pp. 41-124.

848 _____. Hawthorne. Boston: Osgood, 1876.

849 FINKEL, Jan M. "Techniques of Portraying the Grotesque Character in Selected Writings of Nathaniel Hawthorne, Sherwood Anderson, and Joseph Heller." Ph. D. diss., Indiana, 1973. DA, 34 (1974), 7750A-7751A.

850 FINN, Helena Kane. "Design of Despair: The Tragic Heroine and the Imagery of Artifice in Novels by Hawthorne, James, and Wharton." Ph. D. diss., St. John's (New York), 1976. DA, 37 (1977), 5827A.

851 FISHER, Arthur W. "Nathaniel Hawthorne: A Study." Ph. D. diss., Cornell, 1907.

852 FISHER, Burton J. "Imagined Redemption in 'Roger Malvin's Burial.'" Studies in American Fiction, 5 (1977), 257-262.

853 FISHER, Marvin. "The Pattern of Conservatism in Johnson's Rasselas and Hawthorne's Tales." Journal of History of Ideas, 19 (April, 1958), 173-176.

854 _____. "Portrait of the Artist in America: 'Hawthorne and His Mosses.'" Southern Review, 11 (1975), 156-166.

855 FITCH, George. "Hawthorne's Somber Puritan Romances," in Fitch, Great Spiritual Writers of American Literature. San Franscisco: P. Elder, 1916, pp. 37-47.

856 FITZPATRICK, W. P. "The Great American Novel and The Night of the Hunter." Bulletin of West Virginia Association of College English Teachers (Marshall

University), 2 (1975), 18-31.

857 FLANAGAN, John T. "The Durable Hawthorne."
     Journal of English and Germanic Philology, 49
     (June, 1950), 88-96.

858 _____. "Point of View in The Marble Faun."
     Die neuren Sprachen (Frankfurt, Germany), 11
     (1962), 218-224. In English.

859 _____, and Arthur P. Hudson. Folklore in Ameri-
     can Literature. Evanston, Ill.: Row, Peterson,
     1958. Hawthorne, passim.

860 FLECK, Richard F. "Industrial Imagery in The House
     of the Seven Gables." Nathaniel Hawthorne Journal,
     4 (1974), 273-276.

861 FLETCHER, Angus. Allegory: The Theory of a
     Symbolic Mode. Ithaca, N.Y.: Cornell University
     Press, 1964. Hawthorne, pp. 88-92 et passim.

862 FLINT, Allen D. "Nathaniel Hawthorne's Political
     and Social Themes." Ph.D. diss., Minnesota, 1965.
     DA, 27 (1966), 1820A.

863 _____. "Hawthorne and the Slavery Crisis." New
     England Quarterly, 41 (September, 1968), 393-408.

864 _____. "'essentially a day-dream, and yet a fact':
     Hawthorne's Blithedale." Nathaniel Hawthorne Jour-
     nal, 2 (1972), 75-83.

865 _____. "'The Saving Grace' of Marriage in Haw-
     thorne's Fiction." Emerson Society Quarterly, 19
     (1973), 112-116.

866 _____. "Review of Nathaniel Hawthorne: Poems."
     Nathaniel Hawthorne Journal, 3 (1973), 255-260.
     Refers to work edited by Richard Peck, published
     by the Bibliographical Society of the University of
     Virginia, 1967.

867 FOERSTER, Norman, and Robert P. Falk, eds.
     Eight American Writers: An Anthology. New York:
     Norton, 1963. Selections and discussions of Haw-
     thorne by Richard H. Fogle, pp. 582-780.

868 FOGARTY, Robert S. "A Utopian Literary Canon."
New England Quarterly, 38 (1965), 386-391. Attitudes toward Hawthorne and Thoreau as expressed
in the Circular of the Oneida Community.

869 FOGLE, Richard Harter. "Ambiguity and Clarity in
Hawthorne's 'Young Goodman Brown.'" New England
Quarterly, 18 (December, 1945), 448-465.

870 _____. "The Problem of Allegory in Hawthorne's
'Ethan Brand.'" University of Toronto Quarterly,
17 (January, 1948), 190-203.

871 _____. "An Ambiguity of Sin or Sorrow?" New
England Quarterly, 21 (September, 1948), 342-349.
Discusses "The Minister's Black Veil."

872 _____. "The World and the Artist: A Study of
Hawthorne's 'The Artist of the Beautiful.'" Tulane
Studies in English, 1 (1949), 31-52. Reprinted in
Kaul, ed., Hawthorne: A Collection (1966), pp. 99-
110.

873 _____. "Simplicity and Complexity in The Marble
Faun." Tulane Studies in English, 2 (1950), 103-
120.

874 _____. Hawthorne's Fiction: The Light and the
Dark. Norman: University of Oklahoma Press,
1952. Revised edition in 1964, with new essays on
"The Birthmark" and "My Kinsman, Major Molineux."

875 _____. "Nathaniel Hawthorne," in Foerster and
Falk, eds., Eight American Writers (1963), pp. 582-
780.

876 _____. "Hawthorne." Review of Current Scholarship in American Literary Scholarship, 1965, pp.
15-27.

877 _____. "Weird Mockery: An Element of Hawthorne's
Style." Style, 2 (1968), 191-202.

878 _____. "Nathaniel Hawthorne: The House of the
Seven Gables," in Cohen, Hennig, ed., Landmarks
in American Writing (1969), pp. 111-120.

879 _____. "Hawthorne's Pictorial Unity." Emerson
Society Quarterly, 55 (1969), 71-76.

880 _____. Hawthorne's Imagery: The 'Proper Light
and Shadow' in the Major Romances. Norman:
University of Oklahoma Press, 1969.

881 _____. "Hawthorne and Coleridge on Credibility."
Criticism, 13 (1971), 234-241.

882 _____. "Priscilla's Veil: A Study of Veil Imagery
in The Blithedale Romance." Nathaniel Hawthorne
Journal, 2 (1972), 59-65. Based on talk given at
MLA meeting, December, 1971.

883 _____. "Nathaniel Hawthorne and the Great English
Romantic Poets." Keats-Shelley Journal, 21-22
(1972-1973), 219-235.

884 _____. "Hawthorne's Variegated Lighting." Bucknell Review, 21 (1973), 83-88.

885 _____. "Coleridge, Hilda, and The Marble Faun."
Emerson Society Quarterly, 19 (1973), 105-111.

886 _____. "'The Artist of the Beautiful,'" excerpt
from Hawthorne's Fiction (1952), in Kaul, ed.,
Hawthorne: A Collection (1966), pp. 99-110.

887 _____. "Byron and Nathaniel Hawthorne," in
Elledge, W. Paul, and Richard L. Hoffman, eds.,
Romantic and Victorian: Studies in Memory of
William H. Marshall. Rutherford, N. J.: Fairleigh
Dickinson University Press, 1971, pp. 181-197.

888 _____. The Permanent Pleasure. Athens: University of Georgia Press, 1974. Includes "Hawthorne, Literary History, and Criticism," pp. 1-16;
"Weird Mockery," pp. 124-136; and other previously
published essays.

889 _____. "Hawthorne, History, and the Human
Heart." Clio, 5 (1976), 175-180.

890 _____. "The Great English Romantics in Hawthorne's Major Romances." Nathaniel Hawthorne

Journal, 6 (1976), 62-68.

891   _____, ed with Introduction.   The House of the
         Seven Gables.   New York: Collier, 1962.

892 FOLEY, Marie L.   " 'The Key of Holy Sympathy':
     Hawthorne's Social Ideal. "   Ph. D.   diss. ,   Tulane,
     1969.   DA, 30 (1970), 4409.

893 FOLEY, Patrick Keven.   American Authors: 1795-1895.
     Boston: Publisher's Printing, 1897.

894 FOLSOM, James King.   "The Principle of Multiplicity
     in Hawthorne's Fiction. "   Ph. D.   diss. ,   Princeton,
     1959.   DA, 20 (1960), 3726.

895   _____. Man's Accidents and God's Purposes: Multi-
         plicity in Hawthorne's Fiction.   New Haven: College
         and University Press, 1963.

896 FORD, Linda Walters.   "Hawthorne's Reflection Images. "
     M. A. thesis, Texas (Arlington), 1973.

897 FOSSUM, Robert H.   "The Inviolable Circle: The
     Problem of Time in Hawthorne's Tales and Sketches. "
     Ph. D. diss. , Claremont, 1962.   DA, 24 (1963), 2477.

898   _____.   "The Shadow of the Past: Hawthorne's
         Historical Tales. "   Claremont Quarterly, 11 (1963),
         45-56.

899   _____.   "Time and the Artist in 'Legends of the
         Province House. ' "   Nineteenth-Century Fiction, 21
         (March, 1967), 337-348.

900   _____.   "The Summons of the Past: Hawthorne's
         'Alice Doane's Appeal. ' "   Nineteenth-Century Fiction,
         23 (March, 1968), 294-303.

901   _____.   Hawthorne's Inviolable Circle: The Problem
         of Time.   Deland, Fla. :   Everett-Edwards, 1972.

902 FOSTER, Charles H.   "Hawthorne's Literary Theory. "
     PMLA, 57 (March, 1942), 241-254.

903 FOSTER, Richard, ed. with Introduction.   Six American
     Novelists of the Nineteenth-Century.   Minneapolis:

University of Minnesota Press, 1968. "Hawthorne,"
by Hyatt Waggoner, pp. 45-81.

904 FRANCIS, Gloria A. "Recent Hawthorne Scholarship,
1970-1971." Nathaniel Hawthorne Journal, 2 (1972),
273-278.

905 _____. "Recent Hawthorne Scholarship, 1971-1972."
Nathaniel Hawthorne Journal, 3 (1973), 269-277.

906 FRANK, Albert J. von, and John R. Byers, Jr. "The
House of the Seven Gables: An Unlikely Source."
PMLA, 89 (1974), 1114-1115. An exchange between
Frank and Byers.

907 FRANK, Frederick Stilson. "Perverse Pilgrimage:
The Role of the Gothic in the Works of Charles
Brockden Brown, Poe, and Nathaniel Hawthorne."
Ph.D. diss., Rutgers University, 1968. DA, 29
(1968), 1866A-1867A.

908 FRANKLIN, Benjamin V. "Hawthorne's Non-Fiction:
His Attitude Toward America." Ph.D. diss., Ohio
State, 1969. DA, 31 (1970), 1226A-1227A.

909 FRANKLIN, Howard Bruce. "Hawthorne and Science
Fiction." Centennial Review, 10 (Winter, 1966),
112-130.

910 _____. Future Perfect: American Science-Fiction
of the Nineteenth-Century. New York: Oxford
University Press, 1966. Revised edition, 1978.
Reprints "Hawthorne and Science Fiction," listed
above, pp. 3-23.

911 FRANKLIN, Rosemary F. "The Cabin by the Lake:
Pastoral Landscapes of Poe, Cooper, Hawthorne,
and Thoreau." Emerson Society Quarterly, 22
(1976), 59-70.

912 FRANZOSA, John Carl. "Hawthorne in America: A
Problem in Identity." Ph.D. diss., State University
of New York (Buffalo), 1977. DA, 38 (1977), 2787A-
2788A.

913 _____. "'The Custom-House,' The Scarlet Letter,
and Hawthorne's Separation from Salem." Emerson
Society Quarterly, 24 (1978), 57-71.

914 FREDERICK, John T. "Hawthorne and the Workhouse
     Baby. " Arizona Quarterly, 24 (1968), 169-173. Dis-
     cusses an essay by Hawthorne, "Outside Glimpses of
     English Poverty, " published in Atlantic Monthly,
     1863.

915 _____. The Darkened Sky: Nineteenth-Century
     American Novelists and Religion. Notre Dame, Ind.:
     University of Notre Dame Press, 1969. Hawthorne,
     pp. 27-78.

916 _____. "Hawthorne's 'Scribbling Women.'" New
     England Quarterly, 48 (1975), 231-240.

917 FREEHAFER, John. "Hawthorne Publications Since
     the Centenary Year." Jahrbuch für Amerikastudien,
     15 (1970), 293-298.

918 _____. "The Marble Faun and the Editing of Nine-
     teenth-Century Texts." Studies in the Novel, 2
     (1970), 487-503.

919 _____. "Greg's Theory of Copy-Text and the
     Textual Criticism in the CEAA Editions." Studies
     in the Novel, 7 (1975), 375-388.

920 FRENCH, Allen. Hawthorne at the Old Manse. Con-
     cord, Mass.: Privately printed, c. 1948. Pamphlet.

921 FRIEDRICH, Gerhard. "A Note on Quakerism and
     Moby-Dick: Hawthorne's 'The Gentle Boy' as a
     Possible Source." Quaker History, 54 (August,
     1965), 94-102.

922 FRIESEN, Menno M. "The Mask in Nathaniel Haw-
     thorne's Fiction." Ph. D. diss., Denver, 1964.
     DA, 25 (1965), 5276.

923 FROESE, Robert Alan. "Hawthorne, the Teller and the
     Tales: A Study of Structure and Process in Haw-
     thorne's Short Fiction." Ph. D. diss., State Uni-
     versity of New York (Albany), 1977. DA, 38 (1978),
     4166A.

924 FRYE, Prosser H. "Hawthorne's Supernaturalism,"
     in Literary Reviews and Criticism. New York and
     London: Putnam, 1908, pp. 114-129.

925 FRYER, Judith J. "The Faces of Eve: A Study of
     Women in American Life and Literature in the Nine-
     teenth Century." Ph.D. diss., Minnesota, 1972.
     DA, 34 (1973), 2558A.

926 _____. The Faces of Eve: Women in the Nineteenth-
     Century American Novel. New York: Oxford Uni-
     versity Press, 1976. Contains the following essays
     related to Hawthorne: "The Temptress: Beatrice
     Rappaccini: The Literary Convention as Allegory,"
     pp.40-47; "The Temptress: Hawthorne's Miriam:
     The Temptress as Jew," pp.62-71; "The Temptress:
     Hester Prynne: The Dark Lady as 'Deviant,'" pp.
     72-84; "The American Princess: The Pale Maiden,"
     pp.87-97 (refers to Hilda and Priscilla); "The New
     Woman: Zenobia: The New Woman as Tragedy-
     Queen," pp.208-220.

927 FULLER, Edmund, and Olga Achtenhagen, eds. Four
     American Novels. New York: Harcourt, Brace,
     1959. Contains The Scarlet Letter.

928 FULLER, Frederick T. (nephew of Margaret Fuller).
     "Hawthorne and Margaret Fuller Ossoli." The Liter-
     ary World, January 10, 1885.

929 FUSSELL, Edwin S. "Hawthorne, James, and 'The
     Common Doom.'" American Quarterly, 10 (Winter,
     1958), 438-454.

930 _____. "Neutral Territory: Hawthorne on the
     Figurative Frontier," in Pearce, Roy Harvey, ed.,
     Centenary Essays (1964), pp.297-314.

931 _____. Frontier: American Literature and the
     American West. Princeton, N.J.: Princeton Uni-
     versity Press, 1965. "Nathaniel Hawthorne," pp.
     69-131; "Indian Summer of the Literary West," pp.
     327-396.

932 FYKES, Beverly J. "'The Fairest Hope of Heaven':
     Love and Marriage in Hawthorne's Works." Ph.D.
     diss., University of Tennessee, 1974. DA, 35
     (1974), 3738A-3739A.

933 GALE, Martha Tyler. "The Marble Faun, an Alle-

gory, with a Key to Its Interpretation." New Englander, 19 (October, 1861), 860-870. Reprinted in New Englander, 56 (January, 1892), 26-36.

934 GALE, Robert L. "Evil and the American Short Story." Annali Instituto Universitario Orientale Napoli Sezione Germanica, 1 (1958), 183-202.

935 _____. "The Marble Faun and The Sacred Fount: A Resemblance." Studi Americani, 8 (1962), 21-33.

936 _____. "Baglioni in 'Rappaccini's Daughter.'" Studi Americani, 9 (1963), 83-87.

937 _____. Plots and Characters in the Fiction and Sketches of Nathaniel Hawthorne. Hamden, Conn.: Archon, 1968. Foreword by Norman H. Pearson.

938 GALLAGHER, Edward J. "History in 'Endicott and the Red Cross.'" Emerson Society Quarterly, 50 Supplement (1968), 62-65.

939 _____. "Sir Kenelm Digby in Hawthorne's 'The Man of Adamant.'" Notes and Queries, 17 (1970), 15-16. Sir Kenelm Digby published an account of a petrified city in the 1650s; this work relates to Hawthorne's story.

940 _____. "Hawthorne's 'Sir William Phipps.'" Emerson Society Quarterly, 19 (1973), 213-218.

941 _____. "The Concluding Paragraph of 'Young Goodman Brown.'" Studies in Short Fiction, 12 (1975), 29-30.

942 GALLAGHER, Kathleen. "The Art of Snake Handling: Lamia [Keats], Elsie Venner [Holmes], and 'Rappaccini's Daughter.'" Studies in American Fiction, 3 (1975), 51-64.

943 GALLOP, Donald C. "On Hawthorne's Authorship of 'The Battle Omen.'" New England Quarterly, 9 (December, 1936), 690-699.

944 GAMBLE, Richard H. "Reflections of the Hawthorne-Melville Relationship in Pierre." American Literature, 47 (1975), 629-632.

945 GANNON, Frederic Augustus. Hawthorne and the Custom House. Salem, Mass.: Salem Book, 1955.

946 GARDNER, John, and Lennis Dunlap. The Forms of Fiction. New York: Random House, 1962. "Wakefield," pp. 60-62.

947 GARGANO, J. W. "Hawthorne's 'The Artist of the Beautiful.'" American Literature, 35 (May, 1963), 225-230.

948 GARLITZ, Barbara. "Pearl: 1850-1955." PMLA, 72 (September, 1957), 689-699.

949 _____. "Teaching All of Hawthorne." Emerson Society Quarterly, 25 (1961), 6-7.

950 GATES, Lewis E. "Hawthorne." Chap-Book, 9 (June 1, 1898), 51-55. Reprinted in Gates, Studies and Appreciations. New York: Macmillan, 1900, pp. 92-109.

951 GATTA, John, Jr. "Busy and Selfish London: The Urban Figure in Hawthorne's 'Wakefield.'" Emerson Society Quarterly, 23 (1977), 164-172.

952 _____. "Progress and Providence in The House of the Seven Gables." American Literature, 50 (1978), 37-48.

953 GAUTREAU, Henry W., Jr. "A Note on Hawthorne's 'The Man of Adamant.'" Philological Quarterly, 52 (1973), 315-317.

954 _____. "Hawthorne, the Master Genius." Southern Libertarian Messenger (Florence, S. C.), 1 (1975), 55-59.

955 GAVIGAN, Walter V. "Hawthorne and Rome." Catholic World, 103 (August, 1932), 555-559.

956 GEIST, Stanley. "Fictitious Americans." Hudson Review, 5 (Summer, 1952), 199-212.

957 GERALDI, Robert. "Biblical and Religious Sources and Parallels in The Scarlet Letter." Language Quarterly, 15 (1976), 31-34.

958 GERBER, John C. "Form and Content in The Scarlet Letter." New England Quarterly, 17 (March, 1944), 25-55.

959 _____. "A Critical Exercise in the Teaching of The House of the Seven Gables." Emerson Society Quarterly, 25 (1961), 8-11.

960 _____, ed. with Introduction. The Scarlet Letter. New York: Random House, 1950. Modern Library Edition.

961 _____, ed. with Introduction. Twentieth-Century Interpretations of The Scarlet Letter: A Collection of Critical Essays. Englewood Cliffs, N. J.: Prentice-Hall, 1968.

962 GEROULD, Gordon Hall. The Patterns of English and American and American Fiction: A History. Boston: Little, Brown, 1942. "Interpreters: I: Hawthorne, Melville, and the Brontes," pp. 341-366.

963 GEROULD, Katharine Fullerton. "Call It Holy Ground." Atlantic, 163 (January, 1939), 74-82.

964 GERSTENBERGER, Donna, and George Hendrick. The American Novel 1789-1959: A Checklist of Twentieth-Century Criticism. Denver: Allan Swallow, 1961. Hawthorne, pp. 105-118.

965 GIBBENS, Victor E. "Hawthorne's Note to 'Dr. Heidegger's Experiment.'" Modern Language Notes, 60 (June, 1945), 408-409.

966 GIBSON, William M. "The Art of Nathaniel Hawthorne: An Examination of The Scarlet Letter," in Hendrick George, ed., American Renaissance: The History of an Era. Frankfurt, Germany: Diesterweg, 1961, pp. 97-106.

967 _____. "Faulkner's The Sound and the Fury." Explicator, 22 (January, 1964), item 33.

968 GICZKOWSKI, William. "Cooper and Hawthorne: American Innovators in the Tradition of Sir Walter Scott." Ph. D. diss., Stanford, 1971. DA, 32 (1971) 5737A.

969 GILKES, Lillian B. "Hawthorne, Park Benjamin, S.
     G. Goodrich: A Three-Cornered Imbroglio." Na-
     thaniel Hawthorne Journal, 1 (1971), 83-112.

970 GILMORE, Michael T. The Middle Way: Puritanism
     and Ideology in American Romantic Fiction. New
     Brunswick, N. J.: Rutgers University Press, 1977.
     Hawthorne, pp. 65-130; Melville, pp. 131-194.

971 GISH, Lillian; Mark Van Doren; and Lyman Bryson.
     "The Scarlet Letter," in Crothers, George D., ed.,
     Invitation to Learning: English and American Novels.
     New York: Basic Books, 1966, pp. 211-222.

972 GLECKNER, Robert F. "James' Madame de Mauves
     and Hawthorne's The Scarlet Letter." Modern
     Language Notes, 73 (December, 1958), 580-586.

973 GLICKSBERG, Charles I. "The Numinous in Fiction."
     Arizona Quarterly, 15 (Winter, 1959), 305-313.
     Hawthorne, passim.

974 GODFREY, Sondra. "The Changing Vision of Evil in
     Hawthorne's Fiction." Ph. D. diss., City University
     of New York, 1976. DA, 36 (1976), 7421A-7422A.

975 GOGGIO, Emilio. "Dante Interests in Nineteenth-
     Century America." Philological Quarterly, 1 (1922),
     192-201.

976 GOLDFARB, Clare R. "The Marble Faun and Emerson-
     ian Self-Reliance." American Transcendental Quar-
     terly, 1 (1969), 19-23.

977 GOLDFARB, Russell M., and Clare R. Goldfarb.
     Spiritualism in Nineteenth-Century Letters. Ruther-
     ford, N. J.: Fairleigh Dickinson University Press,
     1978. Hawthorne, pp. 141-143.

978 GOLDSTEIN, Jesse Sidney. "The Literary Source of
     Hawthorne's Fanshawe." Modern Language Notes,
     60 (January, 1945), 1-8.

979 GOLLIN, Rita Kaplan. "Dream and Reverie in the
     Writings of Nathaniel Hawthorne." Ph. D. diss.,
     Minnesota, 1960. DA, 22 (1961), 1156.

980 _____. "'Dream Work' in The Blithedale Romance."
Emerson Society Quarterly, 19 (1973), 74-83.

981 _____. "Painting and Character in The Marble
Faun." Emerson Society Quarterly, 21 (1975), 1-10.

982 _____. "The Intelligence Offices of Hawthorne and
Melville." American Transcendental Quarterly, 26
Supplement (1975), 44-47.

983 _____. "Hawthorne on Perception, Lucubration,
and Reverie." Nathaniel Hawthorne Journal, 6 (1976),
227-239.

984 _____. "Hawthorne: The Writer as Dreamer,"
in Myerson, ed., Studies: 1977 (1978), pp. 313-326.

985 GOMBRICH, E. H. Art and Illusion. New York:
Pantheon, 1960. Hawthorne, passim.

986 GOODMAN, Paul. "'The Minister's Black Veil':
Mystery and Sublimity," in Goodman, ed., The
Structure of Literature. Chicago: University of
Chicago Press, 1954, pp. 253-257.

987 GOODRICH, Samuel G. Recollections of a Lifetime,
2 vols. New York: Auburn, Miller, Orton and
Mulligan, 1856. Reprinted New York: C. M. Saxton,
1859. Hawthorne, Vol. II, pp. 269-273 et passim.
See article by Lillian B. Gilkes (1971).

988 GOODSPEED, Charles E. "Nathaniel Hawthorne and the
Museum of the East India Marine Society." American Neptune, 5 (October, 1945), 266-272.

989 _____. Nathaniel Hawthorne and the Museum of
the Salem East India Society: or the Gathering of a
Virtuoso's Collection. Salem, Mass.: Peabody
Museum, 1946. See review in New England Quarterly, 19 (1946), 558-559.

990 GORDAN, John D. "Nathaniel Hawthorne, the Years
of Fulfillment: 1804-1853." Bulletin of the New
York Public Library, 59 (March, April, May, June,
1955), 154-165, 198-217, 259-269, 316-321. Cata-
log of the Berg Collection. Later published as a
book, New York: New York Public Library, 1955.

991 _____. "Novels in Manuscript: An Exhibition from
    the Berg Collection." Bulletin of the New York Public
    Library, 69 (May, 1965), 317-329.

992 GORDON, Caroline, and Allen Tate. The House of
    Fiction, 2nd edition. New York: Scribner, 1960.
    "Young Goodman Brown," pp. 36-38.

993 GORDON, I. "Mostly About Books." Hobbies, 53
    (July, 1948), 133-134.

994 GORDON, Joseph T. "Nathaniel Hawthorne and Brook
    Farm." Emerson Society Quarterly, 33 (1963), 51-
    61.

995 GORMAN, Herbert. Hawthorne: A Study in Solitude.
    New York: Doran, 1927. Murray Hill Biographies
    Series. Reprinted New York: Biblo and Tannen,
    1966.

996 GOTTFRIED, Alex, and Sue Davidson. "Utopia's
    Children: An Interpretation of Three Political
    Novels." Western Political Quarterly, 15 (March,
    1962), 17-32. Refers to Hawthorne's The Blithedale
    Romance (1852); Mary McCarthy's The Oasis (1949);
    Harvey Swados's False Coin (1959).

997 GOTTLEIB, Elaine. "Singer and Hawthorne: A Pre-
    valence of Satan." Southern Review (Adelaide,
    Australia), 8 (1972), 359-370.

998 GOTTSCHALK, Jane. "The Continuity of American
    Letters in The Scarlet Letter and 'The Beast in the
    Jungle.'" Wisconsin Studies in Contemporary Liter-
    ary, 9 (1967), 39-45.

999 GRADDY, William E. "Another Error in The Marble
    Faun." Emerson Society Quarterly, 63 (1971), 26-
    27.

1000 GRAHAM, John. "The Restored Passages in the
    Centenary Edition of The Blithedale Romance."
    Humanities Association Bulletin, 24 (1973), 100-114.

1001 GRANGER, Bruce Ingham. "Arthur Dimmesdale as
    Tragic Hero." Nineteenth-Century Fiction, 19
    (September, 1964), 197-203.

1002 GRANT, Douglas. "Sir Walter Scott and Nathaniel Hawthorne." University of Leeds Review, 8 (1962), 35-41.

1003 _____. Purpose and Place: Essays on American Writers. London: Macmillan, 1965. Hawthorne, pp. 21-33.

1004 GRANT, William E. "Nathaniel Hawthorne and Empirical Psychology." Ph.D. diss., Claremont, 1971. DA, 32 (1971), 2686A-2687A.

1005 _____. "Hawthorne's Hamlet: The Archetypal Structure of The Blithedale Romance." Bulletin of the Rocky Mountain Modern Language Association, 31 (1977), 1-15.

1006 GRAY, Maxwell. "Hawthorne, the Mystic." Nineteenth-Century and After, 87 (January, 1920), 118-125.

1007 GREEN, Martin B. "The Hawthorne Myth: A Protest." Essays and Studies (by members of the English Association), 16 (1963), 16-36. Reprinted in Green, Re-appraisals: Some Commonsense Readings in American Literature. New York: Norton, 1966, pp. 61-85.

1008 GREENE, Maxine. "Man Without God in American Fiction." Humanist, 25 (May-June, 1965), 125-128.

1009 GREENWOOD, Douglas. "The Heraldic Device in The Scarlet Letter: Hawthorne's Symbolic Use of the Past." American Literature, 46 (1974), 207-210.

1010 GREET, T.Y.: Charles E. Edge; and John M. Munro; eds. The Worlds of Fiction: Studies in Context. Boston: Houghton Mifflin, 1964. "Rappaccini's Daughter," pp. 129-135.

1011 GRIBBLE, Francis. "Hawthorne from an English Point of View." Critic, 45 (July, 1904), 20-23.

1012 _____. "Two Centenaries: Nathaniel Hawthorne and George Sand." Fortnightly Review, 82 (August, 1904), 260-278.

1013   GRIFFIN, Gerald R.   "Authorship and Attribution:
       An Internal Analysis of the Hawthorne Short Story
       Apocrypha."   Ph.D. diss., Massachusetts, 1971.
       DA, 32 (1971), 1511A.

1014   _____.   "Hawthorne and 'The New England Village':
       Internal Evidence and a New Genesis of The Scarlet
       Letter."   Essex Institute Historical Collections, 107
       (1971), 268-279.

1015   GRIFFITH, Albert J.   "Heart Images in Hawthorne's
       Names."   Emerson Society Quarterly, 43 (1966),
       78-79.

1016   GRIFFITH, Ben W., Jr.   "Hawthorne's The House
       of the Seven Gables."   Georgia Review, 8 (Summer,
       1954), 235-237.

1017   GRIFFITH, Clark.   "Substance or Shadow: Language
       and Meaning in The House of the Seven Gables."
       Modern Philology, 51 (February, 1953), 187-195.

1018   _____.   "'Emersonianism' and 'Poeism':   Some
       Versions of the Romantic Sensibility."   Modern
       Language Quarterly, 22 (June, 1961), 125-134.

1019   _____.   "Caves and Cave Dwellers: The Study of
       a Romantic Image."   Journal of English and Ger-
       manic Philology, 62 (1963), 551-568.

1020   GRIFFITH, Kelley, Jr.   "Form in The Blithedale
       Romance."   American Literature, 40 (1968), 15-26.

1021   GRIFFITHS, Thomas Morgan.   "'Montpelier' and
       'Seven Gables':   Knox's Estate and Hawthorne's
       Novel."   New England Quarterly, 16 (September,
       1943), 432-443.

1022   _____.   Maine Sources in "The House of the Seven
       Gables."   Waterville, Maine: Privately printed for
       the author, 1945.   49p. pamphlet, documented.

1023   GRILLEY, Virginia.   A Brief History of the Hawthorne
       Family and the Ancient Cottage at 27 Union Street
       Where the Great Romancer Nathaniel Hawthorne Was
       Born on July 4, 1804.   Salem, Mass.:   Seven Gables
       Book Shop, 1959.   Sketch for young people.

1024   GRISWOLD, M. J. "American Quaker History in the
       Works of Whittier, Hawthorne, and Longfellow."
       Americana, 34 (April, 1940), 220-263.

1025   GROLIER CLUB, New York. First Editions of the
       Works of Nathaniel Hawthorne. New York: Grolier
       Club, 1905.

1026   GROSS, Robert A. "'The Most Estimable Place in
       All the World': A Debate on Progress in Nineteenth-
       Century Concord," in Myerson, ed., Studies: 1978
       (1978), pp. 1-16.

1027   GROSS, Robert Eugene. "A Study of Hawthorne's
       Fanshawe and The Marble Faun: The Texture of
       Significance." Ph. D. diss., New York University,
       1960. DA, 21 (1961), 2274.

1028   _____. "Hawthorne's First Novel: The Future of
       a Style." PMLA, 78 (March, 1963), 60-68.

1029   GROSS, Seymour L. "The Technique of Nathaniel
       Hawthorne's Short Stories." Ph. D. diss., Illinois,
       1954. DA, 14 (1954), 1720.

1030   _____. "Hawthorne's Revision of 'The Gentle
       Boy.'" American Literature, 26 (May, 1954), 196-
       208.

1031   _____. "Hawthorne's 'Alice Doane's Appeal.'"
       Nineteenth-Century Fiction, 10 (December, 1955),
       232-236.

1032   _____. "Hawthorne's 'Lady Eleanore's Mantle' as
       History." Journal of English and Germanic Philology,
       54 (October, 1955), 549-554. Reprinted in Studies
       by Members of the English Department in Memory of
       John Jay Parry. Urbana: University of Illinois
       Press, 1955, pp. 89-94.

1033   _____. "Hawthorne's 'Vision of the Fountain' as
       a Parody." American Literature, 27 (March, 1955),
       101-105. Based on original version as it appeared
       in the New England Magazine, 1835.

1034   _____. "Hawthorne's Income from The Token."
       Studies in Bibliography, 8 (1956), 236-238.

1035 _____. "Four Possible Additions to Hawthorne's 'Story Teller.'" Papers of the Bibliographical Society of America, 51 (1957), 90-95.

1036 _____. "Hawthorne's 'My Kinsman, Major Molineux': History as Moral Adventure." Nineteenth-Century Fiction, 12 (September, 1957), 97-109.

1037 _____. "Hawthorne and the Shakers." American Literature, 29 (January, 1958), 457-463.

1038 _____. "'Solitude, and Love, and Anguish': The Tragic Design of The Scarlet Letter." College Language Association Journal, 3 (March, 1960), 154-165.

1039 _____. "Hawthorne's Moral Realism." Emerson Society Quarterly, 25 (1961), 11-13.

1040 _____. "Hawthorne versus Melville." Bucknell Review, 14 (December, 1966), 89-109.

1041 _____. "Hawthorne and the London Athenaeum, 1834-1864." Nathaniel Hawthorne Journal, 3 (1973), 35-72. Discusses reviews by Henry Fothergill Chorley.

1042 _____, ed. A Scarlet Letter Handbook. San Francisco: Wadsworth, 1960. Criticism and bibliography.

1043 _____, ed. with Introduction. The House of the Seven Gables. New York: Norton, 1967. Norton Critical Edition.

1044 _____, and Alfred J. Levy. "Some Remarks on the Extant Manuscripts of Hawthorne's Short Stories." Studies in Bibliography, 14 (1961), 254-257.

1045 _____, and Randall Stewart. "The Hawthorne Revival," in Pearce, Roy Harvey, ed., Centenary Essays (1964), pp. 335-366. Lists numerous writings on Hawthorne.

1046 GROSS, Theodore L. "Nathaniel Hawthorne: The Absurdity of Heroism." Yale Review, 57 (Winter, 1968), 182-195. Reprinted in Gross, The Heroic

Ideal in American Literature. New York: Free
Press, 1971, pp. 18-33.

1047   _____, and Stanley Wertheim. Hawthorne, Mel-
ville, and Stephen Crane: A Critical Bibliography.
New York: Free Press, 1971. "Hawthorne," by
Theodore Gross, pp. 1-100.

1048   GROSSMAN, James. "Vanzetti and Hawthorne."
American Quarterly, 22 (1970), 902-907. Refers
to Sacco-Vanzetti Case of 1927. Vanzetti made these
statements before his death: "Our words, our lives,
our pains--nothing! The taking of our lives--lives
of a good shoemaker and a poor fish pedlar--all!
That last moment belongs to us--that agony is our
triumph." Said to be related to Hawthorne's "The
Ambitious Guest."

1049   GRUNES, Dennis. "Allegory versus Allegory in
Hawthorne." American Transcendental Quarterly,
32 (1976), 14-19.

1050   GUILDS, John C. "Miriam of The Marble Faun:
Hawthorne's Subtle Sinner." Cairo Studies in
English, n. v. (1960), 61-68.

1051   GUPTA, Raj Kumar. "Hawthorne's Theory of Art."
American Literature, 40 (1968), 309-324.

1052   _____. "Hawthorne's Ideal Reader." Indian
Journal of American Studies, 1 (1969), 97-99.

1053   _____. "Hawthorne's Treatment of the Artist."
New England Quarterly, 45 (1972), 65-80.

1054   _____. "The Technique of Counter-statement:
Theme and Meaning in Hawthorne's 'The Village
Uncle.'" Nathaniel Hawthorne Journal, 3 (1973),
154-161.

1055   _____. "The Idea and the Image: Some Aspects
of Imagery in the Minor Short Stories of Nathaniel
Hawthorne," in Chander, Jagdish, and Narindar S.
Pradhan, eds., Studies in American Literature:
Essays in Honor of William Mulder. Delhi, India:
Oxford University Press, 1974, pp. 62-76.

1056 GUSTAFSON, Judith Alma. "Parody in The House of
      the Seven Gables." Nathaniel Hawthorne Journal,
      6 (1976), 294-302.

1057 _____. "Strategies of Deception: Hawthorne and
      James and Their Readers." Ph. D. diss., Wayne
      State, 1978. DA, 39 (1978), 1567A.

1058 GWYNN, Frederick L. "Hawthorne's 'Rappaccini's
      Daughter.'" Nineteenth-Century Fiction, 7 (De-
      cember, 1952), 217-219.

1059 H. R. "Hawthorne in More Cheerful Mood." Christian
      Science Monitor, 27 (July 1, 1935), 7.

1060 HABER, Richard. "The English Renaissance Novella
      and Hawthorne's The Scarlet Letter: Toward a
      Theory of Fiction." Ph. D. diss., Massachusetts,
      1976. DA, 37 (1977), 5850A-5851A.

1061 HAEGER, Cherie Ann. "Allegorical Method in Spenser
      and Hawthorne." Ph. D. diss., Duquesne (Pitts-
      burgh), 1974. DA, 36 (1975), 2190A.

1062 HAGOPIAN, John V., and Martin Dolch, eds. In-
      sight I: Analyses of American Literature. Frank-
      furt, Germany: Hirschgraben, 1962. Hawthorne,
      pp. 67-73, 78-81.

1063 HAKUTANI, Yoshinobu. "Hawthorne and Melville's
      'Benito Cereno.'" Hiroshima Studies in English
      Language and Literature, 10 (1963), 58-64.

1064 HALL, Ian Roger. "Murdering the Time: A Study
      of the Temporal Order in Selected Works of Henry
      David Thoreau, Nathaniel Hawthorne, T. S. Eliot,
      and Ezra Pound." Ph. D. diss., Kent State, 1975.
      DA, (1976), 6099A.

1065 HALL, Lawrence Sargent. "Nathaniel Hawthorne as
      a Critic of Nineteenth-Century America." Ph. D.
      diss., Yale, 1941.

1066 _____. "Hawthorne, Critic of Society: The Mak-
      ing of an American Philosophy." Saturday Review

of Literature, 26 (May 22, 1943), 28 et passim.

1067 _____. Hawthorne: Critic of Society. New Haven:
     Yale University Press, 1944.

1068 HALL, Spencer. "Beatrice Cenci: Symbol and Vision
     in The Marble Faun." Nineteenth-Century Fiction,
     25 (1970), 85-95.

1069 HALL, William F. "Hawthorne, Shakespeare, and
     Tess: Hardy's Use of Allusion and Reference."
     English Studies (Ghent, Belgium), 52 (1971), 533-
     542.

1070 _____. "Henry James and the Picturesque Mode."
     English Studies in Canada (Toronto), 1 (1975), 326-
     343.

1071 HALLIBURTON, David G. "The Grotesque in American
     Literature: Poe, Hawthorne, and Melville." Ph.D.
     diss., California (Riverside), 1966. DA, 27
     (1967), 3840A-3841A.

1072 HALLIGAN, John. "Hawthorne and Democracy:
     'Endicott and the Red Cross.'" Studies in Short
     Fiction, 8 (1971), 301-307.

1073 HAMADA, Masijiro. "The Scarlet Letter: A Tale of
     Three Prisoners." Bungaku-Kai Ronshu (Konan
     University, Japan), 1-18. In English.

1074 _____. "Gothic Romance in The House of the
     Seven Gables." Studies in English Literature (Tokyo),
     45 (1968), 49-61. In English.

1075 HAMBLEN, Abigail Ann. "Protestanism in Three
     American Novels." Forum (Houston), 3 (Fall-Winter,
     1960), 40-43. Studies The Scarlet Letter (1850);
     Sons of the Puritans, by Don Marquis (1939); and
     The John Wood Case, by Ruth Suckow (1959).

1076 HAMBLEN, Ellen N. "Adulterous Heroines in Nine-
     teenth-Century Literature: A Comparative Literature
     Study." Ph.D. diss., Florida State, 1977. DA,
     38 (1977), 2761A.

1077 HANENKRAT, Frank Thomas. "An Investigation of

Hawthorne's Psychology: The Themes of Evil and
Love in Selected Short Stories. " Ph.D. diss.,
Emory, 1971. DA, 32 (1971), 2688A.

1078 HANNIGAN, D. F. "Hawthorne's Place in Literature. "
Living Age, 231 (December 14, 1901), 720-724.

1079 HANSCOM, Elizabeth D., ed. The Scarlet Letter.
New York: Macmillan, 1927.

1080 HANSEN, Elaine Tuttle. "Ambiguity and the Narrator
in The Scarlet Letter. " Journal of Narrative Technique, 5 (1975), 147-163.

1081 HANSEN, Sister Regina, O.S.B. "The Atmospherical
Medium: A Study of the Romantic Milieu in Haw-
thorne's Major Fiction. " Ph.D. diss., Marquette
(Milwaukee), 1972. DA, 33 (1973), 5680A.

1082 HARASZTI, Zoltán. "Hawthorne Forecasts Franklin
Pierce's Career. " Boston Public Library Quarterly,
3 (January, 1951), 83-86.

1083 HARDING, Walter. "American History in the Novel,
1585-1900: The Period of Expansion, 1815-1861. "
Midwest Journal, 8 (Spring-Fall, 1956), 393-398.

1084 _____. "Another Source for Hawthorne's 'Egotism;
or, the Bosom Serpent.'" American Literature, 40
(1969), 537-538.

1085 HARDWICK, Elizabeth. "Seduction and Betrayal, "
in Hardwick, Seduction and Betrayal. New York:
Random House, 1974, pp. 175-208. Includes reference
to Hawthorne.

1086 HARMSEL, Henrietta T. "'Young Goodman Brown'
and 'The Enormous Radio.'" Studies in Short Fiction,
9 (1972), 407-408. Refers to story by John Cheever
(1953).

1087 HAROUTUNIAN, Joseph. Piety versus Moralism: The
Passing of New England Theology. New York: Holt,
1932. Reprinted Gloucester, Mass.: Peter Smith,
1965. Hawthorne, passim.

1088 HARRIS, Joel Chandler. "Provinciality in Literature--

A Defense of Boston," in Harris, Julia Collier,
ed., Joel Chandler Harris: Editor and Essayist.
Chapel Hill: University of North Carolina Press,
1931, pp.186-195.

1089 HART, James D. "The Scarlet Letter: One Hundred
Years After." New England Quarterly, 23 (September, 1950), 381-395.

1090 _____. "Hawthorne's Italian Diary." American
Literature, 34 (January, 1963), 562-567.

1091 HARTLEY, L.P. "The Novelist's Responsibility."
Essays and Studies (by Members of the English
Association), 15 (1962), 88-100.

1092 _____. "Nathaniel Hawthorne," in The Writer's
Responsibility. London: Hamish Hamilton, 1967,
pp.56-141.

1093 HARTMANN, Barbara Snow Hengst. "Communion
with the Divided Segments: The Characters of
Hawthorne's Early Fiction and in The Scarlet Letter."
Ph.D. diss., Brandeis, 1977. DA, 38 (1977),
2789A.

1094 HARTWICK, Harry. The Foreground of American
Fiction. New York: American Book, 1934. Hawthorne, passim.

1095 HARWELL, Richard. Hawthorne and Longfellow:
A Guide to an Exhibit. Brunswick, Maine: Bowdoin
College Press, 1966.

1096 HASSELMAYER, Louis A. "Hawthorne and the Cenci."
Neophilologus, 27 (1941), 59-64.

1097 HASKELL, R.I. "Sensings and Realizations on Reading 'The Great Stone Face.'" Education, 43 (May,
1923), 544-550.

1098 _____. "The Great Carbuncle." New England
Quarterly, 10 (September, 1937), 533-535.

1099 HASTINGS, Louise. "An Origin for 'Dr. Heidegger's
Experiment.'" American Literature, 9 (January,
1938), 403-410.

1100   HATHAWAY, Richard D. "Hawthorne and the Paradise
       of Children." Western Humanities Review, 15
       (Spring, 1961). 161-172.

1101   HAUGH, Robert F. "The Second Secret in The Scar-
       let Letter." College English, 17 (February, 1956),
       269-271.

1102   HAVENS, Elmer A. "'The Golden Branch' as Symbol
       in The House of the Seven Gables." Modern Lan-
       guage Notes, 74 (January, 1959), 20-22.

1103   HAVIGHURST, Walter. "Symbolism and the Student."
       College English, 16 (April, 1955), 429-434, 461.

1104   HAWTHORNE, Hildegarde (Julian Hawthorne's daugh-
       ter). "Hawthorne and Melville." Literary Review
       of New York Evening Post, 2 (February 4, 1922),
       406.

1105   _____. Romantic Rebel: The Story of Nathaniel
       Hawthorne. New York: Appleton-Century, 1932.
       For young people.

1106   _____. "The Most Unforgettable Character I've
       Met." Reader's Digest, February, 1950, pp. 21-25.
       Refers to Rose Hawthorne Lathrop, later Mother
       Alphonsa.

1107   HAWTHORNE, Julian (Hawthorne's son, 1846-1934).
       "The Salem of Hawthorne." Century Magazine, 28
       (May, 1884), 3-17.

1108   _____. "Scenes of Hawthorne's Romances."
       Century Magazine, 28 (July, 1884), 380-397.

1109   _____. Nathaniel Hawthorne and His Wife, 2 vols.
       Boston: Osgood, 1884. Life and letters.

1110   _____. "Problems of The Scarlet Letter." At-
       lantic, 57 (April, 1886), 471-485. Reprinted in
       Cameron, ed., Hawthorne Among His Contemporaries
       (1968), pp. 282-289.

1111   _____. "Hawthorne's Philosophy." Century
       Magazine, 32 (May, 1886), 83-93. Reprinted in
       Cameron, ed., Hawthorne Among His Contemporaries
       (1968), pp. 289-296.

1112   . "Nathaniel Hawthorne's 'Elixir of Life'
        and Methods of Work." Lippincott's Magazine, 45
        (1890), 66-69. Reprinted in Cameron, ed., Haw-
        thorne Among His Contemporaries (1968), pp. 156-
        160.

1113   . Hawthorne's Reading: An Essay. Cleve-
        land: The Rowfant Club, 1902. Reprinted Folcroft,
        Pa.: Folcroft, 1969.

1114   . Hawthorne and His Circle. New York:
        Harper and Brothers, 1903.

1115   . "Hawthorne and His Circle." Nation, 77
        (November 19, 1903), 410-411. Comment on book
        above.

1116   . "A Group of Hawthorne Letters." Harper's
        Magazine, 108 (March, 1904), 602-607.

1117   . "Hawthorne's Last Years." Critic, 45
        (July, 1904), 67-71.

1118   . "Books of Memory." Bookman, 61
        (July, 1925), 567-571.

1119   . "Hawthorne, Man of Action." Saturday
        Review of Literature, 3 (April 21, 1927), 727-728.

1120   . "Such Is Paradise." Century, 105 (De-
        cember, 1927), 157-169.

1121   . "A Daughter of Hawthorne." Atlantic,
        142 (September, 1928), 372-377.

1122   . Shapes That Pass. New York: Macmillan,
        1928. Nathaniel Hawthorne, passim.

1123   . "The Making of The Scarlet Letter."
        Bookman, 74 (December, 1931), 401-411.

1124   . "Nathaniel Hawthorne's Blue Cloak: A
        Son's Reminiscences." Bookman, 75 (September,
        1932), 501-506.

1125   . "Rebellious Puritan: Portrait of Mr.
        Hawthorne, by Lloyd Morris (1927)," a review-

article, in Canby, Henry Seidel, et al., eds., De-
signed for Reading. New York: Macmillan, 1934,
pp. 275-281.

1126   _____. Memoirs of Julian Hawthorne. New York:
Macmillan, 1938.

1127   _____, ed. Dr. Grimshawe's Secret. Boston:
Osgood, 1883.

1128   HAWTHORNE, Manning (Hawthorne's great-grandson).
"Hawthorne and 'The Man of God.'" Colophon, n. s.,
2 (Winter, 1937), 262-282. Refers to Horace L.
Conolly, an aquaintance of Hawthorne's.

1129   _____. "Hawthorne's Early Years." Essex Institute Historical Collections, 74 (January, 1938), 1-
21.

1130   _____. "Nathaniel Hawthorne Prepares for College."
New England Quarterly, 11 (March, 1938), 66-88.

1131   _____. "The Friendship Between Hawthorne and
Longfellow." English Journal, 2 (March, 1939), 221-
223. Also in English Leaflet, 39 (February, 1940),
25-30.

1132   _____. "Maria Louisa Hawthorne." Essex Institute Historical Collections, 75 (April, 1939), 103-
134.

1133   _____. "Nathaniel and Elizabeth Hawthorne, Edi-
tors." Colophon 3 (Fall, 1939), 1-12.

1134   _____. "Hawthorne and Utopian Socialism." New
England Quarterly, 12 (December, 1939), 726-730.

1135   _____. "Parental and Family Influences on Hawthorne." Essex Institute Historical Collections, 76
(January, 1940), 1-13.

1136   _____. "Nathaniel Hawthorne at Bowdoin." New
England Quarterly, 13 (June, 1940), 246-279.

1137   _____. "A Glimpse of Hawthorne's Boyhood."
Essex Institute Historical Collections, 83 (April,
1947), 178-184.

1138 _____. "Aunt Ebe: Some Letters of Elizabeth
Hawthorne." New England Quarterly, 20 (June,
1947), 209-231.

1139 _____. "The Concord Writers," in The American
Literary Scene. Bombay, India: Popular Book De-
pot, 1962, pp. 1-13.

1140 _____. "Hawthorne," in Herzberg, Max J. ed.,
The Reader's Encyclopedia of American Literature.
New York: Crowell, 1962, pp. 439-441.

1141 HAWTHORNE, Nathaniel. The Works of Nathaniel
Hawthorne, 12 vols. Edited by George Parsons
Lathrop. Boston and New York: Houghton Mifflin,
1883. Standard Riverside Edition.

1142 HAWTHORNE, Sophia Amelia Peabody (Hawthorne's
wife), ed. Passages from the American Notebooks
of Nathaniel Hawthorne. Boston: Osgood, 1868.

1143 _____, ed. Passages from the English Notebooks.
Boston: Osgood, 1870.

1144 _____, ed. Passages from the French and Italian
Notebooks. Boston: Osgood, 1871. Reprinted
Boston: Houghton Mifflin, 1891.

1145 HAWTHORNE, Una (Hawthorne's daughter), ed. Septimius Felton: or, The Elixir of Life. Boston: Osgood, 1872.

1146 HAYFORD, Harrison M. "Nathaniel Hawthorne and
Melville: A Biographical and Critical Study." Ph.D.
diss., Yale, 1945.

1147 _____. "Hawthorne, Melville, and the Sea." New
England Quarterly, 19 (December, 1946), 435-452.

1148 HAYS, Peter L. "Why Seven Years in The Scarlet
Letter?" Nathaniel Hawthorne Journal, 2 (1972),
251-253.

1149 HAZARD, Lucy L. "The Puritan Frontier," in
Hazard, The Frontier in American Literature. New
York: Crowell, 1927. Reprinted New York: Ungar,
1967, pp. 1-45.

1150 HEDGES, Elaine. "Howells on a Hawthornesque
      Theme." Texas Studies in Literature and Language,
      3 (Spring, 1961), 129-143.

1151 HEDGES, William L. "Hawthorne's Blithedale: The
      Function of the Narrator." Nineteenth-Century Fic-
      tion, 14 (March, 1960), 303-316.

1152 _____. "Irving, Hawthorne, and the Image of the
      Wife." American Transcendental Quarterly, 5 (1970),
      22-26.

1153 HEENEY, Sister Saint Agnes, S.S.J. "The Cathedral
      in Four Major New England Authors: A Study in
      Symbolical Inspiration." Ph.D. diss., Pennsylvania,
      1956. DA, 17 (1957), 1083-1084.

1154 HEILMAN, Robert B. "Hawthorne's 'The Birthmark':
      Science and Religion." South Atlantic Quarterly, 48
      (October, 1949), 575-583.

1155 HEINITZ, Kenneth L. "Nathaniel Hawthorne's Theory
      of Art." Ph.D. diss., Loyola (Chicago), 1963.

1156 HENDERSON, Harry B., III. "Hawthorne and the
      Limits of the Holiest Imagination," in Versions of
      the Past. New York: Oxford University Press,
      1974, pp. 91-126.

1157 HENDRICK, George. "William Sloane Kennedy Looks
      to Emerson and Thoreau." Emerson Society Quarterly,
      26 (1962), 28-31.

1158 HENNELLY, Mark M., Jr. "Hawthorne's Opus Al-
      chymicum: 'Ethan Brand.'" Emerson Society
      Quarterly, 22 (1976), 96-106.

1159 _____. "'Alice Doane's Appeal': Hawthorne's
      Case Against the Artist." Studies in American Fic-
      tion, 6 (1978), 125-140.

1160 HERNDON, Jerry A., and Sidney P. Moss. "The
      Identity and Significance of the German Jewish Show-
      man in Hawthorne's 'Ethan Brand.'" College English,
      23 (February, 1962), 362-363.

1161 _____. "Hawthorne's Dream Imagery." American Literature, 46 (1975), 538-545.

1162 HERRICK, Robert, and Robert W. Bruére, eds. Twice-Told Tales. Chicago: Scott, Foresman, 1903.

1163 HERRING, Thelma. "The Escape of Sir William Heans: Hay's Debt to Hawthorne and Melville." Southerly (Sydney, Australia), 26 (1966), 75-92. Refers to William Hay, Australian novelist.

1164 HERTENSTEIN, Rod. "A Mythic Reading of 'Roger Malvin's Burial, '" in Baldanza, Frank, ed., Itinerary 3: Criticism. Bowling Green, Ohio: Bowling Green State University Press, 1977.

1165 HESFORD, Walter. "Literary Contexts of 'Life in the the Iron Mills.'" American Literature, 49 (1977), 70-85. Refers to a story by Rebecca Harding Davis, 1861, perhaps influenced by the author's reading of several early Hawthorne sketches.

1166 HEWITT, Augustine F. "Hawthorne's Attitude Toward Catholicism." Catholic World, 42 (October, 1885), 21-34. Reprinted in Cameron, ed., Hawthorne Among His Contemporaries (1968), pp. 269-274.

1167 HICKS, Granville. "A Conversation in Boston." Sewanee Review, 39 (April-June, 1931), 129-142. Refers to Margaret Fuller.

1168 _____. The Great Tradition: An Interpretation of American Literature Since the Civil War. New York: Macmillan, 1933. Reprinted Chicago: Quadrangle, 1969. "Heritage," pp. 1-31; Hawthorne, passim.

1169 HIGGINSON, Thomas Wentworth. "Hawthorne's Last Bequest." Scribner's Monthly, 5 (November, 1872), 100-116. Reprinted in part in Cameron, ed., Hawthorne Among His Contemporaries (1968), pp. 156-160.

1170 _____. "A Precursor of Hawthorne." Independent, 40 (c. 1888), 385-386. Refers to William Austin.

1171 _____, ed. The Hawthorne Centenary Celebration at the Wayside, Concord, Mass., July 4-7, 1904.

Boston: Houghton Mifflin, 1905. Contains addresses by Higginson, Charles T. Copeland, Julia Ward Howe, Charles Francis Adams, F.P. Stearns, M.D. Conway, and F.B. Sanborn.

1172 HIJIYA, James A. "Nathaniel Hawthorne's Our Old Home." American Literature, 46 (1974), 363-373.

1173 HILDEBRAND, Anne. "Incomplete Metamorphosis in 'Allegories of the Heart.'" American Transcendental Quarterly, 13 (1972), 28-31.

1174 HILLARD, Katherine. "Hawthorne as an Interpreter of New England." New England Magazine, 12 (c. 1892), 732-735.

1175 HILLMAN, M.V. "Hawthorne and Transcendentalism." Catholic World, 93 (May, 1911), 199-212.

1176 HIMELICK, Raymond. "Hawthorne, Spenser, and Christian Humanism." Emerson Society Quarterly, 21 (1975), 21-28.

1177 HINTON, Earl M. "Hawthorne, the Hippie, and the Square." Studies in the Novel, 2 (1970), 425-439.

1178 HIRSCH, John C. "Zenobia as Queen: The Background Sources of Hawthorne's The Blithedale Romance." Nathaniel Hawthorne Journal, 1 (1971), 182-191.

1179 _____. "The Politics of Blithedale: The Dilemma of the Self." Studies in Romanticism, 11 (1972), 138-146.

1180 HODGE, Bartow Michael. "Unsound Believers: A Study of Three American Writers." Ph.D. diss., State University of New York (Buffalo), 1977. DA, 38 (1978), 5478A-5479A. Studies Cotton Mather, Nathaniel Hawthorne, and T.S. Eliot.

1181 HOELTJE, Hubert H. "Hawthorne's Review of Evangeline." New England Quarterly, 23 (June, 1950), 232-235.

1182 _____. "Captain Nathaniel Hawthorne: Father of the Famous Salem Novelist." Essex Institute Historical Collections, 89 (October, 1953), 329-356.

1183 _____. "The Writing of The Scarlet Letter."
New England Quarterly, 27 (September, 1954), 326-
346.

1184 _____. "A Forgotten Hawthorne Silhouette."
American Literature, 27 (January, 1957), 510, 511.

1185 _____. "Hawthorne as Senior at Bowdoin." Essex
Institute Historical Collections, 94 (July, 1958), 205-
228.

1186 _____. Inward Sky: The Mind and Art of Nathaniel
Hawthorne. Durham, N. C.: Duke University Press,
1962.

1187 _____. "Hawthorne, Melville, and 'Blackness.'"
American Literature, 37 (March, 1965), 41-51.

1188 HOFFMAN, Daniel G. "Yankee Bumpkin and Scapegoat King." Sewanee Review, 69 (January-March,
1961), 48-60.

1189 _____. Form and Fable in American Fiction.
New York: Oxford University Press, 1961. Contains the following essays on Hawthorne:

"Folklore and the Moral Picturesque," pp. 99-112.
"Yankee Bumpkin and Scapegoat King," pp. 113-125.
"'The Maypole of Merry Mount' and the Folklore of
Love," pp. 126-148.
"Just Married! in the Village of Witches," pp. 149-
168.
"Hester's Double Providence: The Scarlet Letter
and the Green," pp. 169-186.
"Paradise Regained at Maule's Well," pp. 187-201.
"The Blithedale Romance: May-Day in a Cold Ar-
cadia," pp. 202-218.

1190 _____. "Myth, Romance, and the Childhood of Man,"
in Pearce, Roy Harvey, ed., Centenary Essays (1964),
pp. 197-219.

1191 HOFFMAN, Michael J. "The Anti-Transcendental
Reaction: Illusion and Role in The Scarlet Letter,"
in The Subversive Vision. Port Washington, N. Y.:

Kennikat, 1972, pp. 70-86.

1192 HOFFMANN, Charles G. "The Development of the
      Short Story in Hawthorne, Melville, and James."
      Ph. D. diss., Wisconsin, 1952.

1193 HOLADAY, Clayton A. "A Re-examination of Feather-
      top and R L R." New England Quarterly, 27 (March,
      1954), 103-105. Believed to refer to Richard L.
      Rogers. See also article by Alfred A. Kern (1937).

1194 HOLLAND, Laurence B. "Authority, Power, and
      Form: Some American Texts." Yearbook of English
      Studies, 8 (1978), 1-14. Emerson, Hawthorne,
      Melville, and Mark Twain.

1195 HOLLISTER, Michael Alton. "Gloom to Glory:
      Hawthorne's Mythology." Ph. D. diss., Stanford,
      1967. DA, 28 (1968), 4632A.

1196 HOLMAN, C. Hugh. The American Novel Through
      Henry James. New York: Appleton-Century-Crofts,
      1944. Hawthorne, pp. 33-39.

1197 HOLMES, Edward M. "Hawthorne and Romanticism."
      New England Quarterly, 33 (December, 1960), 476-
      488.

1198 _____. "Requiem for a Scarlet Nun." Costerus,
      5 (1972), 35-49.

1199 HOLSBERRY, John Edwin, Jr. "Hawthorne and the
      English Romantic Poets." Ph. D. diss., Duke, 1976.
      DA, 37 (1976), 3624A.

1200 HOLTZ, Nancy Ann. "The Great Measures of Time:
      A Study of Cosmic Order in Nineteenth-Century
      American Thought." Ph. D. diss., University of
      Washington, 1977. DA, 38 (1977), 3500A-3501A.

1201 HOMAN, John, Jr. "Hawthorne's 'The Wedding
      Knell' and Cotton Mather." Emerson Society Quar-
      terly, 43 (1966), 66-67.

1202 HONIG, Edwin. "In Defense of Allegory." Kenyon
      Review, 15 (Winter, 1958), 1-9.

1203   _____. Dark Conceit: The Making of Allegory.
        Evanston, Ill.: Northwestern University Press, 1959.
        Hawthorne, pp. 123-136 et passim.

1204   HOPKINS, Vivian C. Prodigal Puritan: A Life of
        Delia Bacon. Cambridge: Harvard University Press,
        1959. Hawthorne, pp. 200-259 et passim.

1205   HORNE, Lewis B. "The Growth of Awareness in the
        Novels of Hawthorne and Hardy." Ph. D. diss.,
        Michigan, 1966. DA, 27 (1967), 2153A-2154A.

1206   _____. "The Heart, the Hand, and 'The Birth-
        mark.'" American Transcendental Quarterly, 1
        (1969), 38-41.

1207   _____. "Place, Time, and Moral Growth in The
        House of the Seven Gables." Studies in the Novel,
        2 (1970), 459-467.

1208   HORWILL, H. W. "Hawthorne's America." Critic,
        45 (July, 1904), 71-73.

1209   HOSMER, Elizabeth R. "Science and Pseudo-Science
        in the Writings of Nathaniel Hawthorne." Ph. D.
        diss., Illinois, 1948.

1210   HOSTETLER, Norman Henry. "The Rhetorical Uses
        of Point of View and Irony in the Works of Nathaniel
        Hawthorne." Ph. D. diss., Pennsylvania, 1973.
        DA, 34 (1973), 1859A.

1211   _____. "'Earth's Holocaust': Hawthorne's Para-
        ble of the Imaginative Process." Kansas Quarterly,
        7 (1975), 85-89.

1212   HOUSTON, Neal Bryan. "Nathaniel Hawthorne and the
        Eternal Feminine." Ph. D. diss., Texas Tech.,
        1965. DA, 26 (1965), 4659-4660.

1213   _____. "Hester Prynne as Eternal Feminine."
        Discourse, 9 (Spring, 1966), 230-244.

1214   HOVEY, Richard B. "Love and Hate in 'Rappaccini's
        Daughter.'" University of Kansas City Review, 29
        (Winter, 1962), 137-145.

1215   HOWARD, Anne Bail. "Hawthorne's Magnetic Chain:
       The Achievement of Humanity." Ph.D. diss., New
       Mexico, 1965. DA, 27 (1966), 1823A.

1216   HOWARD, David. "The Blithedale Romance and a
       Sense of Revolution," in Howard, David; John Lucas;
       and John Goode; eds., Tradition and Tolerance in
       Nineteenth-Century Fiction. London: Routledge and
       Kegan Paul; New York: Barnes and Noble, 1966,
       pp. 55-97.

1217   _____. "The Fortunate Fall and Hawthorne's The
       Marble Faun," in Fletcher, Ian, ed., Romantic
       Mythologies. London: Routledge and Kegan Paul;
       New York: Barnes and Noble, 1967, pp. 97-136.

1218   HOWARD, Leon. Herman Melville: A Biography.
       Berkeley: University of California Press; London:
       Cambridge University Press, 1951. Hawthorne,
       passim.

1219   _____. "Hawthorne's Fiction." Nineteenth-Century
       Fiction, 7 (March, 1953), 237-250. Critique of
       Fogle's Hawthorne's Fiction: The Light and the Dark
       (1952).

1220   _____. Literature and the American Tradition.
       New York: Doubleday, 1960. Hawthorne, pp. 114-128.

1221   _____; Louis Wright; and Carl Bode; eds. Ameri-
       can Heritage: An Anthology and Interpretive Survey
       of Our Literature, 2 vols. Boston: Heath, 1955.
       "Hawthorne, the Romantic Moralist," discussion and
       selections, pp. 525-590.

1222   HOWE, Irving. "Hawthorne and American Fiction."
       American Mercury, 68 (March, 1949), 367-374.

1223   _____. "Hawthorne: Pastoral and Politics."
       New Republic, 133 (September 5, 1955), 17-20.
       Refers to The Blithedale Romance.

1224   _____. "Some American Novelists: The Politics
       of Isolation," in Howe, Politics and the Novel. New
       York: Horizon, 1957, pp. 163-175.

1225   HOWE, M.A. De Wolfe. "The Tale of Tanglewood."

Yale Review, 32 (December, 1942), 323-336.

1226 _____. "With Hawthorne at Tanglewood." Christian Science Monitor, 38 (July 15, 1946), 6.

1227 HOWELL, Roger, Jr. "A Note on Hawthorne's Ambivalence Toward Puritanism: Hawthorne's View of Sir Henry Vane, the Younger." Nathaniel Hawthorne Journal, 2 (1972), 143-146.

1228 _____. "Hawthorne at Bowdoin: A Letter Concerning His Arrival." Nathaniel Hawthorne Journal, 5 (1975), 5-9.

1229 HOWELLS, William Dean. My Literary Passions. New York: Harpers, 1895. Hawthorne, pp. 186-188.

1230 _____. "My First Visit to New England," in Howells, Literary Friends and Acquaintances (1900), edited by Hiatt, David F., and Edwin H. Cady, and reprinted Bloomington: Indiana University Press, 1968, pp. 7-60.

1231 _____. "Hawthorne's Hester Prynn," in Heroines of Fiction, 2 vols. New York: Harpers, 1901. Vol. I, pp. 161-174.

1232 _____. "The Personality of Hawthorne." North American Review, 177 (December, 1903), 872, 882.

1233 HUDSON, Norma Whiteley. "Shakespeare and Hawthorne: A Comparative Study of Imagery." Ph.D. diss., Tulsa, 1978. DA, 39 (1978), 1568A-1569A.

1234 HUFFMAN, Clifford Chalmers. "History in Hawthorne's Custom-House." Clio, 2 (1973), 161-169.

1235 HULL, Ramona E. "Hawthorne Promotes Thoreau as Writer." Emerson Society Quarterly, 33 (1963), 24-28. Letter.

1236 _____. "Hawthorne and the Magic Elixir of Life: The Failure of a Gothic Theme." Emerson Society Quarterly, 18 (1972), 97-107.

1237 _____. "Some Further Notes on Hawthorne and Thoreau." Thoreau Society Bulletin, 121 (Fall, 1972), 7-8.

1238 _____. "British Periodical Printings of Hawthorne's Works, 1835-1900: A Partial Bibliography." Nathaniel Hawthorne Journal, 3 (1973), 73-88

1239 _____. "Bennoch and Hawthorne." Nathaniel Hawthorne Journal, 4 (1974), 48-74. English friend, Francis Bennoch.

1240 _____. "'Scribbling' Females and Serious Males: Hawthorne's Comments from Abroad on Some American Authors." Nathaniel Hawthorne Journal, 5 (1975), 35-58.

1241 _____. "Una Hawthorne: A Biographical Sketch." Nathaniel Hawthorne Journal, 6 (1976), 86-119.

1242 HULL, Richard Jon. "Equality in Hawthorne." Ph.D. diss., University of Washington, 1975. DA, 37 (1976), 968A.

1243 HUMMA, John B. "'Young Goodman Brown' and the Failure of Hawthorne's Ambiguity." Colby Library Quarterly, 9 (1971), 425-431.

1244 HUNGERFORD, Edward B. "Hawthorne Gossips About Salem." New England Quarterly, 6 (September, 1933), 445-469.

1245 HUNSBERGER, Claude. "'Marble and Mud': Dimensions of Time and Self in Hawthorne's Fiction." Ph.D. diss., Wisconsin, 1971. DA, 33 (1972), 1683A-1684A.

1246 HURLEY, Paul J. "Young Goodman Brown's 'Heart of Darkness.'" American Literature, 37 (January, 1966), 410-419.

1247 HUZZARD, John A. "Hawthorne's The Marble Faun." Italica, 35 (June, 1958), 119-124.

1248 HYMAN, Lawrence W. "Moral Values and Literary Experience." Journal of Aesthetics and Art Criticism, 24 (Summer, 1966), 538-547. Hawthorne, passim.

1249 IBERSHOFF, C.H. "Hawthorne's Philosophy of Life."

Outlook, 126 (September 15, 1920), 124-125.

1250 IDOL, John L., Jr. "William Cowper Brann on Nathaniel Hawthorne." Hawthorne Society Newsletter, 1 (1975), 2.

1251 _____. "Nathaniel Hawthorne and Harriet Hosmer." Nathaniel Hawthorne Journal, 6 (1976), 120-128.

1252 INGE, M. Thomas. "Dr. Rappaccini's Noble Experiment." Nathaniel Hawthorne Journal, 3 (1973), 200-201.

1253 IRWIN, John T. "The Symbol of the Hieroglyphics in the American Renaissance." American Quarterly, 26 (1974), 103-126. Refers to Hawthorne, Melville, Emerson, and Thoreau.

1254 IRWIN, W.R. "The Survival of Pan." PMLA, 74 (June, 1961), 159-167.

1255 ISAACS, Neil D., and Louis H. Leiter, eds. Approaches to the Short Story. San Francisco: Chandler, 1963. "Blake's Urizen as Hawthorne's Ethan Brand," by Glenn Pederson, pp. 115-142.

1256 ISANI, Mukhtar Ali. "Hawthorne and the Branding of William Prynne." New England Quarterly, 45 (1972), 182-195.

1257 ITO, Kiyoshi. "Similarity of Wordings in Hawthorne's Two Works," in Araki, Kazuo, ed., Studies in English Grammar and Linguistics: A Miscellany in Honour of Takanobu Otsuka. Tokyo: Kenkyusha, 1958, pp. 275-288. Refers to The Scarlet Letter and The House of the Seven Gables.

1258 IVES, Charles E. "Hawthorne," in Essays Before a Sonata. New York: Knickerbocker, 1920, pp. 46-50. Reprinted with revisions, and edited by Howard Boatwright, New York: Norton, 1962, pp. 39-48.

1259 JACKSON, Edward A. Mather. Nathaniel Hawthorne: A Modest Man. New York: Crowell, 1940.

1260 JACOBSEN, Eric. "'Stationing' in Paradise Lost

and The Scarlet Letter, " in Seyersted, Brita, ed. ,
Americana-Norwegica, IV: Norwegian Contributions
to American Studies Dedicated to Sigmund Skard.
Oslo: Oslo University Publishers, 1973, pp. 107-122.

1261   JACOBSON, Richard Joseph. Hawthorne's Conception
of the Creative Process. Cambridge: Harvard University Press, 1965.

1262   JAFFE, Adrian, and Herbert Weisinger, eds.   The
Laureate Fraternity: An Introduction to Literature.
Evanston, Ill.: Row, Peterson, 1960.   The Scarlet
Letter, pp. 261-263.

1263   JAFFE, David.   "The Miniature That Inspired Clifford
Pyncheon's Portrait. " Essex Institute Historical
Collections, 98 (October, 1962), 278-282.

1264   JAMES, Henry.   Hawthorne.   London: Macmillan,
1879.   English Men of Letters Series.   Reprinted
Ithaca, N. Y.:   Cornell University Press, 1956.   Also
reprinted with Introduction and Notes by Tony Tanner,
London: Macmillan; New York: St. Martin, 1967.

1265   _____.   "Nathaniel Hawthorne, Comment with
Selections, " in The Warner Library, 30 vols. ,
edited by J. W. Cunliffe and A. H. Thorndike.   New
York: United States Publishers Association, 1917.
Vol. 12.

1266   _____.   "Nathaniel Hawthorne, Comment with
Selections, " (same as in Warner Library), in Columbia University Course, edited by J. W. Cunliffe, et
al.   New York: Columbia University Press, 1928-
1929.   Vol. 17.

1267   _____.   "Hawthorne, " excerpt from Hawthorne
(1879), in Wilson, Edmund, ed. , The Shock of
Recognition.   Garden City, N. Y.:   Doubleday, Doran,
1943, pp. 427-565.

1268   _____.   "Hawthorne: The Scarlet Letter, " in
Zabel, Morton D. , ed , The Portable Henry James.
New York: Viking, 1951, pp. 440-453.

1269   _____.   The American Essays of Henry James.
Edited by Leon Edel.   New York: Vintage, 1956.
"Hawthorne, " pp. 3-31.

1270   _____. "Hawthorne: Early Manhood," in Rahv,
        Philip, ed., Literature in America: An Anthology of
        Literary Criticism. New York: Meridian, 1957, pp.
        84-100.

1271   JANSSEN, James George. "Nathaniel Hawthorne's
        Treatment of Pride in His Major Short Stories and
        Novels." Ph.D. diss., Wisconsin, 1966. DA, 28
        (1967), 678A-679A.

1272   _____. "Dimmesdale's 'Lurid Playfulness.'"
        American Transcendental Quarterly, 1 (1969), 30-34.

1273   _____. "Hawthorne's Seventh Vagabond: 'The Out-
        setting Bard.'" Emerson Society Quarterly, 62
        (1971), 22-28. On "The Seven Vagabonds."

1274   _____. "The 'Dismal Merry-Making' in Hawthorne's
        Comic Vision." Studies in American Humor, 1
        (1974), 107-117.

1275   _____. "Pride and Prophecy: The Final Irony of
        The Scarlet Letter." Nathaniel Hawthorne Journal,
        5 (1975), 241-247.

1276   _____. "Fanshawe and Hawthorne's Developing
        Comic Sense." Emerson Society Quarterly, 22
        (1976), 24-27.

1277   _____. "Impaled Butterflies and the Misleading
        Moral in Hawthorne's Short Works." Nathaniel Haw-
        thorne Journal, 6 (1976), 269-275.

1278   JAPP, Alexander Hay (H.A. Page, pseudonym).
        Memoir of Hawthorne with Stories Now First Published
        in This Country [England]. London: H.S. King,
        1872.

1279   JARRETT, David W. "Hawthorne and Hardy as Modern
        Romancers." Nineteenth-Century Fiction, 28 (1974),
        458-471.

1280   JENKINS, R.B. "A New Look at an Old Tombstone."
        New England Quarterly, 45 (1972), 417-421. Refers
        to Hester Prynne.

1281   JEPSON, G.E. "Hawthorne in the Boston Custom

House." Bookman, 19 (August, 1904), 573-580. Reprinted in Cameron, ed., Hawthorne Among His Contemporaries (1968), pp. 514-518.

1282 JOHNSON, Claudia Haselden Durot. "The Regenerative
Descent in the Works of Nathaniel Hawthorne." Ph.
D. diss., Illinois (Urbana-Champaign), 1973. DA,
34 (1973), 727A-728A.

1283 _____. "Hawthorne and Nineteenth-Century Per-
fectionism." American Literature, 44 (1973), 585-
595.

1284 _____. "'Young Goodman Brown' and Puritan Justi-
fication." Studies in Short Fiction, 11 (1974), 200-
203.

1285 JOHNSON, Evelyn C. "Nathaniel Hawthorne and the
Supernatural." Ph.D. diss., Stanford, 1938.

1286 JOHNSON, George W. "Frank Norris and Romance."
American Literature, 33 (march, 1961), 52-63.

1287 JOHNSON, James Mauritz. "Effects of Ideals upon
Characters in Hawthorne's Fiction." Ph.D. diss.,
Syracuse, 1976. DA, 38 (1977), 2790A.

1288 JOHNSON, W. Stacy. "Hawthorne and The Pilgrim's
Progress." Journal of English and Germanic Philology, 50 (April, 1951), 156-166.

1289 _____. "Sin and Salvation in Hawthorne." Hibbert
Journal, 50 (April, 1951), 39-47.

1290 JOHNSTON, Helen. "The American Boy and Nathaniel
Hawthorne--Now." Education Review, 54 (November,
1917), 413-414.

1291 JOHNSTON, Mark Evan. "Augustan Influence on Hawthorne's Narrative Technique." Ph.D. diss., Yale,
1975. DA, 36 (1975), 3653A.

1292 _____. "The Recording Narrator: The Spectator,
The Rambler, and Hawthorne's Shorter Fiction."
Essays in Arts and Sciences, 6 (1977), 20-46.

1293 JONES, Bartlett C. "The Ambiguity of Shrewdness in

'My Kinsman, Major Molineux.'" Midcontinent American Studies Journal, 3 (Fall, 1962), 42-47.

1294   JONES, Buford. "Nathaniel Hawthorne and English
        Renaissance Allegory." Ph. D. diss., Harvard, 1962.

1295   _____. "Melville's Buccaneers and Crébillon's
        Sofa." English Language Notes, 2 (December, 1964),
        122-126.

1296   _____. "The Faery Land of Hawthorne's Romances."
        Emerson Society Quarterly, 48 (1967), 106-124.

1297   _____. "Hawthorne's Coverdale and Spenser's
        Allegory of Mutability." American Literature, 39
        (May, 1967), 215-219.

1298   _____. "'The Hall of Fantasy' and the Early Haw-
        thorne-Thoreau Relationship." PMLA, 83 (1968),
        1429-1438.

1299   _____. A Checklist of Hawthorne Criticism: 1951-
        1966, with Précis. Hartford, Conn.: Transcendental,
        1967. Also published in Emerson Society Quarterly,
        52 Supplement (1968), 1-90.

1300   _____. "Hawthorne Studies: The Seventies."
        Studies in the Novel, 12 (1970), 504-518.

1301   _____. "'The Man of Adamant' and the Moral
        Picturesque." American Transcendental Quarterly,
        14 (1972), 33-41.

1302   _____. "After Long Apprenticeship: Hawthorne's
        Romances." Emerson Society Quarterly, 19 (1973),
        1-7.

1303   _____. "Hawthorne and Spenser: From Allusion
        to Allegory." Nathaniel Hawthorne Journal, 5 (1975),
        71-90.

1304   _____. "Current Hawthorne Bibliography." Haw-
        thorne Society Newsletter, 1 (1975), 4-6; 2 (1976),
        4-10; 3 (1977), 6-10.

1305   JONES, Dennis M. "From Moralist to Psychologist
        to Maker of Myth: A Study of Hawthorne's Use of

Regional History." Ph.D. diss., State University of
Iowa, 1966. DA, 27 (1967), 3011A-3012A.

1306 JONES, Howard Mumford. History and the Contemporary: Essays in Nineteenth-Century Literature. Madison: University of Wisconsin Press, 1964. Hawthorne, passim.

1307 _____, ed. with Introduction. American Prose
Masters: Hawthorne, Emerson, Poe, Lowell, Henry
James. Cambridge: Harvard University Press, 1963.

1308 _____; Ernest E. Leisy; and Richard M. Ludwig;
eds. Major American Writers. New York: Harcourt,
Brace, 1935. Hawthorne, Introduction with selections,
pp. 485-576.

1309 JONES, Joseph. "Introduction." Aesthetic Papers.
Edited by Elizabeth P. Peabody (1849). Gainesville,
Fla.: Scholars' Facsimile and Reprints, 1957.

1310 _____, et al., eds. American Literary Manuscripts: A Checklist of Holdings in Academic, Historical, and Public Libraries in the United States.
Austin: University of Texas Press, 1960, pp. 163-
164.

1311 JONES: Llewellyn. "Mr. Hawthorne's Scarlet Letter."
Bookman (London), 57 (January, 1924), 622-625.

1312 JONES, Madison. "Variations on a Hawthorne Theme."
Studies in Short Fiction, 15 (1978), 277-283.

1313 JONES, Marga Cottino. "The Marble Faun and a
Writer's Crisis." Studi Americana, 16 (1970), 81-
123.

1314 JONES, Phyllis M. "Hawthorne's Mythic Use of Puritan History." Cithara, 12 (1972), 59-73.

1315 JONES, Victor H. "Laughter in Hawthorne's Fiction."
College Literature, 5 (1978), 57-61.

1316 JONES, Wayne Allen. "New Light on Hawthorne and
the Southern Rose." Nathaniel Hawthorne Journal,
4 (1974), 31-46.

1317 _____. "Sometimes Things Just Don't Work Out: Hawthorne's Income from Twice-Told Tales (1837), and Another 'Good Thing' for Hawthorne." Nathaniel Hawthorne Journal, 5 (1975), 11-26.

1318 _____. "The Hawthorne-Goodrich Relationship and a New Estimate of Hawthorne's Income from The Token." Nathaniel Hawthorne Journal, 5 (1975), 91-140.

1319 _____. "Recent Hawthorne Scholarship, 1973-1974, with Supplemental Entries from Other Years Added." Nathaniel Hawthorne Journal, 5 (1975), 281-316. Review article.

1320 _____. "Two Hawthorne Findings: A Summary." Hawthorne Society Newsletter, 2 (1976), 7.

1321 _____. "A New Love Letter: Hawthorne's Proposal? Discovery of a Sophia Hawthorne Transcript." Nathaniel Hawthorne Journal, 6 (1976), 10-13.

1322 _____. "Checklist of Recent Hawthorne Scholarship, 1974-1975." Nathaniel Hawthorne Journal, 6 (1976), 313-320.

1323 _____. "Hawthorne's First Published Review." American Literature, 48 (1977), 492-500. Refers to work by Goodrich, Outcast and Other Poems (1836).

1324 JONES, William B. "Nathaniel Hawthorne and English Renaissance Allegory." Ph.D. diss., Harvard, 1962.

1325 JORDON, Alice Mabel. "Dawn of Imagination in American Books for Children," in Jordon, From Rollo to Tom Sawyer. Boston: Horn Book, 1948, pp. 92-101.

1326 JORDON, Gretchen Graf. "Hawthorne's 'Bell': Historical Evolution Through Symbol." Nineteenth-Century Fiction, 19 (September, 1964), 123-139.

1327 JOSEPH, Brother. "Art and Event in 'Ethan Brand.'" Nineteenth-Century Fiction, 15 (December, 1960), 249-257.

1328 JOSEPH, Sister M. Evelyn, I.H.M. "Substance as

Suggestion: Ambiguity in Hawthorne." Renascence,
17 (Summer, 1965), 216-220.

1329 JOSEPHS, Lois. "One Approach to the Puritans."
English Journal, 50 (March, 1961), 183-187.

1330 JOSIPOVICI, G. D. "Hawthorne's Modernism." Critical Quarterly (Manchester, England), 8 (Winter, 1966),
351-360.

1331 JOYNER, Nancy. "Bondage in Blithedale." Nathaniel
Hawthorne Journal, 5 (1975), 227-231.

1332 JUNKINS, Donald. "Hawthorne's House of the Seven
Gables: A Prototype of the Human Mind." Literature
and Psychology, 17 (1967), 103-210.

1333 JUSTUS, James H. "Beyond Gothicism: Wuthering
Heights and an American Tradition." Tennessee
Studies in Literature, 5 (1960), 25-33. Includes
Hawthorne, Melville, and Faulkner.

1334 _____. "Hawthorne's Coverdale: Character and
Art in The Blithedale Romance." American Literature,
47 (1975), 21-36.

1335 KAFTAN, Robert Alexander. "A Study of the Gothic
Technique in the Novels of Nathaniel Hawthorne."
Ph. D. diss., Michigan State, 1967. DA, 29 (1968),
1899A.

1336 KAMAN, John Michael. "The Lonely Hero in Hawthorne, Melville, Twain, and James." Ph. D. diss.,
Stanford, 1973. DA, 34 (1974), 5974A-5975A.

1337 KAMOGAWA, Takahiro. "Rome in The Marble Faun."
Kyushu American Literature (Fukuoka, Japan), 11
(1968), 32-43.

1338 _____. "On the Family Name 'Pyncheon' in The
House of the Seven Gables." Hiroshima Studies in
English Literature and Language, 16 (1969), 41-47.
In Japanese; abstract of article in English.

1339 _____. "Textual Editing of the Centenary Marble
Faun." Kyushu American Literature, 17 (1976), 42-
65.

1340   KANE, Carolyn.   "Nathaniel Hawthorne in His World:
       The Author in Relation to His Time and Place."
       Ph.D. diss., Arkansas, 1973.   DA, 34 (1973), 3346A.

1341   KANE, Patricia.   "The Fallen Woman as Free-Thinker
       in The French Lieutenant's Woman and The Scarlet
       Letter."   Notes on Contemporary Literature, 2 (1972),
       8-10.   Refers to novel by John Fowles.

1342   KANE, Robert J.   "Hawthorne's 'The Prophetic Pic-
       tures' and James' 'The Lion.'"   Modern Language
       Notes, 65 (April, 1950), 257-258.

1343   KANTZER, Ruth Marie.   "The Significance of the Heart
       in the Works of Nathaniel Hawthorne."   Ph.D. diss.,
       State University of Iowa, 1976.   DA, 37 (1977), 7751A-
       7752A.

1344   KAPLAN, Elizabeth Ann.   "Hawthorne and Romanticism:
       A Study of Hawthorne's Literary Development in the
       Context of the American and European Romantic
       Movements."   Ph.D. diss., Rutgers, 1970.   DA,
       31 (1971), 6061A.

1345   _____.   "Hawthorne's 'Fancy Pictures' on Film,"
       in Peary, Gerald, and Roger Shatzin, eds., The
       Classic American Novel and the Movies.   New York:
       Ungar, 1977, pp.30-41.   Refers to The House of the
       Seven Gables.

1346   KAPLAN, Harold.   "Hawthorne: The Need to Become
       Human," in Kaplan, Democratic Humanism and Ameri-
       can Literature.   Chicago and London: University of
       Chicago Press, 1972, pp.129-158.

1347   KARIEL, Henry S.   "Man Limited: Nathaniel Haw-
       thorne's Classicism."   South Atlantic Quarterly, 52
       (October, 1953), 528-542.

1348   KARLOW, Martin Peter.   "'Practical Extravagance':
       A Study of Hawthorne's Study of Schizophrenia as a
       Creative Process."   Ph.D. diss., Yale, 1975.   DA,
       36 (1975), 2822A-2823A.

1349   KARRFALT, David H.   "Anima in Hawthorne and Hag-
       gard."   American Notes and Queries, 2 (June, 1964),
       153.   Jungian elements in "Rappaccini's Daughter" and

the novel She.

1350 KASEGAWA, Koh. "Emerson, Thoreau, Melville."
      Aoyama Journal of General Education (Tokyo), 5
      (November, 1964), 15-24.

1351 KATZ, Joseph. "The Centenary Edition of the Works
      of Nathaniel Hawthorne: Our Old Home." Nathaniel
      Hawthorne Journal, 1 (1971), 287-289. Review of
      1970 publication.

1352 KATZ, Seymour. "'Character,' 'Nature,' and Alle-
      gory in The Scarlet Letter." Nineteenth-Century
      Fiction, 23 (1968), 3-17.

1353 KAUL, A.N. The American Vision: Actual and Ideal
      Society in Nineteenth-Century Fiction. New Haven:
      Yale University Press, 1963. "Nathaniel Hawthorne:
      Heir and Critic of the Puritan Tradition," pp.139-214.

1354 _____. "The Blithedale Romance," excerpt from
      American Vision (1963), in Kaul, ed., Hawthorne
      (1966), pp.153-163.

1355 _____. "Character and Motive in The Scarlet
      Letter." Critical Quarterly (England), 10 (1968),
      373-384.

1356 _____, ed. with Introduction. Hawthorne: A Col-
      lection of Critical Essays. Englewood Cliffs, N.J.:
      Prentice-Hall, 1966. Introduction, pp.1-10.

1357 KAY, Carol McGinnis. "Hawthorne's Use of Clothing
      in His Short Stories." Nathaniel Hawthorne Journal,
      2 (1972), 245-249.

1358 KAY, Donald. "Hawthorne's Use of Laughter in Se-
      lected Short Stories." Xavier University Studies,
      10 (1971), 27-32.

1359 _____. "Five Acts of The Blithedale Romance."
      American Transcendental Quarterly, 13 (1972), 25-
      28.

1360 _____. "English Fruits, Yankee Turnips: Another
      Look at Hawthorne and England." Nathaniel Haw-
      thorne Journal, 4 (1974), 150-161.

1361   KAZIN, Alfred.   On Native Grounds.   New York:
       Reynal and Hitchcock, 1942.   Reprinted, abridged,
       with a new Postscript,   Garden City, N.Y.:   Double-
       day/Anchor, 1956.   Hawthorne, passim.

1362   _____.   "Hawthorne: The Artist of New England."
       Atlantic, 218 (December, 1966), 109-113.

1363   _____.   "On Hawthorne."   New York Review, 11
       (October 24, 1968), 26-28.

1364   _____, ed. with Introduction.   Selected Short Stories
       of Nathaniel Hawthorne.   Greenwich, Conn.:   Fawcett,
       1966.   Essentially the same as 1966 article above.

1365   KEARNS, Francis E.   "Margaret Fuller as a Model
       for Hester Prynne."   Jahrbuch für Amerikastudien,
       10 (1965), 161-197.

1366   _____.   "The Theme of Experience in Hawthorne's
       Blithedale Romance," in Weber, Alfred, and Hartmut
       Grandel, eds., Geschichte und Fiction.   Göttingen:
       Vondenhoeck and Ruprecht, 1972, pp.64-84.

1367   KEATING, L. Clark.   "Julien Green and Nathaniel
       Hawthorne."   French Review, 28 (May, 1955), 485-
       492.

1368   KEHL, D.G.   "Hawthorne's 'Vicious' Circles: The
       Sphere-Circle Imagery in the Four Major Novels."
       Bulletin of the Rocky Mountain Modern Language
       Association, 23 (1969), 9-20.

1369   KEHLER, Dorothea.   "Hawthorne and Shakespeare."
       American Transcendental Quarterly, 22 (1974), 104-
       105.

1370   KEHLER, Harold F.   "The Making of the Scarlet A:
       A Study of Hawthorne's Technique of the Central
       Symbol."   Ph.D. diss., Ohio, 1968.   DA, 29 (1969),
       3143A-3144A.

1371   KEHLER, Joel R.   "House, Home and Hawthorne's
       Psychology of Habitation."   Emerson Society Quarterly,
       21 (1975), 142-153.

1372   KELLER, J.C.   Literature and Religion.   Peterborough,

N. H. : Richard R. Smith, 1956. Chapter on Emerson, Hawthorne, and the Puritan Soul, pp. 48-50.

1373 KELLY, George. "Poe's Theory of Unity. " Philological Quarterly, 37 (January, 1958), 34-44.

1374 KELLY, Richard. "Hawthorne's 'Ethan Brand.'" Explicator, 28 (1970), item 47.

1375 KELTON, William J. "'Of Marble and Mud': The Politics of Nathaniel Hawthorne." Ph. D. diss., Vanderbilt, 1971. DA, 32 (1971), 2645A.

1376 KEMPTON, Kenneth. The Short Story. Cambridge: Harvard University Press, 1947. "The Birthmark," pp. 74-78 et passim; "Rappaccini's Daughter, " pp. 83-86.

1377 KERMODE, Frank. "Hawthorne's Modernity." Partisan Review, 41 (1974), 428-441.

1378 KERN, Alexander C. "A Note on Hawthorne's Juveniles." Philological Quarterly, 39 (April, 1960), 242-246.

1379 KERN, Alfred A. "The Sources of Hawthorne's 'Feathertop.'" PMLA, 46 (December, 1931), 1253-1259.

1380 _____. "Hawthorne's 'Feathertop' and 'R. L. R.'" PMLA, 52 (June, 1937), 503-510. Probably refers to Richard L. Rogers.

1381 KERR, Howard. Mediums and Spirit-Rappers, and Roaring Radicals: Spiritualism in American Literature, 1850-1900. Urbana: University of Illinois Press, 1972. Hawthorne, passim.

1382 KESSELRING, Marion L. "Hawthorne's Reading, 1828-1850. " Bulletin of the New York Public Library, 53 (February, March, April, 1949), 55-71, 121-138, 173-194. Published as a book, Hawthorne's Reading, 1828-1850. New York: New York Public Library Press, 1949.

1383 KESTERSON, David Bert. "Nature in the Life and Works of Nathaniel Hawthorne." Ph. D. diss., Arkansas, 1964. DA, 26 (1965), 1023.

1384 _____. "Hawthorne and Nature: Thoreauvian Influence?" English Language Notes, 4 (March, 1967),
200-206.

1385 _____. "Nature and Theme in 'Young Goodman
Brown.'" Dickinson Review, 2 (1970), 42-46.

1386 _____. "Journey to Perugia: Dantean Parallels in
The Marble Faun." Emerson Society Quarterly, 19
(1973), 94-104.

1387 _____. "Nature and Hawthorne's Religious Iso-
lationists." Nathaniel Hawthorne Journal, 4 (1974),
196-208.

1388 _____. "The Founding of the Nathaniel Hawthorne
Society." Nathaniel Hawthorne Journal, 5 (1975),
253-258.

1389 _____, ed. with Preface. Studies in The Marble
Faun. Columbus, Ohio: Merrill, 1971. Merrill
Studies Series; 118p. reprinted criticism.

1390 KETTERER, David. New Worlds for Old: The
Apocalyptic Imagination, Science Fiction, and Ameri-
can Literature. Bloomington: Indiana University
Press, 1973. Hawthorne, passim.

1391 KHATTAB, E. A. "Children in Nathaniel Hawthorne's
Fiction." University of Riyadh Bulletin (Saudi
Arabia), 2 (1971-1972), 7-30.

1392 KIM, Yong-Chol. "A Note on Hawthorne's 'My Kinsman, Major Molineux.'" English Language and
Literature (Korea), 19 (August, 1966), 85-88.

1393 KIMBALL, LeRoy E. "Miss (Delia) Bacon Advances
Learning." Colophon, 2 n.s. (Summer, 1937), 338-
354. Three letters with references to Emerson and
Hawthorne.

1394 KIMBROUGH, Robert. "The Actual and the Imaginary:
Hawthorne's Concept of Art in Theory and Practice."
Transactions of the Wisconsin Academy of Sciences,
Arts, and Letters, 50 (1961), 277-293.

1395 KIMMEY, John L. "Pierre and Robin: Melville's

Debt to Hawthorne." Emerson Society Quarterly, 38
(1965), 90-92.

1396 KINGERY, R.E. "Disastrous Friendship." Hobbies,
45 (January, 1941), 98.

1397 KIRK, Russell. "The Moral Conservation of Hawthorne."
Contemporary Review (London), No. 1044 (December,
1952), 361-366.

1398 _____. "Transitional Conservatism in New England
Sketches," in Kirk, The Conservative Mind from Burke
to Santayana. Chicago: Regnery, 1953, pp. 196-226.

1399 KISNER, Madeleine. "Color in the Worlds and Works
of Poe, Hawthorne, Crane, Anderson, and Welty."
Ph.D. diss., Michigan, 1975. DA, 36 (1975), 3714A.

1400 KJØRVEN, Johannes. "Hawthorne and the Significance
of History." Americana-Norvegica, edited by Skard,
Sigmund, and Henry H. Wasser. Oslo: Gyldenhal
Norsk Forlag, 1966, pp. 110-160.

1401 KLEIMAN, E. "The Wizardry of Nathaniel Hawthorne:
Seven Gables as Fairy Tale and Parable." English
Studies in Canada, 4 (1978), 289-304.

1402 KLIGERMAN, Jack. "A Stylist Approach to Hawthorne's
'Roger Malvin's Burial.'" Language and Style, 4
(1971), 188-194.

1403 KLING, Carlos. "Hawthorne's View of Sin." Personalist, 13 (April, 1932), 119-130.

1404 KLINKOWITZ, Jerome F. "The Significance of the
Ending to The House of the Seven Gables." Ph.D.
diss., Wisconsin, 1969. DA, 31 (1970), 392A.

1405 _____. "In Defense of Holgrave." Emerson Society
Quarterly, 62 (1971), 4-8.

1406 _____. "Ending the Seven Gables: Old Light on a
New Problem." Studies in the Novel, 4 (1972), 396-
401. See also article by Frank Battaglia (1967).

1407 _____. "Hawthorne's Sense of an Ending." Emerson
Society Quarterly, 19 (1973), 43-49.

1408 _____. "The Hawthorne-Fields Letterbook: A Census and Description." Nathaniel Hawthorne Journal, 4 (1974), 92-103.

1409 KLOECKNER, Alfred J. "The Flower and the Fountain: Hawthorne's Chief Symbols in 'Rappaccini's Daughter.'" American Literature, 38 (November, 1966), 323-336.

1410 KNIGHT, Grant C. "Nathaniel Hawthorne," in American Literature and Culture. New York: Long and Smith, 1932, pp. 203-214.

1411 KNOX, George. "The Hawthorne-Lowell Affair." New England Quarterly, 29 (December, 1956), 493-502.

1412 KOISUMI, Ichiro. "The 'Artist' in Hawthorne." Studies in English Literature (Tokyo), 40 (February, 1964), 35-43.

1413 KORNFELD, Milton H. "A Darker Freedom: The Villain in the Novels of Hawthorne, James, and Faulkner." Ph.D. diss., Brandeis, 1970. DA, 31 (1970), 2883A.

1414 KOSKENLINNA, Hazel Marion. "Sir Walter Scott and Nathaniel Hawthorne: Parallels and Divergencies." Ph.D. diss., Wisconsin, 1968. DA, 28 (1968), 5059A.

1415 _____. "Setting, Image, and Scott and Hawthorne." Emerson Society Quarterly, 19 (1973), 50-59.

1416 KOUWENHOVEN, John A. "Hawthorne's Notebooks and Doctor Grimshawe's Secret." American Literature, 5 (January, 1934), 349-358.

1417 KOZIKOWSKI, Stanley J. "'My Kinsman, Major Molineux' as Mock-Heroic." American Transcendental Quarterly, 31 (1976), 20-21.

1418 KRAFT, Quentin G. "The Central Problem of James' Fictional Thought: From The Scarlet Letter to Roderick Hudson." English Literary History, 36 (1969), 416-489.

1419 KRAUSE, Sydney J., ed. Essays on Determinism in American Literature. Kent, Ohio: Kent State University Press, 1964. Hawthorne, passim

1420   KREUTER, Kent Kirby. "The Literary Response to
       Science, Technology, and Industrialism: Studies in
       the Thought of Nathaniel Hawthorne, Melville, Whitman,
       and Twain." Ph.D. diss., Wisconsin (History), 1963.
       DA, 24 (1964), 2446.

1421   KRIEGER, Murray. The Tragic Vision. New York:
       Holt, Rinehart, and Winston, 1960. Does not deal
       with Hawthorne but offers good insights into other
       tragic writers, including Melville.

1422   _____. "The Marble Faun and the International
       Theme," in Krieger, The Play and Place of Criticism.
       Baltimore: Johns Hopkins University Press, 1967,
       pp. 79-90.

1423   _____, ed. with Afterword. The Marble Faun; or
       the Romance of Monte Beni. New York: New Ameri-
       can Library, 1961.

1424   KRIER, William J. "A Pattern of Limitations: The
       Heroine's Novel of the Mind." Ph.D. diss., Indiana,
       1972. DA, 34 (1973), 277A-278A.

1425   KRUMPELMANN, John T. "Hawthorne's 'Young Good-
       man Brown' and Goethe's Faust." Die neueren
       Sprachen, 11 (1956), 516-521.

1426   KUHLMANN, Susan. "The Window of Fiction." CEA
       Critic, 30 (November, 1967), 15-16.

1427   _____. Knave, Fool, and Genius: The Confidence
       Man as He Appears in Nineteenth-Century American
       Fiction. Chapel Hill: University of North Carolina
       Press, 1973. Hawthorne, pp. 75-90.

1428   KUMMINGS, Donald D. "Hawthorne's 'The Custom-
       House' and the Conditions of Fiction in America."
       CEA Critic, 33 (1971), 15-18.

1429   KUSHENS, Betty. "Love's Martyrs: The Scarlet
       Letter as Secular Cross." Literature and Psychology,
       22 (1972), 108-120.

1430   LABAREE, Benjamin W., and Benjamin Bernard Cohen.
       "Hawthorne and the Essex Institute." Essex Institute

Historical Collections, 94 (July, 1958), 297-30. List of special holdings.

1431 LAMONT, Dr. John H. (M.D.). "Hawthorne's Unfinished Works." *Harvard Medical Alumni Bulletin,* 36 (Summer, 1962), 13-20.

1432 LANE, Lauriat, Jr. "Allegory and Character in *The Scarlet Letter.*" *Emerson Society Quarterly,* 25 (1961), 13-16.

1433 LANG, Andrew. "Letters to Dead Authors: To Nathaniel Hawthorne." *Chap-Book,* 8 (February 15, 1898), 276-277.

1434 _____. "Nathaniel Hawthorne," in Lang, *Adventures Among Books.* New York: Longmans, Green, 1905, pp. 211-223.

1435 _____. "Hawthorne's Tales of Old Greece." *Independent,* 62 (April 4, 1907), 792-794.

1436 LANG, Eleanor Marianne. "Hawthorne and Faulkner: The Continuity of a Dark American Tradition." Ph.D., diss., Lehigh, 1970. *DA,* 31 (1971), 5410A.

1437 LANG, Hans-Joachim. "How Ambiguous Is Hawthorne?" in Hammond, Lewis; Dieter Sattler; and Emil Lehnarte; eds., *Geist einer freien Gesellschaft: Festschrift für Senator William Fulbright.* Heidelberg: Quelle and Meyer, 1962, pp. 195-220. Reprinted in Kaul, ed., *Hawthorne* (1966), pp. 86-98.

1439 _____. "*The Blithedale Romance*: A History of Ideas Approach," in Helmcke, Hans; Klaus Lubbers; and Renate Schmidt-von Bardeleben; eds., *Literature und Sprache.* Heidelberg, Germany: Winter, 1969, pp. 88-106.

1440 LANGEMANN, J.K. "Husband to the Month of May." *Christian Science Monitor,* 38 (July 13, 1946), 4-5.

1441 LAPE, Denis Allison. "*The Masks of Dionysus*: An Application of Friederich Nietzsche's Theory of Tragedy to the Works of Hawthorne and Melville." Ph.D. diss., Minnesota, 1970. *DA,* 32 (1972), 5188A-5189A.

129   La Regina

1442 LA REGINA, Gabriella. "'Rappaccini's Daughter': The
      Gothic as a Catalyst for Hawthorne's Imagination."
      Studi Americani, 7 (1971), 29-74.

1443 LASER, Marvin. "Nathaniel Hawthorne and the Craft
      of Fiction: A Study in Artistic Development." Ph.D.
      diss., Northwestern, 1948.

1444 _____. "'Head,' 'Heart,' and 'Will,' in Hawthorne's
      Psychology." Nineteenth-Century Fiction, 10 (Sep-
      tember, 1955), 130-140. Character influence by
      Thomas C. Upham, 1799-1872.

1445 LASSER, Michael L. "Mirror Imagery in The Scarlet
      Letter." English Journal, 56 (February, 1967), 274-
      277.

1446 LATHROP, George Parsons. "A History of Hawthorne's
      Last Romance." Atlantic Monthly, 30 (October, 1872),
      452-460.

1447 _____. A Study of Hawthorne. Boston: Osgood,
      1876.

1448 _____. "Poe, Irving, Hawthorne." Scribner's
      Monthly, 11 (April, 1876), 799-808.

1449 _____. "The Hawthorne Manuscripts." Atlantic
      Monthly, 51 (March, 1883), 363-375. Reprinted in
      Cameron, ed., Hawthorne Among His Contemporaries
      (1968), pp.232-239.

1450 _____. "The Scarlet Letter," a libretto for the
      opera by Walter Damrosch, 1896.

1451 _____, ed. with Introduction and Notes. The
      Complete Works of Nathaniel Hawthorne, 12 vols.
      Boston and New York: Houghton Mifflin, 1883.
      Standard Riverside Edition.

1452 _____, ed. with Biographical Introduction. Tales,
      Sketches, and Papers. Boston and New York:
      Houghton Mifflin, 1884.

1453 LATHROP, Rose Hawthorne (Mrs. G.P. Lathrop).
      Memories of Hawthorne. Boston: Osgood, 1879.
      Reprinted Boston: Houghton Mifflin, 1897.

1454 _____. "My Father's Literary Methods." Ladies'
Home Journal, 11 (March, 1894), 1-2. Reprinted in
Cameron, ed., Hawthorne Among His Contemporaries
(1968), pp. 371-374.

1455 LATIMER, George D. "The Tales of Poe and Hawthorne." New England Magazine, 30 (August, 1904),
693-703.

1456 LAUBER, John. "Hawthorne's Shaker Tales."
Nineteenth-Century Fiction, 18 (June, 1963), 82-86.

1457 LAVERTY, Carroll D. "Some Touchstones of Hawthorne's
Style." Emerson Society Quarterly, 60 (1970), 30-
36.

1458 LAWRENCE, D. H. "Hawthorne: Studies in Classic
American Literature." English Review, 28 (May,
1919), 404-417.

1459 _____. Studies in Classic American Literature.
New York: Thomas Seltzer, 1923. Reprinted New
York: Doubleday/Anchor, 1953. Hawthorne, pp. 92-
120.

1460 _____. "Nathaniel Hawthorne and The Scarlet
Letter," in Studies (1923), pp. 121-147. Reprinted
in Wilson, Edmund, ed., The Shock of Recognition
(1943), pp. 984-1001.

1461 _____. "Hawthorne's Blithedale Romance," in
Studies (1923), pp. 148-162. Reprinted in Wilson,
Edmund, ed., The Shock of Recognition (1943), pp.
1002-1011.

1462 _____. Phoenix: The Posthumous Papers of D. H.
Lawrence, edited by Edward D. McDonald. New
York: Viking, 1936.

1463 _____. Selected Literary Criticism. Edited by
Anthony Beal. New York: Viking, 1956. Reprints
"Nathaniel Hawthorne and The Scarlet Letter," from
Studies (1923), pp. 347-363.

1464 _____. The Symbolic Meaning: The Uncollected
Versions of "Studies in Classic American Literature."
Edited by Arnold Armin. Arundel, England: Centaur,

1962. "Nathaniel Hawthorne, I," and "Nathaniel Hawthorne, II," pp. 121-146, 147-158.

1465 _____. "The Transcendental Element in American
Literature: A Study of Some Unpublished D. H. Lawrence Manuscripts." Modern Philology, 60 (1962),
41-46.

1466 _____. Phoenix II: Uncollected, Unpublished, and
Other Prose Works, edited by Warren Roberts and
Harry T. Moore. New York: Viking, 1968; London:
Heinemann, 1968.

1467 LAWSON, Alvin H. "Hawthorne and the Limits of
Intellect." Ph. D. diss., Stanford, 1966. DA, 27
(1967), 4257A.

1468 LAWTON, William C. The New England Poets: A
Study of Emerson, Hawthorne, Longfellow, Whittier,
Lowell, Holmes. London: Macmillan, 1898. Re-
printed Plainview, N. Y.: Books for Libraries, 1972.
"Emerson: The Philosophic Poet," pp. 21-47, Haw-
thorne, passim; Hawthorne, pp. 48-104.

1469 LE, Van-Diem. "Puritan Idealism and the Transcendental Movement." Ph. D. diss., Minnesota, 1960.
DA, 21 (1961), 1929.

1470 LEAF, Munro. "The House of the Seven Gables by
Nathaniel Hawthorne Who Had Ghosts in His Own
Garrett." American Magazine, 131 (March, 1941),
62. For young readers.

1471 LEARY, Lewis Gaston. American Literature: A
Study and Research Guide. New York: St. Martin,
1976. Hawthorne, pp. 101-104.

1472 _____, ed. Articles on American Literature, 1900-
1950. Durham, N. C.: Duke University Press, 1954.
Hawthorne, pp. 128-134.

1473 _____, ed. American Literary Essays. New York:
Crowell, 1960. Excerpt from Melville's "Hawthorne
and His Mosses," pp. 90-92.

1474 _____, ed. The Teacher and American Literature.
Champaign, Ill.: National Council of Teachers of

English, 1965. "Recent Scholarship on Hawthorne and Melville," by Arlin Turner, pp. 95-109.

1475   , ed. Articles on American Literature, 1950-1967. Durham: Duke University Press, 1970. Hawthorne, pp. 236-259.

1476   , ed. with John Auchard. Articles on American Literature, 1968-1975. Durham: Duke University Press, 1979. Hawthorne, pp. 234-254.

1477 LEASE, Benjamin. "Hawthorne and Blackwoods' in 1849: Two Unpublished Letters." Jahrbuch für Amerikastudien, 14 (1969), 152-154. Letters by Horatio Bridge and John Jay.

1478   . "Hawthorne and a 'Certain Venerable Personage': New Light on 'The Custom-House.'" Jahrbuch für Amerikastudien, 15 (1970), 201-207.

1479   . "Diorama and Dream: Hawthorne's Cinematic Vision." Journal of Popular Culture, 5 (1971), 315-323.

1480   . "Salem vs. Hawthorne: An Early Review of The Scarlet Letter." New England Quarterly, 44 (1971), 110-117. Reprint of a review in Salem Registrar, March 21, 1850.

1481   . "'The Whole Is a Prose Poem': An Early Review of The Scarlet Letter." American Literature, 44 (1972), 128-130.

1482 LEAVIS, Queenie Dorothy. "Hawthorne as Poet," 2 parts. Sewanee Review, 59 (April-June, 1951), 179-205; and 59 (July-September, 1951), 426-458. Reprinted in Feidelson, Charles, and Paul Brodtkorb, eds., Interpretations of American Literature. New York: Oxford University Press, 1959, pp. 30-50. Also reprinted in Kaul, Hawthorne (1966), pp. 25-63.

1483 LEAVITT, Charles Loyal. "Hawthorne's Use of Pageantry." Ph.D. diss., Wisconsin, 1960. DA, 22 (1961), 871-872.

1484 LEE, Young-Oak. "After the Fall: Tragic Themes in the Major Works of Nathaniel Hawthorne and Robert

133 Lee

Penn Warren." Ph.D. diss., Hawaii, 1977. <u>DA</u>,
38 (1978), 6195A-6196A.

1485 LEDGER, Marshall A. "George Eliot and Nathaniel
Hawthorne." <u>Notes and Queries</u>, 11 (June, 1964),
225-226.

1486 LEFCOWITZ, Allan. "Apologia pro Roger Prynne:
A Psychological Study." <u>Literature and Psychology</u>,
24 (1974), 34-44.

1487 _____, and Barbara Lefcowitz. "Some Rents in the
Veil: New Light on Priscilla and Zenobia in <u>The
Blithedale Romance.</u>" <u>Nineteenth-Century Fiction</u>,
21 (December, 1966), 263-275.

1488 LE GALLIENNE, Richard. "Re-reading Hawthorne,"
in <u>Attitudes and Avowals</u>. London: John Lane, 1910,
pp. 267-284.

1489 LEIB, Amos P. "Nathaniel Hawthorne as Scenic Artist." Ph.D. diss., Tulane, 1963. <u>DA</u>, 24 (1964),
3338-3339.

1490 LEIBOWITZ, Herbert A. "Hawthorne and Spenser:
Two Sources." <u>American Literature</u>, 30 (January,
1959), 459-466.

1491 LEITMAN, Carolyn Laura. "Romantic Self-Conscious-
ness in Certain Novels of Hawthorne, Conrad, and
Durrell." Ph.D. diss., Case Western, 1976. <u>DA</u>,
37 (1977), 5110A-5111A.

1492 LENHART, C.S., ed. <u>Nathaniel Hawthorne: The
House of the Seven Gables.</u> New York: Barnes and
Noble, 1966. Book Notes Series.

1493 LENTZ, Vern B., and Allen F. Stein. "The Black
Flower of Necessity: Structure in <u>The Blithedale
Romance.</u>" <u>Essays in Literature</u> (University of Den-
ver), 3 (1976), 86-96.

1494 LESSER, M.X. "Dimmesdale's Wordless Sermon."
<u>American Notes and Queries,</u> 12 (1974), 93-94.

1495 LESSER, Simon O. "The Image of the Father: A
Reading of 'My Kinsman, Major Molineux' and 'I

Want to Know Why.'" Partisan Review, 22 (Summer,
1955), 372-390. Relates to Sherwood Anderson. Reprinted in Lesser, Fiction and the Unconscious.
Boston: Beacon, 1957, pp. 212-224 et passim. Also
reprinted in Phillips, William, ed., Art and Psychoanalysis. New York: Criterion, 1957, pp. 226-246.

1496   _____. "The Attitude of Fiction." Modern Fiction
Studies, 2 (May, 1956), 52-55.

1497   _____. "The Image of the Father," excerpt from
Fiction and the Unconscious (1957), in Scott, Wilbur
Stewart, ed., Five Approaches of Literary Criticism.
New York: Macmillan, 1962, pp. 99-120.

1498   _____. "Hawthorne and Anderson: Conscious and
Unconscious Perception," excerpt from Fiction and the
Unconscious (1957), in Malin, Irving, ed., Psychoanalysis and American Fiction. New York: Dutton,
1965, pp. 87-110.

1499   _____. "Hawthorne's 'My Kinsman, Major Molineux,'" excerpt from Fiction and the Unconscious
(1957), in Sprich, Robert, and Richard W. Noland,
eds., The Whispered Meanings. Amherst: University
of Massachusetts Press, 1977, pp. 44-53.

1500   LEVI, Joseph. "Hawthorne's The Scarlet Letter: A
Psychoanalytical Interpretation." American Imago,
10 (1953), 291-306.

1501   LEVIN, David. History as Romantic Art. Stanford,
Calif.: Stanford University Press, 1959. Hawthorne,
passim.

1502   _____. "Shadows of Doubt: Specter Evidence in
Hawthorne's 'Young Goodman Brown.'" American
Literature, 34 (November, 1962), 344-352.

1503   _____. "Nathaniel Hawthorne: The Scarlet Letter,"
in Stegner, Wallace E., ed., The American Novel
from Cooper to Faulkner. New York: Basic Books,
1965, pp. 13-24.

1504   _____. In Defense of Historical Literature. New
York: Hill and Wang, 1967, pp. 98-117.

1505   _____, ed. with Introduction. The Scarlet Letter.
          New York: Dell, 1960.

1506   _____, ed. with Introduction. The House of the
          Seven Gables. New York: Dell, 1960.

1507   _____, ed. with Introduction. The Blithedale Romance.
          New York: Dell, 1960.

1508   _____, ed. with Introduction. The Marble Faun.
          New York: Dell, 1960.

1509   _____, ed with Introduction. What Happened in
          Salem? New York: Harcourt, Brace, 1960. Re-
          printed materials on the Salem witch trials.

1510   LEVIN, Harry. The Power of Blackness: Hawthorne,
          Poe, and Melville. New York: Knopf, 1958. Re-
          printed New York: Vintage, 1960. Hawthorne, pp.
          34-102.

1511   _____. "Statues from Italy: The Marble Faun,"
          in Levin, Refractions: Essays in Comparative Liter-
          ature. New York: Oxford University Press, 1966,
          pp. 192-211. Reprinted in Pearce, Roy Harvey, ed.,
          Centenary Essays (1964), pp. 119-140.

1512   _____, ed. with Introduction. The Scarlet Letter.
          Boston: Houghton Mifflin, 1960. Riverside Edition.

1513   _____, ed. with Introduction. The Scarlet Letter
          and Other Tales of the Puritans. Boston: Houghton
          Mifflin, 1961.

1514   _____, ed. with Introduction and Notes. The House
          of the Seven Gables. Columbus, Ohio: Merrill, 1969.
          Merrill Edition.

1515   LEVY, Alfred Jacob. "Nathaniel Hawthorne's Attitude
          Toward Total Depravity and Evil." Ph.D. diss.,
          Wisconsin, 1956. DA, 17 (1957), 1751.

1516   _____. "'Ethan Brand' and the Unpardonable Sin."
          Boston University Studies in English, 5 (August, 1961),
          185-190.

1517   _____. "The House of the Seven Gables: The

Religion of Love." Nineteenth-Century Fiction, 16
(December, 1961), 189-203.

1518   LEVY, Leo B. "Hawthorne's 'The Canal Boat': An
        Experiment in Landscape." American Quarterly,
        16 (Summer, 1964), 211-215.

1519   _____. "Hawthorne's 'Middle Ground.'" Studies
        in Short Fiction, 2 (1964), 56-60. Between natural
        and unnatural lines in "The Canterbury Pilgrims."

1520   _____. "The Mermaid and the Mirror: Hawthorne's
        'The Village Uncle.'" Nineteenth-Century Fiction,
        19 (September, 1964), 205-211.

1521   _____. "Hawthorne, Melville, and the Monitor."
        American Literature, 37 (March, 1965), 33-40.

1522   _____. "Picturesque Style in The House of the
        Seven Gables." New England Quarterly, 39 (June,
        1966), 147-160.

1523   _____. "Hawthorne and the Sublime." American
        Literature, 37 (January, 1966), 391-402.

1524   _____. "The Temple and the Tomb: Hawthorne's
        'The Lily's Quest.'" Studies in Short Fiction, 3
        (Spring, 1966), 334-342.

1525   _____. "Criticism Chronicle: Hawthorne, Melville,
        and James." Southern Review, 2 (Spring, 1966),
        427-442.

1526   _____. "Hawthorne and the Idea of 'Bartleby.'"
        Emerson Society Quarterly, 47 (1967), 66-69.

1527   _____. "The Blithedale Romance: Hawthorne's
        'Voyage Through Chaos.'" Studies in Romanticism,
        8 (1968), 1-15.

1528   _____. "The Landscape Modes of The Scarlet
        Letter." Nineteenth-Century Fiction, 23 (1969), 377-
        392.

1529   _____. "The Marble Faun: Hawthorne's Landscape
        of the Fall." American Literature, 42 (1970), 139-
        156.

1530   _____. "Fanshawe: Hawthorne's World of Images."
        Studies in the Novel, 2 (1970), 440-448.

1531   _____. "'Time's Portraiture': Hawthorne's Theory
        of History." Nathaniel Hawthorne Journal, 1 (1971),
        192-200.

1532   _____. "The Notebook Source and the Eighteenth-
        Century Context of Hawthorne's Theory of Romance."
        Nathaniel Hawthorne Journal, 3 (1973), 120-129.

1533   _____. "The Problem of Faith in 'Young Goodman
        Brown.'" Journal of English and Germanic Philology,
        74 (1975), 375-387.

1534   _____. "'Lifelikeness' in Hawthorne's Fiction."
        Nathaniel Hawthorne Journal, 5 (1975), 141-145.

1535   LEWIN, Walter. "Nathaniel Hawthorne." Bookman
        (London), 26 (July, 1904), 121-128.

1536   _____. Nathaniel Hawthorne. London: Hodder
        and Stoughton, 1906. Reprinted Folcroft, Pa.: Fol-
        croft, 1977.

1537   LEWIS, Paul. "Victor Frankenstein and Owen Warland:
        The Artist as Satan and God." Studies in Short Fic-
        tion, 14 (1977), 279-282.

1538   LEWIS, R.W.B. "The Danger of Innocence: Adam
        as Hero in American Literature." Yale Review, 29
        (Spring, 1950), 473-490.

1539   _____. "The Return into Time: Hawthorne," in
        Lewis, The American Adam: Innocence, Tragedy,
        and Tradition in the Nineteenth Century. Chicago:
        University of Chicago Press, 1955, pp. 110-126. Re-
        printed in Kaul, ed., Hawthorne (1966), pp. 72-85.

1540   _____. "'Hold on Hard to the Huckleberry Bushes.'"
        Sewanee Review, 67 (1959), 462-477. Reprinted in
        Lewis, Trials of the Word (1965), pp. 97-111. Quo-
        tation from Emerson refers to a hold on reality,
        which Emerson is said not to have, and Hawthorne
        has.

1541   _____. "The Tactics of Sanctity: Hawthorne and

James," in Pearce, Roy Harvey, ed., Centenary Essays (1964), pp. 271-295.

1542 _____. Trials of the Word. New Haven: Yale University Press, 1965. Reprints 1959 article listed above; and "Hawthorne and James: The Matter of the Heart," pp. 77-96, similar to essay in Centenary Essays (1964).

1543 LEWISOHN, Ludwig. Expressionism in America. New York: Harper Brothers, 1932. Hawthorne, pp. 168-186. Revised and reissued as The Story of American Literature. New York: Harper Brothers, 1937. Reprinted New York: Random House, 1939. Modern Library Edition.

1544 LIEBMAN, Sheldon W. "The Design of The Marble Faun." New England Quarterly, 40 (March, 1967), 61-78.

1545 _____. "Hawthorne and Milton: The Second Fall in 'Rappaccini's Daughter.'" New England Quarterly, 41 (December, 1968), 521-535.

1546 _____. "Ambiguity in 'Lady Eleanor's Mantle.'" Emerson Society Quarterly, 58 (1970), 97-101.

1547 _____. "Robin's Conversion: The Design of 'My Kinsman, Major Molineux.'" Studies in Short Fiction, 8 (1971), 443-457.

1548 _____. "Hawthorne's Comus: A Miltonic Source for 'The Maypole of Merrymount.'" Nineteenth-Century Fiction, 27 (1972), 345-351.

1549 _____. "The Forsaken Maiden in Hawthorne's Stories." American Transcendental Quarterly, 19 (1973), 13-19.

1550 _____. "The Fearful Sympathy: A Critical Study of Selected Works of Nathaniel Hawthorne." Ph.D. diss., Pennsylvania, 1972. DA, 33 (1973), 5731A-5732A.

1551 _____. "Point of View in The House of the Seven Gables." Emerson Society Quarterly, 19 (1973), 203-212.

1552 _____. "Ethan Brand and the Unpardonable Sin."
American Transcendental Quarterly, 24 Supplement
(1974), 9-14.

1553 _____. "Moral Choice in 'The Maypole of Merry
Mount.'" Studies in Short Fiction, 11 (1974), 173-180.

1554 _____. "'Roger Malvin's Burial': Hawthorne's
Allegory of the Heart." Studies in Short Fiction, 12
(1975), 253-260.

1555 _____. "The Reader in 'Young Goodman Brown.'"
Nathaniel Hawthorne Journal, 5 (1975), 156-169.

1556 _____. "Hawthorne's Romanticism: 'The Artist of
the Beautiful.'" Emerson Society Quarterly, 22
(1976), 85-95.

1557 LIMPRECHT, Nancy Silverman. "Repudiating the Self-
Justifying Fiction: Charles Brockden Brown, Nathaniel
Hawthorne, and Herman Melville as Anti-Romancers."
Ph.D. diss., California (Berkeley), 1977. DA, 39
(1978), 886A.

1558 LIND, Sidney E. "Emily Dickinson's 'Further in
Summer Than the Birds,' and Nathaniel Hawthorne's
The Old Manse." American Literature, 39 (May,
1967), 163-169.

1559 LINK, Franz H. "Hawthorne's Skizzen." Die neueren
Sprachen, 8 (December, 1959), 537-546. Study of the
Sketches; in German.

1560 LISCHER, Tracy Kenyon. "The Passive Voice in
American Literature: Vehicle for Tragedy in Charles
B. Brown, Hawthorne, O'Neill, Wharton, and Frost."
Ph.D. diss., Saint Louis, 1977. DA, 39 (1978),
1573A.

1561 LITTLE, George Thomas. "Hawthorne's Fanshawe
and Bowdoin's Past." Bowdoin Quill, 8 (June, 1904),
179-186.

1562 LITZINGER, Boyd. "Mythmaking in America: 'The
Great Stone Face' and Raintree County." Tennessee
Studies in Literature, 8 (1963), 81-84.

1563 LLOYD, Michael. "Hawthorne, Ruskin, and the Hostile
      Tradition." English Miscellany (Rome, Italy), 6
      (1955), 109-133. Refers to hostility to Italy.

1564 LOFGREN, Hans Borje. "Democratic Skepticism:
      Literary-Historical Point of View in Cooper, Haw-
      thorne, and Melville." Ph. D. diss., California
      (Santa Cruz), 1977. DA, 38 (1978), 6714A-6715A.

1565 LOGAN, Samuel T., Jr. "Hermeneutics and American
      Literature." Ph. D. diss., Emory, 1971. DA, 33
      (1972), 2897A.

1565a LOGGINS, Vernon. The Hawthornes: The Story of
      Seven Generations of an American Family. New
      York: Columbia University Press, 1951.

1566 LOHMANN, Christoph K. "Nathaniel Hawthorne: The
      American Janus." Ph. D diss., Pennsylvania, 1968.
      DA, 30 (1969), 1172A.

1567 _____. "The Burden of the Past in Hawthorne's
      American Romances." South Atlantic Quarterly, 66
      (Winter, 1967), 92-104.

1568 _____. "The Agony of the English Romance."
      Nathaniel Hawthorne Journal, 2 (1972), 219-229.

1569 _____. "A Review of Alfred Weber's Work on Haw-
      thorne." Nathaniel Hawthorne Journal, 2 (1972), 267-
      270. Weber's work in German; has not been translated.

1570 LOMBARD, Charles M. "Hawthorne and French Ro-
      manticism." Rivista di Letteratura Moderne e Com-
      parate, 24 (1971), 311-316.

1571 LONG, Robert Emmet. "The Society and the Masks:
      The Blithedale Romance and The Bostonians." Nine-
      teenth-Century Fiction, 19 (September, 1964), 105-122.

1572 _____. "The Ambassadors and the Genteel Tradi-
      tion: James' Correction of Hawthorne and Howells."
      New England Quarterly, 42 (1969), 44-64.

1573 _____. "The Theatre of Political Moralism: Lowell,
      Hawthorne, and Melville." Modern Poetry Studies, 1
      (1970), 207-224.

1574   _____. "Transformations: The Blithedale Romance
        to Howells and James." American Literature, 47
        (1976), 552-571.

1575   _____. "Henry James' Apprenticeship--The Haw-
        thorne Aspect." American Literature, 48 (1976),
        194-216.

1576   _____. "James' Roderick Hudson: The End of
        Apprenticeship--Hawthorne and Turgenev." American
        Literature, 48 (1976), 312-326.

1577   LONG, William J. Outlines of American Literature
        with Readings. New York: Ginn, 1925. Hawthorne,
        pp. 145-153.

1578   LONGFELLOW, Henry W. "Review of Twice-Told
        Tales." North American Review, 54 (April, 1842),
        496-499. Reprinted in Richardson, L. N. , ; G. H.
        Orians; and H. R. Brown; eds. , Heritage of American
        Literature, 2 vols. Boston: Ginn, 1951. Vol. I,
        pp. 720-722. Also reprinted in Cohen, Benjamin
        Bernard, ed. , Recognition (1969), pp. 9-12.

1579   LONGFELLOW, Samuel. Life of Henry W. Longfellow.
        Boston: Houghton Mifflin, 1887. Hawthorne's letters
        referred to.

1580   LORING, George Bailey, M. D. "Hawthorne's Scarlet
        Letter." The Massachusetts Quarterly Review, 3
        (September, 1850), 484-500. Reprinted in Miller,
        Perry, ed. , The Transcendentalists. Cambridge:
        Harvard University Press, 1950, pp. 475-482. Also
        reprinted in Cohen, Benjamin Bernard, ed. Recog-
        nition (1969), pp. 41-49.

1581   _____. "Hawthorne," in Papyrus Leaves. Edited
        by William F. Gill. New York: R. Worthington,
        1880, pp. 249-268. Reprinted in Cameron, ed. ,
        Hawthorne Among His Contemporaries (1968), pp.
        213-218.

1582   LOUVRE, Alfred W. "The Limits of Living in Style."
        Ph. D. diss. , Cornell, 1973. DA, 34 (1974), 7238A.

1583   LOVECRAFT, H. P. Supernatural Horror in Literature.
        New York: Ben Abramson, 1945. Discusses The

House of the Seven Gables, pp. 63-65.

1584   LOVEJOY, David S. "Lovewell's Fight and Hawthorne's
       'Roger Malvin's Burial.'" New England Quarterly,
       27 (December, 1954), 527-531.

1585   LOVING, Jerome M. "Melville's Pardonable Sin."
       New England Quarterly, 47 (June, 1974), 262-278.

1586   LOWELL, James Russell. "The Marble Faun."
       Atlantic Monthly, 5 (April, 1860), 509-510. Re-
       printed in Cohen, Benjamin Bernard, ed., Recog-
       nition (1969), pp. 75-78.

1587   LOWELL, Robert. "'My Kinsman, Major Molineux.'"
       Partisan Review, 31 (Fall, 1964), 495-514, 566-583.
       Drama based on Hawthorne's story.

1588   _____. "Hawthorne," a poem, in Pearce, ed.,
       Roy Harvey, Centenary Essays (1964), pp. 3-4.
       Slightly different version in Lowell, For the Union
       Dead. New York: Farrar, Straus, and Giroux,
       1964, pp. 38-39.

1589   _____. The Old Glory. New York: Farrar,
       Straus, and Giroux, 1964, 1968. Contains "Haw-
       thorne," a poem, and Lowell's play based on Mel-
       ville's Benito Cereno.

1590   LOZYNSKY, Artem. "Whitman the Man and Hawthorne
       the Artist: An English Evaluation." Nathaniel Haw-
       thorne Journal, 5 (1975), 270-271.

1591   LUBBERS, Klaus. "Metaphorical Patterns in Haw-
       thorne's The House of the Seven Gables," in Helmcke,
       Hans; Klaus Lubbers; and Renate Schmidt-von Bar-
       deleben; eds., Literature und Sprache. Heidelberg,
       Germany: Winter, 1969, pp. 107-116.

1592   LUCKE, Jessie Ryon. "The Inception of 'The Beast
       in the Jungle.'" New England Quarterly, 26 (De-
       cember, 1953), 529-532. Relates James to Haw-
       thorne.

1593   _____. "Hawthorne's Madonna Image in The Scarlet
       Letter." New England Quarterly, 38 (September,
       1965), 391-392.

143   Luecke

1594   LUECKE, Sister Jane Marie, O.S.B. "Villains and
       Non-Villains in Hawthorne's Fiction." PMLA, 78
       (December, 1963), 551-558.

1595   LUEDERS, Edward G. "The Melville-Hawthorne
       Relationship in Pierre and The Blithedale Romance."
       Western Humanities Review, 4 (August, 1950), 323-
       334.

1596   LUEDTKE, Luther. "Hawthorne on Architecture:
       Sources for Parley's Universal History and The Ameri-
       can Notebooks." Papers of the Bibliographical Society
       of America, 71 (1977), 88-98.

1597   LUNDBLAD, Jane. "Nathaniel Hawthorne and the
       Tradition of Gothic Romance." Studia Neophilologica,
       19 (1946), 1-92. Also published as book by Essays
       and Studies in American Language and Literature, No.
       4, American Institute at Uppsala, 1946.

1598   _____. Nathaniel Hawthorne and European Literary
       Tradition. Essays and Studies in American Language
       and Literature, No. 6, American Institute at Uppsala,
       1947; Cambridge: Harvard University Press, 1947.
       Based on Ph.D. diss., Uppsala, 1947.

1599   LYCETTE, Ronald L. "Diminishing Circumferences:
       Feminine Responses in Fiction to New England's
       Decline." Ph.D. diss., Purdue, 1970. DA, 31
       (1971), 1764A.

1600   LYNCH, James J. "The Devil in the Writings of
       Irving, Hawthorne, and Poe." New York Folklore
       Quarterly, 8 (Summer, 1952), 111-131.

1601   _____. "Structure and Allegory in 'The Great Stone
       Face.'" Nineteenth-Century Fiction, 15 (September,
       1960), 137-146.

1602   LYND, Robert. "Hawthorne," in Books and Authors.
       London: Dent, 1922. Reprinted New York: Dent, 1952.
       pp.140-148. Reprinted in Rhys, Ernest, ed., Modern
       English Essays. New York: Dutton, 1922, pp.10-16.

1603   LYNN, Kenneth S., ed. The Scarlet Letter: Text, Sources,
       and Criticism. New York: Harcourt, Brace, and World,
       1961.

1604 LYTTLE, David J. "'Giovanni! My Poor Giovanni!'" Studies in Short Fiction, 2 (Winter, 1965), 145-156.

1605 MABIE, Hamilton Wright. "Nathaniel Hawthorne." North American Review, 179 (July, 1904), 12-23.

1606 _____. "Hawthorne in the New World," in Mabie, Backgrounds of Literature. New York: Macmillan, 1904, pp. 303-328.

1607 McALEER, J. J. "Hester Prynne's Grave." Descant, 5 (Winter, 1961), 29-33.

1608 McCABE, Bernard. "Narrative Technique in 'Rappaccini's Daughter.'" Modern Language Notes, 74 (March, 1959), 213-217.

1609 McCALL, Dan Elliott. "Citizen of Somewhere Else: The Achievement of The Scarlet Letter." Ph. D. diss., Columbia, 1966. DA, 28 (1967), 1790A.

1610 _____. "Robert Lowell's 'Hawthorne.'" New England Quarterly, 39 (June, 1966), 237-239.

1611 _____. "The Design of Hawthorne's 'Custom House.'" Nineteenth-Century Fiction, 21 (March, 1967), 349-358.

1612 _____. "Hawthorne's 'Familiar Kind of Preface.'" English Literary History, 35 (1968), 422-439.

1613 _____. "'I Felt a Funeral in My Brain' and 'The Hollow of the Three Hills.'" New England Quarterly, 42 (1969), 432-435.

1614 MacCARTHY, Sir Desmond. "Nathaniel Hawthorne," in MacCarthy, ed., Humanities. Preface by Lord David Cecil. New York: Oxford University Press, 1954, pp. 167-171.

1615 McCARTHY, Harold T. "Hawthorne's Dialogue with Rome: The Marble Faun." Studi Americani, 14 (1968), 97-112. Reprinted in McCarthy, The Expatriate Perspective: American Novelists and the Idea of America. Rutherford, N.J.: Fairleigh Dickinson University Press, 1974, pp. 62-78.

1616 McCARTHY, Paul E. "The Extraordinary Man as
      Idealist in Novels by Hawthorne and Melville," in
      Cook. Reginald L. , ed. , <u>Themes, Tones, and Motifs
      in the American Renaissance</u>. Hartford, Conn. :
      Transcendental, 1968, pp.43-51. Also published as
      <u>Emerson Society Quarterly</u>, 54 (1969), 43-51.

1617 _____. "A Perspective in Hawthorne's Novels."
      <u>Ball State University Forum</u>, 13 (1972), 46-58.

1618 McCOLGAN, Kristin Pruitt. "The World's Slow
      Stain: The Theme of Initiation in Selected American
      Novels." Ph.D. diss. , North Carolina (Chapel Hill),
      1974. <u>DA</u>, 36 (1975), 279A.

1619 McCORQUODALE, Marjorie Kimball. "Melville's
      Pierre as Hawthorne." <u>University of Texas Studies
      in English</u>, 33 (1954), 97-102.

1620 McCULLEN, Joseph T. , Jr. "Young Goodman Brown:
      Presumption and Despair." <u>Discovery</u>, 2 (July,
      1959), 145-157.

1621 _____. "Zenobia: Hawthorne's Scornful Sceptic."
      <u>Discovery</u>, 4 (Winter, 1961), 72-80.

1622 _____. "Ancient Rites for the Dead and Hawthorne's
      'Roger Malvin's Burial.'" <u>Southern Folklore Quarterly,</u>
      30 (1966), 313-322.

1623 _____. "Influences on Hawthorne's 'The Artist of
      the Beautiful.'" <u>Emerson Society Quarterly</u>, 50
      supplement (1968), 43-46.

1624 _____, and John C. Guilds. "The Unpardonable
      Sin in Hawthorne: A Re-examination." <u>Nineteenth-
      Century Fiction</u>, 15 (December, 1960), 221-237.

1625 McDONALD, John Joseph. "Hawthorne at the Old
      Manse." Ph.D. diss. , Princeton, 1971. <u>DA,</u>
      (1972), 6439A.

1626 _____. "'The Old Manse' and Its Mosses: The
      Inception and Development of <u>Mosses from an Old
      Manse</u>." <u>Texas Studies in Literature and Language,</u>
      16 (1974), 77-108.

1627   _____. "The Old Manse Period Canon." Nathaniel
        Hawthorne Journal, 2 (1972), 13-39.

1628   _____. "A Guide to Primary Source Materials for
        the Study of Hawthorne's Old Manse Period," in
        Myerson, ed., Studies: 1977 (1978), pp. 261-312.

1629   _____, ed. "A Sophia Hawthorne Journal, 1843-
        1844." Nathaniel Hawthorne Journal, 4 (1974), 1-
        30.

1630   McDOWELL, Tremaine. "Nathaniel Hawthorne and the
        Witches of Colonial Salem." Notes and Queries,
        166 (March 3, 1934), 152.

1631   McELDERRY, Bruce R., Jr. "The Transcendental
        Hawthorne." Midwest Quarterly, 2 (Summer, 1961),
        307-323.

1632   McELROY, John Harmon. "Images of the Seventeenth-
        Century Puritan in American Novels, 1823-1860."
        Ph.D. diss., Duke, 1966.

1633   _____. "The Brand Metaphor in 'Ethan Brand.'"
        American Literature, 43 (1972), 633-637.

1634   _____. "The Hawthorne Style of American Fiction."
        Emerson Society Quarterly, 19 (1973), 117-123.

1635   McHANEY, Thomas L. "The Textual Editions of
        Hawthorne and Melville." Studies in the Literary
        Imagination, 2 (1969), 27-41.

1636   McINERNEY, Thomas Joseph. "Nathaniel Hawthorne,
        1825-1850: Literary Apprentice, Magazinist, and
        Experimental Craftsman." Ph.D. diss., University
        of Washington, 1958. DA, 20 (1959), 1026.

1637   _____. "A Tribute to Rose Hawthorne from Her
        Niece." Essex Institute Historical Collections, 111
        (1975), 35-36.

1638   McINTIRE, Mary Beth. "The Buried Life: A Study
        of The Blithedale Romance, The Confidence Man,
        and The Sacred Fount." Ph.D. diss., Rice, 1975.
        DA, 36 (1975), 2183A.

1639 McINTOSH, James M. "Hawthorne's Search for a
Wider Public and a Select Society." Forum (Houston),
13 (1976), 4-7.

1640 MACK, Stanley Thomas. "Portraits and Portraitists
in Hawthorne and James." Ph.D. diss., Lehigh,
1976. DA, 37 (1977), 7131A-7132A.

1641 McKEITHAN, Dan M. "Hawthorne's 'Young Goodman
Brown': An Interpretation." Modern Language Notes,
67 (February, 1952), 93-96.

1642 _____. "Poe and the Second Edition of Hawthorne's
Twice-Told Tales." Nathaniel Hawthorne Journal,
4 (1974), 257-269.

1643 McKIERNAN, John Thomas. "The Psychology of
Nathaniel Hawthorne." Ph.D. diss., Pennsylvania
State, 1956. DA, 17 (1957), 3019.

1644 MacLEAN, Hugh Norman. "Hawthorne's Scarlet Letter:
The Dark Problem of This Life." American Literature, 27 (March, 1955), 12-24.

1645 McMURRAY, William. "Point of View in Howell's
The Landlord at Lion's Head." American Literature,
34 (May, 1962), 207-214. Relates to influence of
Hawthorne.

1646 McNALLIE: Robin M. "Nathaniel Hawthorne and England: His Views on British History and Institutions."
Ph.D. diss., Princeton, c.1965.

1647 McNAMARA, Anne Marie. "The Character of Flame:
The Function of Pearl in The Scarlet Letter."
American Literature, 27 (January, 1956), 537-553.

1648 McNAMARA, Leo F. "Subject, Style, and Narrative
Technique in 'Bartleby' and 'Wakefield.'" Michigan
Academician, 3 (1971), 41-46.

1649 McPHERSON, Hugo Archibald. "Hawthorne and the
Greek Myths: A Study in Imagination." Ph.D. diss.,
Toronto, 1956.

1650 _____. "Hawthorne's Major Source for His Mythological Tales." American Literature, 30 (November, 1958), 364-365.

1651 _____. "Hawthorne's Mythology: A Mirror for Puritans." University of Toronto Quarterly, 28 (April, 1959), 267-278.

1652 _____. Hawthorne as Myth-Maker: A Study in Imagination. Toronto: University of Toronto Press, 1969. University of Toronto Department of English Studies and Texts, No. 16.

1653 MacSHANE, Frank. "The House of the Dead: Hawthorne's Custom House and The Scarlet Letter." New England Quarterly, 35 (March, 1962), 93-101.

1654 McWILLIAMS, John P., Jr. "'Thorough-Going Democrat' and 'Modern Tory': Hawthorne and the Puritan Revolution of 1776." Studies in Romanticism, 15 (1976), 549-571.

1655 _____. "Fictions of Merry Mount." American Quarterly, 29 (1977), 3-30.

1656 McWILLIAMS, Wilson Carey. The Idea of Fraternity in America. Berkeley: University of California Press, 1973. Hawthorne, pp. 301-327.

1657 MACY, John Albert. The Spirit of American Literature. New York: Boni and Liveright, 1908. Reprinted New York: Random House, 1913. Hawthorne, pp. 77-96.

1658 _____, ed. American Writers on American Literature. New York: Liveright, 1931. "Hawthorne," by Louis Bromfield, pp. 97-104.

1659 MADDEN, Edward H. "George W. Curtis: Practical Transcendentalist." Personalist, 40 (Autumn, 1959), 369-379.

1660 MAES-JELINCK, Hena. "Roger Chillingworth: An Example of the Creative Process in The Scarlet Letter." English Studies, 49 (1968), 341-348.

1661 MAGALANER, Marvin, and Edmond L. Volpe, eds. Twelve Short Stories. New York: Macmillan, 1961.

"Young Goodman Brown," discussion, pp. 7-11.

1662   MAGINNIS, Mary Amelia. "Nathaniel Hawthorne's
       Comments on the Arts as Evidence of an Aesthetic
       Theory." Ph. D. diss., North Carolina, 1948.

1663   _____. "Hawthorne on Church Architecture."
       Florida State University Studies (Tallahassee), 11
       (1963), 54-74.

1664   MAGRETTA, Joan. "The Coverdale Translation:
       Blithedale and the Bible." Nathaniel Hawthorne
       Journal, 4 (1974), 250-256.

1665   MAHAN, Helen R. "Hawthorne's The Marble Faun:
       A Critical Introduction and Annotation." Ph. D.
       diss., Rochester, 1965. DA, 27 (1966), 1341A.

1666   MALE, Roy R., Jr. "Criticism of Bell's 'Hawthorne's
       Fire-Worship: Interpretation and Source.'" Ameri-
       can Literature, 25 (March, 1953), 85-87.

1667   _____. "Hawthorne and the Romantic Concept of
       Sympathy." PMLA, 68 (March, 1953), 138-149.

1668   _____. "'From the Innermost Germ': The Or-
       ganic Principle in Hawthorne's Fiction." Journal
       of English Literary History, 20 (September, 1953),
       218-236.

1669   _____. "The Dual Aspects of Evil in 'Rappaccini's
       Daughter.'" PMLA, 69 (March, 1954), 99-109.

1670   _____. "Toward The Wasteland: The Theme of
       The Blithedale Romance." College English, 16
       (February, 1955), 277-283.

1671   _____. Hawthorne's Tragic Vision. Austin:
       University of Texas Press, 1957.

1672   _____. "Hawthorne's Allegory of Guilt and Re-
       demption." Emerson Society Quarterly, 25 (1961),
       16-18.

1673   _____. "Review of The Sins of the Fathers by
       Frederick Crews (1966)." Nineteenth-Century
       Fiction, 21 (1966), 193-196.

1674 _____. "Hawthorne." Review of Current Scholarship in American Literary Scholarship, 1968, 1969,
pp. 19-29, 19-32.

1675 _____. "Hawthorne's The Blithedale Romance."
Explicator, 28 (1970), item 56.

1676 _____. "Hawthorne's Fancy, or the Medium of
The Blithedale Romance." Nathaniel Hawthorne
Journal, 2 (1972), 67-73. Based on talk given at
MLA, December, 1971.

1677 _____, and Frederick Crews. "Exchange of
Opinion." Nineteenth-Century Fiction, 22 (June,
1967), 101-110.

1678 MALIN, Irving, ed. Psychoanalysis and American
Fiction. New York: Dutton, 1965. "Robin Molineux
on the Analyst's Couch: A Note on the Limits of
Psycho-analytic Criticism," by Roy Harvey Pearce,
pp. 309-316.

1679 MANI, Lakshmi. "The Apocalypse in Cooper, Hawthorne, and Melville." Ph.D. diss., McGill, 1972.
DA, 34 (1973), 783A.

1680 MANIERRE, William R. "Some Apparent Confusions
in The Scarlet Letter." CEA Critic, 33 (1971), 9-
13.

1681 _____. "The Role of Sympathy in The Scarlet
Letter." Texas Studies in Literature and Language,
13 (1971), 497-507.

1682 MANLEY, Seon. Nathaniel Hawthorne: Captain of
the Imagination. New York: Vanguard, 1967.

1683 MANN, Charles W. "D.H. Lawrence: Notes on
Reading Hawthorne's The Scarlet Letter." Nathaniel
Hawthorne Journal, 3 (1973), 8-25.

1684 MANN, Robert W. "After Thoughts on Opera and The
Scarlet Letter." Studi Americani, 5 (1959), 339-350.
Followed by "The Scarlet Letter: A Libretto in Four
Acts and Nine Scenes," by Robert W. Mann, pp. 351-
381.

1685   MANNING, C. A.   "Hawthorne and Dostoevsky."
       Slavonic Review, 14 (January, 1936), 417-424.

1686   MANNING, Elizabeth.   "The Boyhood of Hawthorne."
       Wide Awake, November, 1891, pp. 500-518.   Re-
       printed in Chandler, Elizabeth Lathrop, ed.   "Haw-
       thorne's Spectator."   New England Quarterly, 4
       (April, 1931), 288-330.

1687   MANSFIELD, Luther S.   "The Emersonian Idiom and
       the Romantic Period in American Literature."
       Emerson Society Quarterly, 34 (1964), 23-28.   Haw-
       thorne, passim.

1688   MARBLE, Annie R.   "Gloom and Cheer in Hawthorne."
       Critic, 45 (July, 1904), 28-36.

1689   MARCUS, Fred H.   "The Scarlet Letter: The Power
       of Ambiguity."   English Journal, 51 (October, 1962),
       449-458.

1690   MARENCO, Franco.   "Nathaniel Hawthorne e il
       Blithedale Romance."   Studi Americani, 6 (1960),
       135-182.   In Italian.

1691   MARIANO, Josefina T.   "Nathaniel Hawthorne's
       Symbolism of Black and White as a Synthesis of
       Permanence and Change in The House of the Seven
       Gables and The Marble Faun."   Diliman Review
       (Philippine Islands), 18 (1970), 268-283.

1692   MARKS, Alfred H.   "Irony and Romantic Irony in
       Nathaniel Hawthorne."   Ph. D. diss., Syracuse, 1953.

1693   _____.   "German Romantic Irony in Hawthorne's
       Tales."   Symposium, 7 (November, 1953), 274-305.

1694   _____.   "Who Killed Judge Pyncheon?   The Role
       of the Imagination in The House of the Seven Gables."
       PMLA, 71 (June, 1956), 355-369.

1695   _____.   "Hawthorne's Daguerreotypist: Scientist,
       Artist, Reformer."   Ball State Teachers College
       Forum, 3 (Spring, 1962), 61-74.   Refers to Hol-
       grave of The House of the Seven Gables.

1696   _____.   "Two Rodericks and Two Worms: 'Ego-

tism; or, The Bosom Serpent' as Personal Satire. "
PMLA, 74 (December, 1959), 607-612.   Refers to
Poe's character   Roderick Usher.

1697   _____.   "Ironic Inversion in The Blithedale Romance. "
Emerson Society Quarterly, 55 (1969), 95-102.

1698   MARKS, Barry A.   "The Origin of Original Sin in
Hawthorne's Fiction. "   Nineteenth-Century Fiction,
14 (March, 1960), 359-362.

1699   MARKS, Margaret Louise.   "Flannery O'Connor's
American Models: Her Work in Relation to That of
Hawthorne, James, Faulkner, and West. "   Ph. D.
diss. , Duke, 1977.   DA, 38 (1978), 4830A.

1700   MARKS, William S. , III.   "The Psychology of the
Uncanny in Lawrence's 'The Rocking Horse Winner. '"
Modern Fiction Studies, 11 (Winter, 1965-1966),
381-392.

1701   MARKUS, Manfred.   "Hawthorne's 'Alice Doane's
Appeal':   An Anti-Gothic Tale. "   Germanisch-
romanische Monatsschrift, 25 (1975), 338-349.

1702   MAROVITZ, Sanford E.   "Roderick Hudson: James'
Marble Faun. "   Texas Studies in Literature and
Language, 11 (1970), 1427-1443.

1703   MARSH, Philip.   "Hawthorne and Griswold. "   Modern
Language Notes, 63 (February, 1948), 132-134.

1704   MARTIN, Harold C.   "The Development of Style in
Nineteenth-Century American Fiction. "   English
Institute Essays.   New York: Columbia University
Press, 1958, pp. 114-141.   Hawthorne, passim.

1705   MARTIN, Terence.   The Instructed Vision: Scottish
Common Sense Philosophy and the Origin of American
Fiction.   Bloomington: Indiana University Press,
1961.   Hawthorne, passim.

1706   _____.   "Adam Blair and Arthur Dimmesdale:
A Lesson from the Master. "   American Literature,
34 (May, 1962), 274-279.   Refers to Adam Blair,
a novel by John Gibson Lockhart (1822).   Similarity
first remarked upon by Henry James.

1707 _____. "The Method of Hawthorne's Tales," in
Pearce, Roy Harvey, ed., Centenary Essays (1964),
pp. 7-30.

1708 _____. Nathaniel Hawthorne. New York: Twayne,
1965. Twayne United States Authors Series.

1709 _____. "The Imagination at Play: Edgar Allan
Poe." Kenyon Review, 28 (March, 1966), 194-209.

1710 _____. "Dimmesdale's Ultimate Sermon." Arizona Quarterly, 27 (1971), 230-240.

1711 _____. "Hawthorne's Public Decade and the
Values of Home." American Literature, 46 (1974),
141-152.

1712 MARTINEAU, Stephen Francis. "Opposition and
Balance: A Characteristic of Structure in Hawthorne,
Melville, and James." Ph.D. diss., Columbia,
1967. DA, 28 (1967), 1441A.

1713 MARVIN, Frederic Rowland. "Ethan Brand," in
Excursions of a Book Lover. New York: Sherman,
French, 1910, pp. 129-151.

1714 MARX, Leo. "The Machine in the Garden." New
England Quarterly, 29 (March, 1956), 27-42. Discusses "Ethan Brand."

1715 _____. The Machine in the Garden: Technology
and the Pastoral Ideal in America. New York:
Oxford University Press, 1964. Hawthorne, pp.
1-33, 265-277.

1716 _____, ed. with Introduction. The Scarlet Letter.
New York: New American Library, 1959.

1717 MASBACK, Frederic Joseph. "The Child Character
in Hawthorne and James." Ph.D. diss., Syracuse,
1960.

1718 MASHECK, J.D.C. "Samuel Johnson's Ultoxeter
Penance in the Writings of Hawthorne." Hermathena,
11 (Spring, 1971), 51-54.

1719 MASON, Miriam P. "Hawthorne Agonistes." The
Dial, 3 (February, 1883), 222-224.

1720 MASON, Ronald Charles. "Melville and Hawthorne:
A Study in Contrasts." Wind and the Rain, 4
(Autumn, 1947), 93-100.

1721 _____. Spirit Above the Dust: A Biography of
Herman Melville. London: John Lehmann, 1951.
Second edition, with a new Foreword by Howard P.
Vincent. Mamaroneck, N.Y.: Paul P. Appel, 1972.
Chapter 8, "Melville and Hawthorne," pp. 96-110.

1722 MATENKO, Percy. "Tieck, Poe, and Hawthorne,"
in Matenko, Ludwig Tieck and America. Chapel
Hill: University of North Carolina Press, 1954,
pp. 71-88.

1723 MATHER, Jackson Edward Arthur. Nathaniel Hawthorne: A Modest Man. New York: Crowell, 1940.

1724 MATHERLY, E.P. "Poe and Hawthorne as Writers
of the Short Story." Education, 40 (January, 1920),
294-306.

1725 MATHESON, Terence J. "Feminism and Femininity
in The Blithedale Romance." Nathaniel Hawthorne
Journal, 6 (1976), 215-226.

1726 MATHEWS, J. Chesley. "Hawthorne's Knowledge of
Dante." University of Texas Studies in English, 20
(1940), 157-165.

1727 _____. "The Interest in Dante Shown by Nineteenth-
Century Men of Letters." Studi Americani, 11
(1965), 77-104.

1728 MATHEWS, James W. "Hawthorne and the Chain of
Being." Modern Language Quarterly, 18 (December,
1957), 283-294.

1729 _____. "Hawthorne and Howells: The Middle Way
in American Fiction." Ph.D. diss., Tennessee,
1960. DA, 21 (1961), 1941-1942.

1730 _____. "The Heroines of Hawthorne and Howells."
Tennessee Studies in Literature, 7 (1962), 37-46.

1731 _____. "Antinomianism in 'Young Goodman Brown.'"
Studies in Short Fiction, 3 (Fall, 1965), 73-75.

1732 _____. "The House of Atreus and The House of the Seven Gables." Emerson Society Quarterly, 63 (1971), 31-36.

1733 _____. "Hawthorne and the Periodical Tale: From Popular Lore to Art." Papers of the Bibliographical Society of America, 68 (1974), 149-162.

1734 MATHY, Francis. "The Magnetic Chain of Humanity-- A Study of Alienation and Involvement in Hawthorne." English Language and Literature Studies (Hiroshima), 7 (1970), 82-109.

1735 _____. "The Three Johns: Portraits of Emerson, Thoreau, Hawthorne, and Holmes." English Language and Literature Studies, 10 (1973), 163-181.

1736 MATLOCK, James H. "Hawthorne and Elizabeth Barstow Stoddard." New England Quarterly, 50 (1977), 278-302. Refers to a novel, The Morgesons (1862), by Richard Henry Stoddard and his wife, Elizabeth Barstow Stoddard.

1737 MATSUYAMA, Nobunao. "Hawthorne's The House of the Seven Gables and Nature." Studies in Humanities (Doshisha University, Japan), 75 (July, 1964), 58-90.

1738 _____. "Solitude in Hawthorne." Studies in English Literature (Tokyo), 42 (March, 1966), 171-192.

1739 _____. "Nature in Hawthorne's Major Novels." Jumbungaku, 43 (January, 1967), 41-49.

1740 MATTFIELD, Mary S. "Hawthorne's Juvenile Classics." Discourse, 12 (1969), 346-364.

1741 MATTHIESSEN, Francis O. American Renaissance: Art and Expression in the Age of Emerson and Whitman. New York: Oxford University Press, 1941. Hawthorne, pp. 179-368. Reissued in paperback, 1967.

1742 _____. "Nathaniel Hawthorne," in The Responsibility of the Critic. New York: Oxford University Press, 1952. Pp. 209-211.

1743 _____. "The House of the Seven Gables," excerpts
from American Renaissance (1941), in Kaul, ed.,
Hawthorne (1966), pp. 141-152.

1744 MAURIAC, François. Mémoires intérieurs. Trans-
lated from French by Gerard Hopkins. New York:
Farrar, Straus, and Cudahy, 1961. Hawthorne and
The Scarlet Letter, pp. 114-118.

1745 MAUROIS, André. "Un-Puritan." Nouvelles Litté-
raires, 1311 (October, 1952), 1, 5. In French.

1746 MAXWELL, Desmond E. S. "The Tragic Phase:
Melville and Hawthorne," in Maxwell, American
Fiction: The Intellectual Background. New York:
Columbia University Press, 1963, pp. 141-191.

1747 MAY, Charles E. "Pearl as Christ and Anti-Christ."
American Transcendental Quarterly, 24 Supplement
(1974), 8-11.

1748 MAY, John Rollo. Toward a New Earth: Apocalypse
in the American Novel. Notre Dame and London:
University of Notre Dame Press, 1972. "The Possi-
bility of Renewal: The Ideal and the Real in Hawthorne, Melville, and Twain," pp. 42-91. Refers to
The Blithedale Romance.

1749 _____. Power and Innocence: A Search for the
Sources of Violence. New York: Norton, 1972.
Hawthorne, passim.

1750 MAYER, David, R. S. V. D. "Symbolic Action in Hawthorne's Parable: 'The Minister's Black Veil.'"
Fu Jen Studies (Republic of China), 7 (1974), 25-31.

1751 MAYNARD, Theodore. A Fire Was Lighted. New
York: Appleton-Century, 1948. Biography of Rose
Hawthorne Lathrop, later Mother Alphonsa.

1752 _____. "Hawthorne Year." Catholic World, 168
(January, 1949), 283-286.

1753 MEATHENIA, Jack. "A Study of the Functional Aspects of Humor in the Works of Nathaniel Hawthorne."
Ph. D. diss., Duke, 1971. DA, 33 (1972), 1146A.

1754 MEHTA, R. N. "'Mr. Higginbotham's Catastrophe':

An Unusual Story," in Mukherjee, S., and D. V. K.
Raghavcharyulu, eds., Indian Essays in American
Literature: Papers in Honor of Robert E. Spiller.
Bombay: Popular Prakashan, 1969, pp. 113-119.

1755   MEIXSELL, Anne Bruch. "Symbolism in The Marble
Faun." Ph. D. diss., Pennsylvania State, 1968. DA,
30 (1969), 1174A.

1756   MELCHIORI, Giorgio. "The English Novelist and the
American Tradition." Translated by Barbara Melchiori Arnett. Sewanee Review, 68 (1960), 502-515.
Originally published in Italian, in Studi Americani, 1
(1955), 55-71.

1757   _____. "Locksley Hall Revisited: Tennyson and
Henry James." Review of English Literature, 6
(October, 1965), 9-25. Discusses relationship of
Our Old Home.

1758   MELVILLE, Herman. "Hawthorne and His Mosses."
Literary World, 7 (August 17 and 24, 1850), 125-
127 and 145-147. Published by "A Virginian Spend-
ing His Summer [July] in Vermont," pseudo. Has
been frequently reprinted, as in the following:

Wilson, Edmund, ed. The Shock of Recognition
(1943), pp. 187-204.
Richardson, Lyon Norman, et al., eds. Heritage
of American Literature, 2 vols. New York:
Ginn, 1951. Vol. I, pp. 797-802.
Brown, Clarence A., ed. Achievement of American
Criticism. New York: Ronald, 1954, pp. 289-
301.
Fiedler, Leslie A., ed. The Art of the Essay
(1958), pp. 571-584.
Miller, Perry, ed. The Golden Age (1959), pp.
407-419.
Leary, Lewis G., ed. American Literary Essays
(1960), pp. 90-92. Excerpt.
Trask, Georgianna Sampson, and Charles Burkhart,
eds. Storytellers and Their Art. New York:
Doubleday, 1963, pp. 259-278.
Cohen, B. Bernard, ed. Recognition (1969), pp. 29-41.

1759   MERIVALE, Patricia. "The Raven and the Bust of
Pallas: Classical Artifacts and Gothic Tale." PMLA,
89 (1974), 960-966.

1760   MERRILL, L. J. "The Puritan Policeman." American-
       Sociological Review, 10 (December, 1945), 766-776.

1761   MERRILL, Walter M., ed. with Introduction. "Spe-
       cial Hawthorne Issue." Essex Institute Historical
       Collections, 94 (July, 1958), 169-308. Contains
       articles by the following: Merrill, p. 169; Pearson,
       pp. 170-190; Adams, pp. 191-193; Cummings, pp. 196-
       204; Hoeltje, pp. 205-228; Pearson, pp. 229-242; Ryan,
       pp. 243-255; Pearson, pp. 256-274; Stewart, pp. 275-
       281; Cohen, pp. 282-296; and Larabee and Cohen, pp.
       297-308.

1762   METZDORF, Robert F. "Hawthorne's Suit Against
       Ripley and Dana." American Literature, 12 (May,
       1940), 235-241.

1763   METZGER, Charles R. "Effictio and Notatio: Haw-
       thorne's Technique of Characterization." Western
       Humanities Review, 14 (Spring, 1960), 224-226.

1764   MEYER, John Rodney. "Hawthorne in Tocqueville's
       America: A Speculative Biographical and Critical
       Essay." Ph. D. diss., Minnesota, 1975. DA, 36
       (1975), 3716A.

1765   MEYERS, Jeffrey. "Guido Reni and The Marble
       Faun," in Meyers, Painting and the Novel. New
       York: Barnes and Noble, 1975, pp. 6-18.

1766   MICHAUD, Régis. "How Nathaniel Hawthorne Exor-
       cised Hester Prynne," in The American Novel Today:
       A Social and Psychological Study. Boston: Little,
       Brown, 1928, pp. 25-46.

1767   MICHEL, Pierre. "Hawthorne Rehabilitated."
       English Studies, 45 (February, 1964), 44-48. On
       the Centenary edition of Hawthorne and the need for
       accurate editions of novels.

1768   MILLER, Edwin Haviland. "'My Kinsman, Major
       Molineux': The Playful Art of Nathaniel Hawthorne."
       Emerson Society Quarterly, 24 (1978), 145-151.

1769   MILLER, Harold P. "Hawthorne as a Satirist." Ph. D.
       diss., Yale, 1936. DA, 31 (1971), 4728A.

1770   _____. "Hawthorne Surveys His Contemporaries."

American Literature, 12 (May, 1940), 228-241. Refers to "The Hall of Fantasy."

1771   MILLER, James E., Jr. "Hawthorne and Melville: The Unpardonable Sin." PMLA, 70 (March, 1955), 91-114. Reprinted in Miller, Quests (1967), pp. 209-238.

1772   _____. "Uncharted Interiors: The American Romantics Revisited." Emerson Society Quarterly, 35 (1964), 34-39.

1773   _____. "Hawthorne and Melville: No! in Thunder," in Miller, Quests, Surd and Absurd. Chicago: University of Chicago Press, 1967, pp. 186-208.

1774   MILLER, Paul W. "Hawthorne's 'Young Goodman Brown': Cynicism or Meliorism." Nineteenth-Century Fiction, 14 (December, 1959), 255-264.

1775   MILLER, Perry. The Raven and the Whale: The War of Words and Wits in the Era of Poe and Melville. New York: Harcourt, Brace, 1956. Hawthorne, pp. 280-285 et passim.

1776   _____. Nature's Nation. Cambridge: Harvard University Press, 1967. Hawthorne, passim. Posthumous publication.

1777   _____, ed. with Introduction. The Transcendentalists: An Anthology. Cambridge: Harvard University Press, 1950. "The Scarlet Letter," by G.B. Loring, pp. 475-482.

1778   _____, ed. with Introduction. The Golden Age of American Literature. New York: Braziller, 1959. Reprints Melville's "Hawthorne and His Mosses," pp. 407-419.

1779   MILLER, Raymond Andrew, Jr. "Representative Tragic Heroines in the Work of Brown, Hawthorne, Howells, James, and Dreiser." Ph.D. diss., Wisconsin, 1956. DA, 17 (1957), 2612-2613.

1780   MILLER, William B. "A New Review of the Career of Paul Akers, 1825-1861." Colby Library Quarterly, 7 (1966), 227-256. Refers to sculptor; article relates to The Marble Faun.

Mills   160

1781   MILLS, Barriss. "Hawthorne and Puritanism." New
       England Quarterly, 21 (March, 1948), 78-102.

1782   MILLS, Nicolaus C.   "Nathaniel Hawthorne and George
       Eliot," in Mills, American and English Fiction in the
       Nineteenth-Century: An Anti-genre Critique and
       Comparison. Bloomington: Indiana University Press,
       1973, pp. 52-73.

1783   MILNE, Gordon. George William Curtis and the
       Genteel Tradition. Bloomington: Indiana University
       Press, 1956. Hawthorne, passim.

1784   MILTON, John R. "The American Novel: The Search
       for Home, Tradition, and Identity." Western Hu-
       manities Review, 16 (Spring, 1962), 169-180.

1785   MINOCK, Daniel W. "Hawthorne and the Rumor About
       the Governor's Lady." American Notes and Queries,
       13 (1975), 87-88.

1786   MINTER, David L. "Definition of a Fictional Form:
       Hawthorne's The Blithedale Romance," in The Inter-
       preted Design as a Structural Principle in American
       Prose. New Haven: Yale University Press, 1969,
       pp. 137-160.

1787   MITFORD, Mary R. Recollections of a Literary
       Life. New York and London: Richard Bentley,
       1852. Hawthorne, passim.

1788   MIZENER, Arthur. "The Scarlet Letter," in Mizener,
       Twelve Great American Novels. New York: New
       American Library, 1967.

1789   MOLDENHAUER, Joseph J. "'Bartleby' and 'The
       Custom House.'" Delta English Studies, 7 (1978),
       21-62.

1790   MOLLINGER, Shernaz. "Dualism in Nathaniel Haw-
       thorne and D. H. Lawrence." Nassau Review, 3
       (1978), 23-32.

1791   _____. "Hawthorne, Language and Reality." Ph.D.
       diss., Columbia, 1978. DA, 39 (1978), 2276A-
       2277A.

1792   MONKE, Arthur, and C. E. Frazer Clark, Jr. "Haw-
        thorne's 'Moonlight.'" <u>Nathaniel Hawthorne Journal,</u>
        3 (1973), 27-35. Refers to poems "The Ocean" and
        "Moonlight" in <u>Salem Gazette,</u> 1825.

1793   MONTEIRO, George. "Hawthorne, James, and the
        Destructive Self." <u>Texas Studies in Literature and</u>
        <u>Language,</u> 4 (Spring, 1962), 58-71. Discusses the
        hero of "The Beast in the Jungle," and possible
        influence by Hawthorne.

1794   _____. "Hawthorne's 'The Minister's Black Veil.'"
        <u>Explicator,</u> 22 (October, 1963), item 9.

1795   _____. "First Printing of a Hawthorne Letter."
        <u>American Literature,</u> 36 (November, 1964), 346.

1796   _____. "Maule's Curse and Julian Hawthorne."
        <u>Notes and Queries,</u> 14 (1967), 62-63.

1797   _____. "Hawthorne Letters in Old Catalogs."
        <u>American Transcendental Quarterly,</u> 1 (1969), 122.

1798   _____. "A Non-Literary Source for Hawthorne's
        'Egotism; or, the Bosom Serpent.'" <u>American</u>
        <u>Literature,</u> 41 (1970), 575-577.

1799   _____. "Elizabeth Shaw Melville as Censor."
        <u>Emerson Society Quarterly,</u> 62 (1971), 32-33. On
        her attempted censorship of some Melville letters
        to Hawthorne.

1800   _____. "Hawthorne in Portuguese," 3 parts.
        <u>Nathaniel Hawthorne Journal,</u> 1 (1971), 228-231; 2
        (1972), 263-264; 4 (1974), 280-281.

1801   _____. "The Full Particulars of the Minister's
        Behavior--According to Hale." <u>Nathaniel Hawthorne</u>
        <u>Journal,</u> 2 (1972), 173-182.

1802   _____. "Hawthorne's Emblematic Serpent."
        <u>Nathaniel Hawthorne Journal,</u> 3 (1973), 134-142.

1803   _____. "Hawthorne in the English Press."
        <u>Nathaniel Hawthorne Journal,</u> 4 (1974), 162-178.
        Reprints 5 reviews and a long essay on Hawthorne's
        death.

1804   _____.   "'The Items of High Civilization': Haw-
          thorne, Henry James, and George Parsons Lathrop."
          Nathaniel Hawthorne Journal, 5 (1975), 146-155.

1805   MONTGOMERY, Judith H.   "The American Galatea."
          College English, 32 (1971), 890-899.   A feminist
          interpretation of The Blithedale Romance, The Por-
          trait of a Lady, and The House of Mirth.

1806   MONTGOMERY, Marion.   "Style and the Difference
          Grace Makes: Reflections on Hawthorne."   Thought,
          53 (1978), 5-14.

1807   _____.   "The Artist as 'A Very Doubtful Jacob':
          A Reflection on Hawthorne and O'Connor."   Southern
          Quarterly, 16 (1978), 95-103.   Refers to Flannery
          O'Connor.

1808   MOORE, Helen-Jean.   "The American Criticism of
          Nathaniel Hawthorne, 1938-1948."   Ph.D. diss.,
          Pittsburgh, 1952.

1809   MOORE, John Brooks, ed.   Selections from Poe's
          Literary Criticism.   New York: Crofts, 1926.
          "Nathaniel Hawthorne" (1847), pp. 111-147.

1810   MOORE, L. Hugh, Jr.   "Hawthorne's Ideal Artist
          as Presumptious Intellectual."   Studies in Short
          Fiction, 2 (Spring, 1965), 278-283.   Owen Warland
          in "The Artist of the Beautiful."

1811   MOORE, Robert.   "Hawthorne's Folk-Motifs and The
          House of the Seven Gables."   New York Folklore
          Quarterly, 28 (1972), 221-233.

1812   MORE, Paul Elmer.   "The Solitude of Nathaniel
          Hawthorne."   Atlantic, 88 (November, 1901), 588-
          599.   Reprinted in More, Shelburne Essays: First
          Series.   New York: Putnam, 1904, pp. 22-50.
          Excerpt reprinted in Shelburne Essays on American
          Literature.   Selected from the eleven series of
          Shelburne essays (1904-1921), and edited by Daniel
          Aaron.   New York: Harcourt, Brace, 1963, pp.
          107-125.   Published posthumously; More died in
          1937.

1813   _____.   "The Origins of Hawthorne and Poe."

Independent, 54 (October, 1902), 2453-2460. Reprinted in Shelburne Essays: First Series (1904), pp. 51-70. Excerpt reprinted in Aaron, ed., Shelburne Essays on American Literature (1963), pp. 86-98.

1814 _____. "Hawthorne: Looking Before and After." Independent, 56 (June, 1904), 1489-1494. Reprinted in Shelburne Essays: Second Series. New York: Putnam, 1905, pp. 173-187. Also reprinted in Rahv, Philip, ed., Literature in America: An Anthology of Literary Criticism. New York: Meridian, 1957, pp. 101-109. Excerpt reprinted in Aaron, ed., Shelburne Essays on American Literature (1963), pp. 126-135.

1815 MORGAN, Edmund S. The Puritan Family. Boston: Trustees of the Boston Public Library, 1956. Hawthorne, passim. Reprinted from the February, March, April, and September, 1942; and January and May, 1943, issues of More Books, the bulletin of the Boston Public Library.

1816 MORGAN, Ellen E. "The Veiled Lady: The Secret Love of Miles Coverdale." Nathaniel Hawthorne Journal, 1 (1971), 169-181.

1817 MORISON, Samuel Eliot, ed. "Melville's 'Agatha' Letter to Hawthorne." New England Quarterly, 2 (April, 1929), 296-307.

1818 MOROOKA, Aiko. "A Man of Solitude: Nathaniel Hawthorne." Kamereon, 5 (August, 1962), 17-25. Article in Japanese; abstract in English.

1819 _____. "Hawthorne: The Trial of Romance in The Scarlet Letter," in Takamura, Katsuji, and Iwao Iwamoto, eds., The Development of American Novels. Tokyo: Shohakusha, 1976, pp. 55-63. In Japanese; abstract in English.

1820 MORRIS, Lloyd R. The Rebellious Puritan: Portrait of Mr. Hawthorne. New York: Harcourt, Brace, 1927.

1821 MORROW, Patrick. "A Writer's Workshop: Hawthorne's 'The Great Carbuncle.'" Studies in Short Fiction, 6 (1969), 157-164.

1822   MORSBERGER, Katharine M.   "Hawthorne's 'Border-
       line':   The Locale of the Romance."   Costerus, 7
       (1973), 93-112.

1823   MORSBERGER, Robert E.   "Wakefield in the Twilight
       Zone."   American Transcendental Quarterly, 14
       (1972), 6-8.

1824   _____.   "'The Minister's Black Veil':   Shrouded in
       a Blackness Ten Times Black."   New England Quar-
       terly, 46 (1973), 454-463.

1825   _____.   "The Woe That Is Madness: Goodman
       Brown and the Face of the Fire."   Nathaniel Haw-
       thorne Journal, 3 (1973), 177-182.

1826   MORSE, James Herbert.   "Nathaniel Hawthorne Again."
       Century, 4 (June, 1883), 309-311.

1827   MOSES, W. R.   "A Further Note on 'The Custom
       House.'"   College English, 23 (February, 1962),
       396.   Related to Baskett article (1961).

1828   MOSKOWITZ, Sam.   Seekers of Tomorrow: Masters
       of Modern Science Fiction.   Cleveland: World, 1966.
       Hawthorne, p. 333 et passim.

1829   MOSS, Sidney P.   Poe's Literary Battles: The Critic
       in the Context of His Literary Milieu.   Durham,
       N. C.:   Duke University Press, 1963.   Hawthorne,
       passim.

1830   _____.   "The Problem of Theme in The Marble
       Faun."   Nineteenth-Century Fiction, 18 (March,
       1964), 393-399.

1831   _____.   "A Reading of 'Rappaccini's Daughter.'"
       Studies in Short Fiction, 2 (Winter, 1965), 145-156.

1832   _____.   "The Mountain God of Hawthorne's 'The
       Ambitious Guest.'"   Emerson Society Quarterly,
       47 (1967), 74-75.

1833   _____.   "The Symbolism of the Italian Background
       in The Marble Faun."   Nineteenth-Century Fiction,
       23 (1968), 332-336.

1834 _____. "Hawthorne and Melville: An Inquiry into
Their Art and the Mystery of Their Friendship."
Literary Monographs, 7 (1975), 47-84.

1835 MOTODA, Shuichi. "The Witches' Sabbath in 'Young
Goodman Brown.'" Studies in English Literature
(Tokyo), 42 (October, 1966), 73-86.

1836 MOTTRAM, Richard Allen. "Hawthorne's Men: Their
Dominant Influence." Ph.D. diss., Tulane, 1974.
DA, 35 (1975), 5419A.

1837 MOUNTS, Charles Eugene. "Hawthorne's Echoes of
Spenser and Milton." Nathaniel Hawthorne Journal,
3 (1973), 162-171.

1838 MOWAT, Robert Balmain. "Americans and English
in the Eighteen-Fifties," in Mowat, Americans in
England. Boston: Houghton Mifflin, 1935, pp.155-
185. Hawthorne, passim.

1839 MOYER, Patricia. "Time and the Artist in Kafka
and Hawthorne." Modern Fiction Studies, 4 (Winter,
1958), 295-306.

1840 MUGRIDGE, Donald H., and Blanche P. McCrum.
A Guide to the Study of the United States of America:
Representative Books Reflecting the Development of
American Life and Thought. Washington, D.C.:
Library of Congress Publication, 1960. Bibliography
relative to Hawthorne, pp.37-39.

1841 MULDER, Arnold. "An Immoral Moral." Freeman,
5 (August 9, 1922), 517-518.

1842 MULLINS, Patricia Ann. "The Shadow of Satan: A
Study of the Devil Archetype in Selected American
Novels from Hawthorne to the Present Day." Ph.D.
diss., Texas (Austin), 1971. DA, 32 (1972), 6457A.

1843 MUMFORD, Lewis. The Golden Day. New York:
Boni and Liveright, 1926. "Twilight: Hawthorne,"
pp.138-142, et passim.

1844 _____. "The Writing of Moby-Dick." American
Mercury, 15 (December, 1928), 482-490. Reprinted
in Withim, R.A., ed., Essays of Today. Boston:

Houghton Mifflin, 1931, pp. 281-288.   Deals with the
influence of Hawthorne on Melville.

1845   . Herman Melville: A Study of His Life and
        Vision. New York: Literary Guild, 1929.   Revised
        edition New York: Harcourt, Brace, and World,
        1963. Hawthorne, pp. 137-147 et passim.

1846 MUNDY, Jacqueline Sue Sexton.   "Hawthorne's Per-
        vasive Child." Ph. D. diss., Indiana, 1975. DA,
        36 (1976), 7424A.

1847 MUNGER, Theodore Thornton.   "Notes on The Scarlet
        Letter." Atlantic, 93 (April, 1904), 521-535.   Re-
        printed in Essays for the Day. Boston: Houghton
        Mifflin, 1904, pp. 103-153.

1848   . "The Centenary of Nathaniel Hawthorne."
        Century, 68 (July, 1904), 482-483.

1849 MURAKAMI, Fujio. "Hawthorne and Transcendentalism."
        Studies in Humanities (Osaka City University), 13
        (May, 1962), 105-124.

1850 MURPHY, Denis M.   "Poor Robin and Shrewd Ben:
        Hawthorne's Kinsman." Studies in Short Fiction,
        15 (1978), 185-190.

1851 MURPHY, John J.   "The Function of Sin in Hawthorne's
        Novels." Emerson Society Quarterly, 50 Supplement
        (1968), 65-71.

1852   . "Willa Cather and Hawthorne: Significant
        Resemblances." Renascence, 27 (1975), 161-175.

1853 MURPHY, Morris. "Wordsworthian Concepts in 'The
        Great Stone Face.'" College English, 23 (February,
        1962), 364-365.

1854 MURRAY, Peter B. "Mythopoesis in The Blithedale
        Romance." PMLA, 75 (December, 1960), 591-596.

1855   . "Myth in The Blithedale Romance," in
        Vickery, J. B., ed., Myth and Literature: Contempo-
        rary Theory and Practice. Lincoln: University of
        Nebraska Press, 1966, pp. 213-220.

1856 MYERS, Gustave. "Hawthorne and the Myths About
      Puritans." American Spectator, 2 (April, 1934), 1.

1857 MYERS, Henry Alonzo. Are Men Equal? An Inquiry
      into the Meaning of American Democracy. New
      York: Putnam, 1945. Hawthorne, pp. 46-51.

1858 MYERS, Joan S. "Dualism and Duplicity in the Works
      of Nathaniel Hawthorne: A Study of Artistic Conflict."
      Ph. D. diss., Rutgers, 1970. DA, 31 (1971), 6019A.

1859 MYERSON, Joel, ed. with Introduction. "Hawthorne
      Letter to William B. Pike." Nathaniel Hawthorne
      Journal, 3 (1973), 3-8.

1860 _____, ed. with Introduction. "Sarah Clarke's
      Reminiscences of the Peabodys and Hawthorne."
      Nathaniel Hawthorne Journal, 3 (1973), 130-133.

1861 _____, ed. Studies in the American Renaissance:
      1977. Boston: Twayne, 1978. Contains "A Guide
      to Primary Source Materials for the study of Haw-
      thorne's Old Manse Period," by John J. McDonald,
      pp. 261-312; and "Hawthorne: The Writer as Dreamer,"
      by Rita K. Gollin, pp. 313-325.

1862 _____, ed. Studies in the American Renaissance:
      1978. Boston: Twayne, 1978. Contains "An An-
      notated Edition of Nathaniel Hawthorne's Official Dis-
      patches to the State Department, 1853-1857," Part
      I, by Mark F. Sweeney, pp. 331-386.

1863 _____, ed. Studies in the American Renaissance:
      1979. Boston: Twayne, 1979. Contains Part II,
      "Official Dispatches...," by Mark F. Sweeney, pp.
      355-398.

1864 NAKATA, Yuji. "The House of the Seven Gables: A
      Study in Isolation with an Emphasis on Name Symbol-
      ism." Kyushu American Literature (Fukuoka, Japan),
      11 (1968), 11-31.

1865 NAPIER, Elizabeth R. "Aylmer as 'Scheidekünstler':
      The Pattern of Union and Separation in Hawthorne's
      'The Birthmark.'" South Atlantic Bulletin, 41 (1976),
      32-35.

1866   NAPLES, Diane C.   " 'Roger Malvin's Burial':   A
       Parable for Historians?"   American Transcendental
       Quarterly, 13 (1972), 45-48.

1867   NASH, Deanna C.   "The Web as an Organic Metaphor
       in The Marble Faun, Middlemarch, and The Golden
       Bowl: The Growth of Contextualism as an Aesthetic
       Theory in the Nineteenth-Century."   Ph.D. diss.,
       North Carolina (Chapel Hill), 1970.   DA, 31 (1971),
       4131A.

1868   NATALE, Eleonora Taglioné.   "Solitudine di Haw-
       thorne."   Nuova Antologia, No. 391 (1964), 373-386.
       In Italian.

1869   NATHANIEL HAWTHORNE JOURNAL.   Established
       1971, published annually by the Bruccoli-Clark
       Publishers, 1490 Sodon Lake Drive, Bloomfield Hills,
       Michigan 48013.   Editor, Matthew J. Bruccoli,
       Department of English, University of South Carolina,
       Columbia, South Carolina   29208.

1870   NAYYAR, Sewak.   "Sin and Redemption in The Scarlet
       Letter," in Maini, Darshan Singh, ed.   Variations
       on American Literature.   New Delhi: U.S. Educa-
       tional Foundation in India, 1968, pp. 53-57.

1871   NEFF, Merlin.   "Symbolism and Allegory in the
       Writing of Nathaniel Hawthorne."   Ph.D. diss.,
       University of Washington, 1939.

1872   NELSON, Truman.   "The Matrix of Place."   Essex
       Institute Historical Collections, 95 (April, 1959),
       176-185.   Life in Salem during Hawthorne's period.

1873   NEVINS, Winfield S.   "Nathaniel Hawthorne's Removal
       from the Salem Custom House."   Essex Institute
       Historical Collections, 53 (April, 1917), 97-132.

1874   NEVIUS, B.R.   "The Hawthorne Centenary."   Nine-
       teenth-Century Fiction, 19 (September, 1964), 103-
       104.

1875   NEWBERRY, Frederick Henry.   " 'The Gray Champi-
       on':   Hawthorne's Ironic Criticism of Puritan Re-
       bellion."   Studies in Short Fiction, 13 (1976), 363-
       370.

169   Newberry

1876 _____. "The English Past and the American Scene
in Hawthorne's Works." Ph.D. diss., Washington
State (Pullman), 1977. DA, 38 (1977), 1393A-1394A.

1877 _____. "The Demonic in 'Endicott and the Red
Cross.'" Papers on Language and Literature, 13
(1977), 251-259.

1878 _____. "Tradition and Disinheritance in The Scarlet
Letter." Emerson Society Quarterly, 23 (1977), 1-
26.

1879 NEWLIN, Paul Arthur. "The Uncanny in the Supernatural Short Fiction of Poe, Hawthorne, and James."
Ph.D. diss., California (Los Angeles), 1967. DA,
28 (1968), 5064A-5065A.

1880 _____. "'Vague Shapes of the Borderland': The
Place of the Uncanny in Hawthorne's Gothic Vision."
Emerson Society Quarterly, 18 (1972), 83-96.

1881 NEWMAN, Franklin B. "'My Kinsman, Major Molineux': An Interpretation." University of Kansas
City Review, 21 (March, 1955), 203-212.

1882 NIESS, Robert J. "Hawthorne and Zola--An Influ-
ence?" Revue de Littérature Comparée, 27 (October-
December, 1953), 446-449. Refers to The Scarlet
Letter and Thérèse Raquin.

1883 NILON, Charles H. Bibliography of Bibliographies
in American Literature. New York: Bowker, 1970.
Hawthorne, pp.92-95. Includes primary and secondary materials.

1884 NILSEN, Hedge N. "Hawthorne's 'My Kinsman,
Major Molineux,'" in Seyersted, Brita, ed.,
Americana-Norvegica: Norwegian Contribution to
American Studies Dedicated to Sigmund Skard.
Oslo: Oslo University, 1973, pp.123-136.

1885 NINETEENTH-CENTURY FICTION, 19 (September,
1964), 103-211. Special Hawthorne Centenary Issue:

Nevius, Blake R. "The Hawthorne Centenary,"
pp.103-104.
Long, Robert E. "The Society and the Masks: The

Blithedale Romance and The Bostonians,"
pp. 105-122.
Jordan, Gretchen G.   "Hawthorne's 'Bell':   His-
torical Evolution through Symbol," pp. 123-139.
Thorslev, Peter L., Jr.   "Hawthorne's Determinism:
An Analysis," pp. 141-157.
Wheeler, Otis B.   "Hawthorne and the Fiction of
Sensibility," pp. 159-170.
Broes, Arthur T.   "Journey into Moral Darkness: 'My
Kinsman, Major Molineux,' as Allegory," pp.
171-184.
Evans, Oliver.   "Allegory and Incest in 'Rappaccini's
Daughter,'" pp. 185-195.
Granger, Bruce I.   "Arthur Dimmesdale as Tragic
Hero," pp. 197-203.
Levy, Leo B.   "The Mermaid and the Mirror: Haw-
thorne's 'The Village Uncle,'" pp. 205-211.

1886   NIRENBERG, Morton.   "Hawthorne's Reception in
Germany."   Jahrbuch für Amerikastudien, 15 (1970),
141-161.

1887   NITZSCHE, J. C.   "House Symbolism in Hawthorne's
'My Kinsman, Major Molineux.'"   American Transcendental Quarterly, 38 (1978), 167-175.

1888   NOBLE, David W.   "The Jeremiahs: James Fenimore
Cooper, Nathaniel Hawthorne, Herman Melville,"
in Noble, The Eternal Adam and the New World
Garden: The Central Myth in the American Novel
Since 1830.   New York: Braziller, 1968, pp. 1-47.

1889   _____.   "The Analysis of Alienation by Twentieth-
Century Social Scientists and Nineteenth-Century
Novelists: The Example of Hawthorne's The Scarlet
Letter," in Kalin, Berkley, and Clayton Robinson,
eds., Myths and Realities: Conflicting Values in
America.   Memphis, Tenn.:   John Willard Brister
Library of Memphis State University, 1972, pp. 5-19.

1890   NOLTE, William H.   "Hawthorne's Dimmesdale's:
A Small Man Gone Wrong."   New England Quarterly,
38 (1965), 168-186.

1891   NORFORD, Don Parry.   "Rappaccini's Garden of
Allegory."   American Literature, 50 (1978), 167-
186.

1892 NORIGUCHI, Shinichiro. "Allegory in Hawthorne's
      Short Stories." Kyushu American Literature (Fukuoka,
      Japan), 17 (1976), 66-74.

1893 NORMAND, Jean. Nathaniel Hawthorne: An Approach
      to an Analysis of Artistic Creation. Paris: Presses
      Universitaires de France, 1964. Translated from
      French by Derek Coltman, with Foreword by Henri
      Peyre. Cleveland: Case Western Reserve Univer-
      sity Press, 1970.

1894 _____. "Thoreau et Hawthorne à Concord--Les
      Ironies de la solitude." Europe, 45 (July-August,
      1967), 162-169. In French.

1895 NOYES, Russell. "Hawthorne's Debt to Charles
      Lamb." Charles Lamb Bulletin, 4 (1973), 69-77.

1896 O'BRIEN, Edward. The Short Story Case Book. New
      York: Farrar and Rinehart, 1935. "The Gray
      Champion," text and discussion, pp. 212-227.

1897 O'BRIEN, Frank. Pennant Key-Indexed Study Guide
      to The Scarlet Letter. Paterson, N.J.: Littlefield
      and Adams, 1968.

1898 O'CONNOR, Evangelina Maria Johnson. An Analytical
      Index to the Works of Nathaniel Hawthorne. Boston:
      Houghton Mifflin, 1882. Reprinted with new Intro-
      duction by C. E. Frazer Clark. Detroit: Gale, 1967.
      Includes proper names and topics.

1899 O'CONNOR, Flannery. "Mary Ann, the Story of a
      Little Girl." Jubilee, 9 (May, 1961), 28-35. Re-
      lates to Rose Hawthorne, founder of the society for
      aid to victims of incurable cancer; lived 1851-1926.

1900 O'CONNOR, William Van. "Conscious Naivete in The
      Blithedale Romance." Revue des Langues Vivantes
      (Brussels), 20 (February, 1954), 37-45.

1901 _____. "Hawthorne and Faulkner: Some Common
      Ground." Virginia Quarterly Review, 33 (Winter,
      1957), 105-123. Reprinted in O'Connor, The Gro-
      tesque: An American Genre and Other Essays.
      Carbondale: Southern Illinois University Press, 1962,
      pp. 59-77.

1902   _____. "The Narrator as Distorting Mirror," in O'Connor, The Grotesque (1962), pp. 78-91.

1903   _____. "The Hawthorne Museum: Dialogue," in O'Connor, The Grotesque (1962), pp. 193-231.

1904   O'DONNELL, Charles Robert. "The Mind of the Artist: Cooper, Thoreau, Hawthorne, Melville." Ph.D. diss., Syracuse, 1956. DA, 17 (1957), 1752.

1905   _____. "Hawthorne and Dimmesdale: The Search for the Realm of Quiet." Nineteenth-Century Fiction, 14 (March, 1960), 317-332.

1906   O'DONNELL, Thomas F. "Theron Ware, the Irish Picnic, and Comus." American Literature, 46 (1975), 528-537. Refers to "The Maypole of Merry Mount."

1907   OGDEN, Merlene Ann. "Nathaniel Hawthorne and John Bunyan." Ph.D. diss., Nebraska, 1963. DA, 25 (1964), 2964-2965.

1908   OKAMOTO, Katsumi. "The Scarlet Letter: Struggle Toward Integrity." Studies in English Literature (Japan), 46 (1969), 45-61.

1909   OLDHAM, Ellen M., ed. "Letter of Mrs. Hawthorne to Mrs. Fields." Boston Public Library Quarterly, 9 (July, 1957), 143-154.

1910   OLSEN, Frederick Bruce. "Hawthorne's Integration of Methods and Materials." Ph.D. diss., Indiana, 1960. DA, 21 (1961), 3458.

1911   OREL, Harold. "The Double Symbol." American Literature, 23 (March, 1951), 1-6.

1912   ORIANS, G. Harrison. "New England Witchcraft in Fiction." American Literature, 2 (March, 1930), 54-71.

1913   _____. "The Angel of Hadley in Fiction: A Study of the Sources of Hawthorne's 'The Gray Champion.'" American Literature, 4 (November, 1932), 257-269.

1914   _____. "Hawthorne and 'The Maypole of Merry-

Mount.'" Modern Language Notes, 53 (March, 1938),
159-167.

1915   _____. "Scott and Hawthorne's Fanshawe." New
England Quarterly, 11 (June, 1938), 388-394.

1916   _____. "The Source of Hawthorne's 'Roger Malvin's
Burial.'" American Literature, 10 (November,
1938), 313-318.

1917   _____. "The Sources and Themes of Hawthorne's
'The Gentle Boy.'" New England Quarterly, 14
(December, 1941), 664-678.

1918   _____. "Hawthorne and Puritan Punishments."
College English, 13 (May, 1952), 424-432.

1919   ORICE, Sherwood R. "The Heart, the Head, and
'Rappaccini's Daughter.'" New England Quarterly,
27 (September, 1954), 399-403.

1920   OSBORN, Robert, and Marijane Osborn. "Another
Look at an Old Tombstone." New England Quarterly,
46 (1973), 278-279. Refers to Hester Prynne's; see
article by Jenkins (1972).

1921   OSBORNE, J.B. "Nathaniel Hawthorne as American
Consul." Bookman, 16 (January, 1903), 461-464.

1922   OSER, Marilyn Schiffman. "Rhetorical Patterns in
Fiction: A Study in the Narrative Art." Ph.D. diss.,
State University of New York (Stony Brook), 1974.
DA, 35 (1975), 6105A-6106A. Includes The Scarlet
Letter and The Red Badge of Courage.

1923/24 OWENS, Louis. "Paulding's 'The Dumb Girl,' A
Source of The Scarlet Letter." Nathaniel Hawthorne
Journal, 4 (1974), 240-249.

PAGE, H.A., Pseudonym see JAPP, Alexander

1925   PANCOST, David W. "Hawthorne's Epistemology and
Ontology." Emerson Society Quarterly, 19 (1973),
8-13.

1926   _____. "Evidence of Editorial Additions to Hawthorne's 'Fragments from the Journal of a Solitary Man.'" Nathaniel Hawthorne Journal, 5 (1975), 210-226.

1927 PANDEYA, Prabhat K. "The Drama of Evil in 'The Hollow of Three Hills.'" Nathaniel Hawthorne Journal, 5 (1975), 177-181.

1928 PANNWITT, Barbara, ed. The Art of Short Fiction. Boston: Ginn, 1964. "The Man of Adamant," pp. 334-335.

1929 PARCHER, Adrian. "Hawthorne's The Scarlet Letter." Explicator, 21 (February, 1963), item 48.

1930 PARIS, Bernard J. "Optimism and Pessimism in The Marble Faun." Boston University Studies in English, 2 (Summer, 1956), 95-112.

1931 PARKER, Hershel. "Regularizing Accidentals: The Latest Form of Infidelity." Proof, 3 (1973), 1-20.

1932 _____. "Aesthetic Implications of Authorial Excisions: Examples from Nathaniel Hawthorne, Mark Twain, and Stephen Crane," in Millgate, Jane, ed., Editing Nineteenth-Century Fiction. New York: Garland, 1978, pp. 99-119. Based on a Conference at University of Toronto, November, 1977.

1933 _____, ed. Shorter Works of Hawthorne and Melville. Columbus, Ohio: Merrill, 1972.

1934 _____, and Bruce Bebb. "The 'CEAA': An Interim Assessment." Papers of the Bibliographic Society of America, 68 (1974), 129-148.

1935 PARKES, Henry Bamford. The American Experience: An Interpretation of the History and Civilization of the American People. New York: Knopf, 1947. Hawthorne and Melville, pp. 198-205 et passim.

1936 _____. "Poe, Hawthorne, Melville: An Essay in Sociological Criticism." Partisan Review, 16 (February, 1949), 157-165.

1937 PARKS, Edd W., et al. "Problems of the Complete or Collected Edition." Mississippi Quarterly, 15

(Summer, 1962), 97-99. "Editing Hawthorne," by
Randall Stewart.

1938 PARRINGTON, Vernon Louis. "Nathaniel Hawthorne:
Skeptic," in Main Currents in American Thought, 3
vols. New York: Harcourt, Brace, 1927-1930.
Combined one-volume edition published in 1939.
Vol. I, pp. 442-450.

1939 _____. "Foufouville, Excelsior, and Blithedale,"
in Parrington, American Dreams. Providence, R. I.:
Brown University Press, 1947. Brown University
Studies in Americana Series. Posthumous publication; Parrington died in 1929.

1940 PASSERINI, Edward M. "Hawthornesque Dickens."
Dickens Studies, 2 (1966), 18-25.

1941 PATTEE, Fred Lewis. A History of American Literature. Boston: Silver Burdett, 1896. Revised and
reissued New York: Century, 1909, 1915. Hawthorne,
pp. 240-256.

1942 _____. Side-Lights on American Literature. New
York: Century, 1922. Hawthorne, passim.

1943 _____. The Development of the American Short
Story: An Historical Survey. New York and London:
Harper, 1923. Reprinted New York: Biblo and
Tannen, 1966. Hawthorne and Melville, pp. 91-128.

1944 _____. The New American Literature, 1890-1930.
New York: Century, 1930. Hawthorne, passim.

1945 _____. The First Century of American Literature,
1770-1870. New York and London: Appleton-Century,
1935. Hawthorne, pp. 537-550. Reprinted New York:
Cooper Square, 1966.

1946 PATTERSON, Kent R. "The Uncertain Light."
Ph. D. diss., Kentucky, 1971. DA, 32 (1972),
5196A.

1947 PATTISON, Joseph C. "The Guilt of the Innocent
Donatello." Emerson Society Quarterly, 31 (1963),
66-68.

1948 _____. "Point of View in Hawthorne." PMLA,
82 (October, 1967), 363-369.

1949 _____. "'The Celestial Railroad' as Dream-Tale."
American Quarterly, 20 (1968), 224-236. Extends
1967 article, listed above.

1950 PAUL, Louis. "A Psychoanalytical Reading of Hawthorne's 'Major Molineux': The Father Manqué and
the Protégé Manqué." American Imago, 18 (Fall,
1961), 279-288.

1951 PAUL, Sherman. "Hawthorne's Debt to Ahab." Notes
and Queries, 196 (June 9, 1951), 255-257.

1952 PAULITS, Walter J. "Ambivalence in 'Young Goodman
Brown.'" American Literature, 41 (1970), 577-584.

1953 PAULY, Thomas H. "The Travel Sketch-Book and the
American Author: A Study of the European Travelogues of Irving, Longfellow, Hawthorne, etc...."
Ph.D. diss., California (Berkeley), 1970. DA, 32
(1971), 928A.

1954 _____. "'Mr. Higginbotham's Catastrophe': The
Story-Teller's Disaster." American Transcendental
Quarterly, 14 (1972), 171-174.

1955 _____. "The Literary Sketch in Nineteenth-Century
America." Texas Studies in Literature and Language, 17 (1975), 489-503.

1956 _____. "Hawthorne's Houses of Fiction." American Literature, 48 (1976), 271-291.

1957 PAYNE, L. Warren. History of American Literature.
New York: Rand McNally, 1919. Hawthorne, pp.
154-168.

1958 PEABODY, Elizabeth Palmer. "The Genius of Hawthorne." Atlantic Monthly, 22 (September, 1868),
359-374. Reprinted in Cameron, ed., Hawthorne
Among His Contemporaries (1968), pp. 99-108.

1959 _____. "The Two Hawthornes." Western, 1
(June, 1875), 352-359.

1960 _____. "The Genius of Hawthorne," in Peabody, The Last Evening with Allston and Other Papers. Boston: Lothrop, 1886, pp.293-330. Extended version of 1868 article, listed above.

1961 PEARCE, Howard D. "Hawthorne's Old Moodie: The Blithedale Romance and Measure for Measure." South Atlantic Bulletin, 38 (1973), 11-15.

1962 PEARCE, Roy Harvey. "Hawthorne and the Twilight of Romance." Yale Review, 27 (Spring, 1948), 487-506. Reprinted in Pearce, Historicism Once More (1969), pp.175-199. Refers to The Marble Faun.

1963 _____. "Hawthorne and the Sense of the Past, or the Immortality of Major Molineux." Journal of English Literary History, 21 (December, 1954), 327-349.

1964 _____. "Robin Molineux on the Analyst's Couch: A Note on the Limits of Psycho-analytic Criticism." Criticism, 1 (Spring, 1959), 83-90. Reprinted in Malin, ed., Psychoanalysis (1965), pp.309-316. Also reprinted in Pearce, Historicism Once More (1969), pp.96-106.

1965 _____. "Romance and the Study of History," in Pearce, ed., Centenary Essays (1964), pp.221-244.

1966 _____. "General Introduction," in Charvat, William, et al., eds., The Blithedale Romance and Fanshawe. Columbus: Ohio State University Press, 1964. Volume III, Centenary Edition of Hawthorne.

1967 _____. Historicism Once More. Princeton, N.J.: Princeton University Press, 1969. Reprints articles on Hawthorne, including "Hawthorne and the Sense of the Past," pp.137-174, expanded version of 1954 article.

1968 _____. "Historical Introduction," in Bowers, Fredson, ed., True Stories from History and Biography. Columbus: Ohio State University Press, 1972. Volume VI, Centenary Edition of Hawthorne.

1969 _____. "General Introduction," in Bowers, Fred-

son, ed., <u>A Wonder Book and Tanglewood Tales.</u>
Columbus: Ohio State University Press, 1972.
Volume VII, Centenary Edition of Hawthorne.

1970 _____. "Day-Dream and Fact: The Import of <u>The</u>
<u>Blithedale Romance,</u>" in Baldwin, Kenneth H., and
David K. Kirby, eds. <u>Individual and Community.</u>
Durham, N.C.: Duke University Press, 1975, pp.
49-63.

1971 _____, ed. with Introduction. <u>Nathaniel Hawthorne:</u>
<u>Twice-Told Tales.</u> New York: Dutton; London:
Dent, 1955. Everyman's Library Edition.

1972 _____, ed. with Introduction. <u>The Scarlet Letter.</u>
New York: Dutton; London: Dent, 1957. Every-
man's Library Edition.

1973 _____, ed. <u>Hawthorne Centenary Essays.</u> Colum-
bus: Ohio State University Press, 1964. Essays by
Terence Martin, pp.7-30; Charles Feidelson, Jr.,
pp.31-77; Marcus Cunliffe, pp.79-101; Robert C.
Elliott, pp.103-117; Harry Levin, pp.119-140; Edward
H. Davidson, pp.141-163; Hyatt H. Waggoner, pp.
167-195; Daniel Hoffman, pp.197-219; Roy H. Pearce,
pp.221-244; Larzer Ziff, pp.245-269; R.W.B. Lewis,
pp.271-295; Edwin Fussell, pp.297-314; Edwin H.
Cady, pp.317-334; Seymour L. Gross and Randall
Stewart, pp.335-366; Roger Asselineau, pp.367-385;
Matthew J. Bruccoli, pp.387-400; Fredson Bowers,
pp.401-425; Lionel Trilling, pp.429-458.

1974 PEARSON, Norma Holmes. "A Sketch by Hawthorne."
<u>New England Quarterly,</u> 6 (March, 1933), 136-144.
Refers to "A Good Man's Miracle," published in <u>The</u>
<u>Child's Friend,</u> February, 1844.

1975 _____. "Nathaniel Hawthorne's French and Italian
Notebooks." Ph.D. diss., Yale, 1941.

1976 _____. "Anonymous Editor." <u>Saturday Review</u>
<u>of Literature,</u> 24 (July 26, 1941), 18 et passim.

1977 _____. "Hawthorne's Usable Truth" and Other
<u>Papers Presented at the Fiftieth Anniversary of New</u>
<u>York Lambda Chapter of Phi Beta Kappa.</u> Canton,
N.Y.: St. Lawrence University Press, 1950.

1978 _____. "Hawthorne and the Mannings." <u>Essex Institute Historical Collections</u>, 94 (July, 1958), 169-190.

1979 _____. "Hawthorne's Duel." <u>Essex Institute Historical Collections</u>, 94 (July, 1958), 229-242.

1980 _____. "Elizabeth Peabody on Hawthorne." <u>Essex Institute Historical Collections</u>, 94 (July, 1958), 256-276.

1981 _____. "The American Writer and the Feelings for Community." <u>English Studies</u>, 43 (October, 1962), 403-412.

1982 _____. <u>Hawthorne's Two "Engagements."</u> Northampton, Mass.: Privately printed, 1963. Pamphlet, 14p.

1983 _____. "The Pyncheons and Judge Pyncheon." <u>Essex Institute Historical Collections</u>, 100 (October, 1964), 235-255.

1984 _____. "A 'Good Thing' for Hawthorne." <u>English Institute Historical Collections</u>, 100 (October, 1964), 300-305.

1985 _____. "Hawthorne's Letters and 'French and Italian Notebooks.'" <u>Hawthorne Society Newsletter</u>, 1 (1975), 3-4.

1986 _____, ed. with Introduction. <u>The Complete Novels and Selected Tales</u>. New York: Random House, 1937. Modern Library Giant Edition.

1987 PEARY, Gerald, and Roger Shatzin, eds. <u>The Classic American Novel and the Movies</u>. New York: Ungar, 1977. Includes studies of <u>The Scarlet Letter</u>, <u>The House of the Seven Gables</u>, <u>Moby-Dick</u>, and <u>Billy-Budd</u>.

1988 PEBWORTH, Ted-Larry. "'The Soul's Instinctive Perception': Dream, Actuality, and Reality in Four Tales from Hawthorne's <u>Mosses from an Old Manse</u>." <u>South Central Bulletin</u>, 23 (Winter, 1963), 18-23.

1989 PECK, Harry Thurston. "Hawthorne and <u>The Scarlet</u>

Peck   180

Letter," in Peck, <u>Studies in Several Literatures</u>.
New York: Dodd, Mead, 1909, pp. 117-130.

1990   PECK, Richard E. , ed. <u>Hawthorne's Poems</u> (29).
Kingsport, Tenn.: Kingsport, 1967, for the Bibli-
ographic Society of the University of Virginia,
Charlottesville, Virginia, 1967.

1991   PECKHAM, Morse. "Toward a Theory of Romanticism." <u>PMLA</u>, 66 (1951), 5-23.

1992   _____. "Toward a Theory of Romanticism: II.
Reconsiderations." <u>Studies in Romanticism</u>, 1
(1961), 1-8.

1993   _____. "Hawthorne and Melville as European
Authors," in Vincent, Howard P. , ed. , <u>Melville
and Hawthorne in the Berkshires: A Symposium.</u>
Kent, Ohio: Kent State University Press, 1968,
pp. 42-62. Reprinted in Peckham, <u>The Triumph
of Romanticism.</u> Columbia: University of South
Carolina Press, 1970, pp. 153-175.

1994   PEDERSON, Glenn. "Blake's Urizen as Hawthorne's
Ethan Brand." <u>Nineteenth-Century Fiction</u>, 12
(March, 1958), 304-314. Reprinted in Isaacs and
Leiter, eds. , <u>Approaches to the Short Story</u> (1963),
pp. 115-142.

1995   PEPLE, Edward Cronin, Jr. "The Personal and
Literary Relationship of Hawthorne and Thoreau."
Ph. D. diss. , Virginia, 1970. <u>DA</u>, 31 (1971), 4730A.

1996   _____. "The Background of the Hawthorne-Thoreau
Relationship." <u>Resources for American Literary
Study</u>, 1 (1971), 104-112.

1997   _____. "Hawthorne on Thoreau, 1853-1857."
<u>Thoreau Society Bulletin</u>, 119 (Spring, 1972), 1-3.

1998   _____. "Three Unlisted Reviews of Hawthorne."
<u>Emerson Society Quarterly</u>, 18 (1972), 146-147.
Reprints three brief reviews from <u>The Dial</u>, 1841,
by Margaret Fuller.

1999   _____. "Thoreau and Donatello." <u>Thoreau Jour-</u>
<u>nal Quarterly,</u> 5 (1973), 22-25.

2000 PERKINS, George. "Howells and Hawthorne."
      Nineteenth-Century Fiction, 15 (December, 1960),
      259-262.

2001 PERRY, Bliss. "The Centenary of Hawthorne."
      Atlantic Monthly, 94 (August, 1904), 195-206. Re-
      printed in Perry, Park Street Papers. Boston:
      Houghton Mifflin, 1908, pp. 97-103.

2002 _____. "Hawthorne at North Adams," in Perry,
      The Amateur Spirit. Boston: Houghton Mifflin,
      1904, pp. 117-139. Reprinted in Hastings, William
      Thomson, ed., Contemporary Essays. Boston:
      Houghton Mifflin, 1928, pp. 287-300. Relates to
      "Ethan Brand."

2003 PERRY, Ruth. "The Solitude of Hawthorne's 'Wake-
      field.'" American Literature, 49 (1978), 613-619.

2004 PERSON, Leland S. "Aesthetic Headaches and Euro-
      pean Women in The Marble Faun and The American."
      Studies in American Fiction, 4 (1976), 65-77.

2005 PETERICH, Werner. "Hawthorne and the Gesta
      Romanorum: The Genesis of 'Rappaccini's Daughter'
      and 'Ethan Brand.'" Kleine Beitrage..., 21 (1961),
      11-18. Edited by Hans Galinsky and Hans-Joachim
      Lang. Heidelberg, Germany: Carl Winter, 1961.

2006 PETERS, Leonard J. "Nathaniel Hawthorne and the
      Fall of Man." Ph.D. diss., Tulane, 1953.

2007 PETERSON, Anna Marie Willenbrock. "Hawthorne's
      Double Focus and Its Use in The Blithedale Romance."
      Ph.D. diss., California (Los Angeles), 1965. DA,
      26 (1966), 4637.

2008 PETERSON, Sandra M. "The View from the Gallows:
      The Criminal Confession in American Literature."
      Ph.D. diss., Northwestern, 1971. DA, 33 (1972),
      947A.

2009 PETTISON, Joseph C. "The Guilt of the Innocent
      Donatello." Emerson Society Quarterly, 31 (1963),
      66-68.

2010 PFEIFFER, Karl G. "The Prototype of the Poet in

'The Great Stone Face.'" Research Studies (Washington State University), 9 (June, 1941), 100-108. Possibly Wordsworth.

2011   PHELPS, Austin. "Theology of The Marble Faun," in My Portfolio. New York: Scribner, 1882, pp. 130-139. Reprinted in Cameron, ed., Hawthorne Among His Contemporaries (1968), pp. 227-229.

2012   PHELPS, William Lyon. "Nathaniel Hawthorne and Puritanism." Ladies' Home Journal, 40 (March, 1923), 15 et passim. Reprinted in Phelps, Some Makers of American Literature. Francestown, N.H.: Marshall Jones, 1923, pp. 97-128.

2013   PHILLIPS, John A. "Melville Meets Hawthorne: How a Champagne Picnic on Monument Mountain Led to a Profound Revision of Moby-Dick and Disenchantment." American Heritage, 27 (1975), 16-21, 87-90.

2014   PHILLIPS, Robert S. "The Scarlet Letter: A Selected Checklist of Criticism." Bulletin of Bibliography, 23 (1962), 213-216.

2015   _____; Jack Kligerman; Robert E. Long; and Robert Hastings. "Nathaniel Hawthorne: Criticism of the Four Major Romances: A Selected Bibliography." Thoth, 3 (Winter, 1963), 39-50.

2016   PICKARD, Samuel Thomas. "Hawthorne's First Diary: With An Account of Its Discovery and Loss." Chap-Book, 8 (December 1, 1897), 87. Short discussion of 2018 below.

2017   _____. "Is Hawthorne's First Diary a Forgery?" Dial, 33 (September 16, 1902), 155.

2018   _____, ed. Hawthorne's First Diary, with An Account of Its Discovery and Loss. Boston: Houghton Mifflin, 1897. Diary may not be authentic.

2019   PIETRO, Robert di. "Hawthorne's 'The Birthmark': Puritan Inhibitions and Romantic Appeal in the Context of the Faustian Quest," in Gorlier, Claudio, ed., Studi e ricerche di letteratura inglese e Americana, Vol. II. Milan, Italy: Cisalpino-Goliardica, 1969. In English.

2020 PIKULEFF, Michael Joseph. "The Role of Community
      in the Major Writings of Nathaniel Hawthorne."
      Ph.D. diss., Wisconsin, 1969. DA, 31 (1970),
      1809A-1810A.

2021 PINSKER, Sanford. "Hawthorne's 'Double-Faced
      Fellow': A Note on 'My Kinsman, Major Molineux.'"
      Nathaniel Hawthorne Journal, 2 (1972), 255-256.

2022 _____. "The Scaffold as Hinge: A Note on the
      Structure of The Scarlet Letter." College Literature,
      5 (1978), 144-145.

2023 PLANK, Robert. "Heart Transplant Fiction." Hart-
      ford Studies in Literature, 2 (1970), 102-112. Dis-
      cusses "Ethan Brand."

2024 PLUMSTEAD, Arthur W. "Puritanism and Nineteenth-
      Century American Literature." Queen's Quarterly,
      70 (Summer, 1963), 209-222.

2025 POCHMANN, Henry August. German Culture in
      America: Philosophical and Literary Influences,
      1600-1900. Madison: University of Wisconsin
      Press, 1957. Hawthorne discussed in "Germanic
      Materials and Motifs in the Short Story," pp.381-
      388.

2026 _____. "Hawthorne at Wisconsin." Emerson
      Society Quarterly, 25 (1961), 18-20.

2027 _____, and Gay Wilson Allen. Introduction to
      Masters of American Literature. Carbondale:
      Southern Illinois University Press, 1969. Haw-
      thorne, pp.52-58. Based on material in Pochmann
      and Allen, eds., Masters of American Literature,
      2 vols. New York: Macmillan, 1949.

2028 POE, Edgar Allan. "Review of Twice-Told Tales."
      Graham's Magazine, 20 (May, 1842), 298-300. A
      brief notice of publication had appeared in April,
      1842, p.254. The Review has been frequently re-
      printed, as in the following examples:

      Johnson, A. Theodore, and Allen Tate, eds.
      America Through the Essay. New York: Oxford
      University Press, 1938, pp.289-296.

Wilson, Edmund, ed. The Shock of Recognition (1943), pp. 154-169.

Richardson, Lyon Norman, et al., eds. Heritage of American Literature, 2 vols. New York: Ginn, 1951. Vol. I, pp. 516-520.

Brown, Clarence A., ed. The Achievement of American Criticism. New York: Ronald, 1954, pp. 191-195.

Fiedler, Leslie A., ed. The Art of the Essay (1958), pp. 559-570.

Miller, Perry, ed. The Golden Age of American Literature. New York: Braziller, 1959, pp. 75-81.

Summers, Hollis S., ed. Discussions of the Short Story. Boston: Heath, 1963, pp. 1-4. Discussions of Literature Series.

Hough, Robert L., ed. Literary Criticism of Edgar Allan Poe. Lincoln: University of Nebraska Press, 1965, pp. 133-141.

May, Charles E., ed. Short Story Theories. Athens: Ohio University Press, 1976, pp. 45-51.

2029 _____. "Tale Writing: Mr. Hawthorne." Godey's Lady's Book, 35 (November, 1847), 252-256. Reprinted occasionally, as in the following:

Van Nostrand, Albert D., ed. Literary Criticism in America. New York: Liberal Arts, 1957, pp. 38-49.

Hough, Robert L., ed. Literary Criticism of Edgar Allan Poe (1965), pp. 142-149.

Cohen, Bernard, ed. Recognition (1969), pp. 21-27.

2030 POIRIER, Richard. "From Visionary to Voyeur: Hawthorne and James," in Poirier, A World Elsewhere: The Place of Style in American Literature. New York: Oxford University Press, 1966, pp. 93-143. Reprinted in Lohner, Edgar, ed., Der Amerikanische Roman. Berlin: Eric Schmidt, 1974, pp.

36-48.

2031 POLLIN, Burton R. " 'Rappaccini's Daughter'--Sources and Names." Names, 14 (March, 1966), 30-35.

2032 POND, Wayne Johnston. "The Adverse World: The Closed Society in the Major Romances of Nathaniel Hawthorne." Ph.D. diss., North Carolina (Chapel Hill), 1976. DA, 38 (1977), 789A.

2033 PORTE, Joel. The Romance in America: Studies in Cooper, Poe, Hawthorne, Melville, and James. Middletown, Conn.: Wesleyan University Press, 1969. Hawthorne, pp.95-151; Melville, pp.152-192.

2034 PORTER, John Addison. "The 'Dr. Grimshawe' Manuscript." New Englander, 42 (May, 1883), 339-353.

2035 POULET, Georges. "Timelessness and Romanticism." Journal of the History of Ideas, 15 (1954), 3-22.

2036 _____. Studies in Human Time. Translated by Elliott Coleman. Baltimore: Johns Hopkins University Press, 1956. Hawthorne, pp.326-329.

2037 POWERS, L.H. "Hawthorne and Faulkner and the Pearl of Great Price." Papers of the Michigan Academy of Science, Arts, and Letters, 52 (1967), 391-401.

2038 PRATER, William G. "Nathaniel Hawthorne: A Self-Characterization in the Novels." Ph.D. diss., Ohio, 1968. DA, 30 (1969), 2494A-2495A.

2039 PRAZ, Mario. "Shelley, Lamartine, Hawthorne, Dostoevsky a Firenze." Rivista di Letteratura Moderne e Comparate, 8 (January-March, 1955), 5-20. In Italian. Refers to city of Florence, Italy.

2040 _____. Mnemosyne. Princeton, N.J.: Princeton University Press, 1970. Hawthorne, passim.

2041 PREDMORE, Richard Lionel, Jr. "The Defeated: The Archetypal Hero in Hawthorne's Tales." Ph.D. diss., Florida, 1974. DA, 36 (1975), 1508A-1509A.

2042   _____. "The Hero's Test in 'Rappaccini's Daughter.'"
            English Language Notes, 15 (1978), 284-291.

2043   PRICE, Sherwood R. "The Heart, the Head, and
            'Rappaccini's Daughter.'" New England Quarterly,
            27 (September, 1954), 399-403.

2044   PRIESTLEY, J.B. Literature and Western Man.
            New York: Harper, 1960. "The Novelists," pp.
            222-273. Hawthorne, passim.

2045   PRITCHARD, John Paul. "Hawthorne's Debt to
            Classical Literary Criticism." Classical World,
            29 (December 2, 1935), 41-45.

2046   _____. Return to the Fountains. Durham, N.C.:
            Duke University Press, 1942. Reprinted New York:
            Octagon, 1966. Hawthorne, pp. 68-78.

2047   PRITCHETT, V.S. "Books in General," column.
            New Statesman and Nation, 24 (October, 1942), 275.
            Remarks on Hawthorne.

2048   _____. "Hawthorne at Brook Farm." New States-
            man and Nation, 28 (November, 1944), 323.

2049   PROCHNOW, H.V. "Housekeeper to Genius." Coro-
            net, 27 (December, 1949), 39.

2050   PROSSER, Michael H. "A Rhetoric of Alienation as
            Reflected in the Works of Nathaniel Hawthorne."
            Quarterly Journal of Speech, 54 (1968), 22-28.

2051   PRYCE-JONES, Allan. "Hawthorne in England."
            Life and Letters, 50 (August, 1946), 71-80.

2052   PRYSE, Marjorie L. "The Marked Character in
            American Fiction: Essays in Social and Metaphorical
            Isolation." Ph.D. diss., California (Santa Cruz),
            1973. DA, 35 (1974), 1119A-1120A.

2053   PUTZEL, Max. "The Way Out of the Minister's
            Maze: Some Hints for Teachers of The Scarlet
            Letter." Die neueren Sprachen, 9 (March, 1960),
            127-131.

187   Quatermain

2054 QUATERMAIN, P.A. "Nathaniel Hawthorne and Puritan:
A Study of the Puritan Influence on Nineteenth-Century
New England Literature." Ph.D. diss., Nottingham
(England), 1959.

2055 QUICK, Jonathan R. "Silas Marner as Romance: The
Example of Hawthorne." Nineteenth-Century Fiction,
29 (1974), 287-298.

2056 QUINN, Arthur Hobson, ed. The Literature of the
American People: An Historical and Critical Survey.
New York: Appleton, 1915. Reissued 1951. "The
Establishment of a National Literature," by Arthur
Hobson Quinn, pp. 175-568. Includes Hawthorne.

2057 _____. American Fiction: An Historical and
Critical Survey. New York: Appleton-Century,
1936. Hawthorne and Melville, pp. 132-158.

2058 QUINN, James, and Ross Baldessarini. "Literary
Technique and Psychological Effect in Hawthorne's
'The Minister's Black Veil.'" Literature and Psy-
chology, 24 (1974), 115-123.

2059 RACKHAM, Jeff. "Hawthorne's Method in Moonlight
Madness." Publication of the Arkansas Philological
Association, 3 (1977), 47-52. Discusses "The
Custom House" and The House of the Seven Gables.

2060 RAGAN, James F. "Nature in Nathaniel Hawthorne's
American Novels." Ph.D. diss., Notre Dame, 1955.
DA, 15 (1955), 2214.

2061 _____. "Hawthorne's Bulky Puritans." PMLA,
75 (September, 1960), 420-423.

2062 _____. "The Irony in Hawthorne's Blithedale."
New England Quarterly, 35 (June, 1962), 239-246.

2063 _____. "Social Criticism in The House of the
Seven Gables," in Slote, Bernice, ed., Literature
and Society. Lincoln: University of Nebraska
Press, 1964, pp. 112-120.

2064 RAHV, Philip. "The Dark Lady of Salem." Partisan Review, 8 (September-October, 1941), 362-381.

Reprinted in Rahv, Image and Idea: Twenty Essays
on Literary Themes. Norfolk, Conn.: New Direc-
tions, 1949, pp. 22-41. Also reprinted in Rahv,
Literature and the Sixth Sense. Boston: Houghton
Mifflin, 1969, pp. 55-75. Also reprinted in Porter,
Arabel J., and Andrew J. Dvosin, eds., Essays
on Literature and Politics: 1932-1972. Boston:
Houghton Mifflin, 1978, pp. 25-42.

2065 _____, ed. Discovery of Europe: The Story of
American Experience in the Old World. Boston:
Houghton Mifflin, 1947. "Consular Experiences,"
by Hawthorne, pp. 173-236.

2066 _____, ed. Literature in America: An Anthology
of Literary Criticism. New York: Meridian, 1957.
"Hawthorne: Early Manhood," by Henry James, pp.
84-100.

2067 RALEIGH, John Henry. "Eugene O'Neill." Ramparts,
2 (Spring, 1964), 72-87. Relates to Hawthorne's
sense of tragedy.

2068 RANDALL, David A., and John T. Winterich. "One
Hundred Good Novels: Nathaniel Hawthorne's The
Scarlet Letter." Publishers' Weekly, 137 (March
16, 1940), 1181-1182.

2069 RANDEL, William P. "Hawthorne, Channing, and
Margaret Fuller." American Literature, 10 (January, 1939), 472-476. See article by Cargill (1937).

2070 RANERI, Marietta R. "The Self Behind the Self: The
Americanization of the Gothic." Ph.D. diss.,
Pennsylvania State, 1973. DA, 34 (1974), 5200A-
5201A.

2071 RAWLS, Walton. "Hawthorne's 'Rappaccini's Daughter.'"
Explicator, 15 (April, 1957), item 47.

2072 RAY, Gordon Norton, ed. with Introduction and Foreword. Introduction by C. Waller Barrett. The
American Writer in England. Charlottesville: University Press of Virginia, 1969. Hawthorne, passim.

2073 READ, Sir Herbert Edward. "Hawthorne." Hound
and Horn, 3 (January-March, 1930), 213-229. Simi-

lar article also printed in the following: Read, ed.,
Sense of Glory. New York: Harcourt, Brace, 1930,
pp. 153-177. Read, Collected Essays in Literary
Criticism. London: Faber and Faber, 1938, pp.
265-279. Read, The Nature of Literature. New
York: Horizon, 1956, pp. 265-279.

2074 REECE, James B. "Mr. Hooper's Vow." Emerson
Society Quarterly, 21 (1975), 93-102.

2075 REED, Amy Louise. "Self-Portraiture in the Works
of Nathaniel Hawthorne." Studies in Philology, 23
(January, 1926), 40-54.

2076 REED, P. L. "The Telling Frame of Hawthorne's
'Legends of the Province House.'" Studies in American Fiction, 4 (1976), 105-111.

2077 REED, Richard B., and John D. O'Heru. "Nathaniel
Hawthorne at Bowdoin College." Nathaniel Hawthorne
Journal, 2 (1972), 147-157.

2078 REES, John Owen, Jr. "Nathaniel Hawthorne and the
Emblem." Ph.D. diss., State University of Iowa,
1964. DA, 26 (1965), 357.

2079 _____. "Elizabeth Peabody and 'The Very ABC':
A Note on The House of the Seven Gables." American Literature, 38 (January, 1967), 537-540. Refers to a book published by Elizabeth Peabody, Significance of the Alphabet (1846), by Charles Kraitser,
an attempt to popularize the alphabet.

2080 _____. "Shakespeare in The Blithedale Romance."
Emerson Society Quarterly, 19 (1973), 84-93.

2081 _____. "Hawthorne's Concept of Allegory: A
Reconsideration." Philological Quarterly, 54 (1975),
494-510.

2082 REEVE, Clayton Clark. "Hawthorne's Dilemma: The
Confrontation Between Christian and Romantic Think-
ing in the Tales and Novels." Ph.D. diss., Illinois
(Urbana-Champaign), 1970. DA, 31 (1970), 2397A.

2083 REEVES, George Jr. "Hawthorne's 'Ethan Brand.'"
Explicator, 14 (June, 1956), item 56.

2084 REEVES, Pamela. "Hawthorne's Settings: Forest,
      City, Country, and Garden." Ph.D. diss., Tennessee,
      1974. DA, 35 (1975), 5359A.

2085 REGAN, Robert. "Hawthorne's 'Plagiary': Poe's
      Duplicity." Nineteenth-Century Fiction, 25 (1970),
      281-298. Studies "The Masque of the Red Death"
      and "Legends of Province House."

2086 REID, Alfred S. "The Sources of The Scarlet Letter."
      Ph.D. diss., Florida, 1952.

2087 _____. The Yellow Ruff and The Scarlet Letter:
      A Source of Hawthorne's Novel. Gainesville: Uni-
      versity of Florida Press, 1955.

2088 _____. "A Note on the Date of The Scarlet Letter."
      Furman University Bulletin, 4 (Winter, 1957), 30-39.

2089 _____. "The Role of Transformation in Hawthorne's
      Tragic Vision." Furman Studies, 6 (Fall, 1958), 9-20.

2090 _____. "Hawthorne's Ghost-Soul and the Harmonized
      Life." Furman Studies, 12 (Fall, 1964), 1-10.

2091 _____. "Hawthorne's Humanism: 'The Birthmark'
      and Sir Kenelm Digby." American Literature, 38
      (November, 1966), 337-351. Refers to a British
      scientist-author, 1603-1665, possibly source for
      character of Aylmer; Georgiana from Lady Digby.

2092 _____, ed. Sir Thomas Overbury's Vision (1616)
      by Richard Nicolls and Other English Sources of
      Nathaniel Hawthorne's The Scarlet Letter. Facsimile
      reproduction with an Introduction. Gainesville, Fla.:
      Scholars Facsimiles and Reproductions, 1957. In-
      cludes Loseley Manuscript: Fulke Greville's The
      Five Years of King James (1643), state trials.

2093 REILLY, Cyril A. "On the Dog's Chasing His Own
      Tail in 'Ethan Brand.'" PMLA, 68 (December,
      1953), 975-981.

2094 REISS, John P., Jr. "Problems of the Family Novel:
      Cooper, Hawthorne, and Melville." Ph.D. diss.,
      Wisconsin, 1968. DA, 30 (1969), 1178A-1179A.

2095 RESH, Richard. "Nathaniel Hawthorne's Development

of his Major Character in His Major Novels. " Ph. D.
diss. , Wisconsin, no date available.

2096   REYNOLDS. Donald Martin.   Hiram Powers and His
       Ideal Sculpture.   New York: Garland, 1977.   Haw-
       thorne, p. 97 et passim.   Based on Ph. D. diss. ,
       Columbia (Fine Arts), 1975.   Makes use of Passages
       from the French and Italian Notebooks, ed. by Sophia
       Hawthorne. Boston: Osgood, 1871.

2097   REYNOLDS, Gordon D.   "Psychological Rebirth in
       Selected Works by Nathaniel Hawthorne, Stephen
       Crane, Henry James, William Faulkner, and Ralph
       Ellison. " Ph. D. diss. , California (Irvine), 1973.
       DA, 34 (1974), 7719A.

2098   REYNOLDS, Larry J.   "Melville's Use of 'Young
       Goodman Brown. '" American Transcendental Quar-
       terly, 31 (1976), 12-14.

2099   RIBBENS, Dennis N.   "The Reading Interests of Haw-
       thorne and Lanier. " Ph. D. diss. , Wisconsin, 1969.
       DA, 31 (1970), 777A.

2100   RICE, Nancy Hall.   "Beauty and the Beast and the
       Little Boy: Clues about the Origins of Sexism and
       Racism from Folklore and Literature: Chaucer's
       'The Prioress's Tale, ' Melville's 'Benito Cereno, '
       and Hawthorne's 'Rappaccini's Daughter. '" Ph. D.
       diss. , Massachusetts, 1975. DA, 36 (1975), 875A.

2101   RICHARD, Claude. "Poe et Hawthorne. "   Etudes
       Anglaises, 22 (1969), 351-361. In French.

2102   RICHARDS, Irving T.   "A Note on the Authorship of
       'David Whicher. '" Jahrbuch für Amerikastudien,
       7 (1962), 293-296.

2103   RICHARDSON, R. D. , Jr.   Myth and Literature in the
       American Renaissance. Bloomington: Indiana Uni-
       versity Press, 1978. Hawthorne, pp. 165-194.

2104   RICKS, Beatrice; Joseph J. Adams; and Jack O.
       Hazlerig.   Nathaniel Hawthorne: A Reference
       Bibliography, 1900-1971. Boston: Hall, 1972.

2105   RINGE, Donald A.   "Hawthorne's Psychology of the
       Head and Heart. " PMLA, 65 (March, 1950), 120-132.

2106 _____. "Teaching Hawthorne to Engineering Students." Emerson Society Quarterly, 25 (1961), 24-26.

2107 _____. "Hawthorne's Night Journeys." American Transcendental Quarterly, 10 (1971), 27-32.

2108 RINGLER, Ellin Jane. "The Problem of Evil: A Correlative Study in the Novels of Nathaniel Hawthorne and George Eliot." Ph.D. diss., State University of Iowa, 1967. DA, 28(1968), 5068A.

2109 ROBBINS, J. Albert, ed. American Literary Manuscripts: A Checklist of Holdings in Academic, Historical, and Public Libraries, Museums, and Authors' Homes in the United States. Athens: University of Georgia Press, 1960. Reissued 1977.

2110 ROBERTS, J.E. "Sophia Hawthorne, Editor." Saturday Review of Literature, 29 (December 23, 1939), 9.

2111 ROBERTSON, Patricia R. "Shelley and Hawthorne: A Comparison of Imagery and Sensibility." South Central Bulletin, 32 (1972), 233-239.

2112 ROBEY, Richard Charles. "The Enchanted Ground: An Approach to the Tales and Sketches of Nathaniel Hawthorne." Ph.D. diss., Columbia, 1966. DA, 29 (1969), 4467A-4468A.

2113 _____, ed. with Foreword. The Life of Franklin Pierce. New York: Garrett, 1970. Refers to campaign biography written by Hawthorne in 1852.

2114 ROBILLARD, Douglas. "Hawthorne's 'Roger Malvin's Burial.'" Explicator, 26 (1968), item 56.

2115 ROBINSON, E. Arthur. "The Vision of Goodman Brown: A Source and an Interpretation." American Literature, 35 (March, 1963), 218-225.

2116 _____. "Thoreau's Buried Short Story." Studies in Short Fiction, 1 (Fall, 1963), 16-20. Refers to "Baker Farm" chapter in Walden; Hawthorne, passim.

2117 ROBINSON, H.A. "Nathaniel Hawthorne in Wirral." Cheshire Life (Manchester, England), 19 (May, 1953), 43.

2118 ROBINSON, H. M. "Materials of Romance." Common-
weal, 10 (October 16, 1929), 622-623.

2119 ROCHE, Arthur J., III. "A Literary Gentleman in
New York: Evert A. Duyckinck's Relationship with
Hawthorne, Melville, Poe, and Simms." Ph.D. diss.,
Duke, 1973. DA, 34 (1974), 4282A.

2120 ROCKS, James E. "Hawthorne and France: In Search
of American Literary Nationalism." Tulane Studies
in English, 17 (1969), 145-157.

2121 RODABAUGH, Delmer J. "Nathaniel Hawthorne's Use
of the English and Italian Past." Ph.D. diss.,
Minnesota, 1952.

2122 RODNON, Stewart. "The House of the Seven Gables
and Absalom! Absalom!: Time, Tradition, and
Guilt," in Grayburn, William F., ed. Studies in
the Humanities. Indiana: Indiana University of
Pennsylvania Press, 1970, pp. 42-46.

2123 RODRIGUEZ, Joe Domingo. "Aspects of Internal
Conflict in Certain Early Tales and Sketches from
Hawthorne." Ph.D. diss., California (San Diego),
1977. DA, 38 (1978), 5484A.

2124 ROGERS, Barbara J. "Entropy and Organization in
Hawthorne's America." Southern Quarterly, 16
(1978), 223-239.

2125 ROHRBERGER, Mary. "Nathaniel Hawthorne and the
Modern Literary Short Story: A Study in Genre."
Ph.D. diss., Tulane, 1961. DA, 22 (1962), 3206-
3207.

2126 _____. "Hawthorne's Literary Theory and the
Nature of His Short Story." Studies in Short Fiction,
3 (1965), 23-30.

2127 _____. Hawthorne and the Modern Short Story:
A Study in Genre. The Hague: Mouton, 1966. Includes Joseph Conrad, Katherine Mansfield, Faulkner, Eudora Welty, etc.

2128 ROPER, Gordon. "The Originality of Hawthorne's
The Scarlet Letter." Dalhousie Review, 29 (April,
1950), 62-79.

2129 _____, ed. with Introduction. The Scarlet Letter
      and Selected Prose Works. New York: Hendricks
      House, 1949.

2130 ROSA, Alfred F. "A Study of Transcendentalism in
      Salem with Special Reference to Nathaniel Hawthorne."
      Ph. D. diss., Massachusetts, 1970. DA, 32 (1971),
      1485A.

2131 ROSE, Harriet. "The First Person Narrator as
      Artist in the Works of Charles Brockden Brown,
      Nathaniel Hawthorne, and Henry James." Ph. D.
      diss., Indiana, 1972. DA, 33 (1973), 6373A.

2132 ROSE, Marilyn Gaddis. "'My Kinsman, Major
      Molineux' and the Theseus Motif." Emerson Society
      Quarterly, 47 (1967), 21-23.

2133 _____. "Miles Coverdale as Hawthorne's Personae."
      American Transcendental Quarterly, 1 (1969), 90-91.

2134 _____. "Julian Green's Hawthorne Essay."
      Nathaniel Hawthorne Journal, 5 (1975), 248-250. Re-
      fers to Un Puritain Homme de lettres: Nathaniel
      Hawthorne, published in French, 1928.

2135 ROSENBERRY, Edward Hoffman. "Hawthorne's
      Allegory of Science: 'Rappaccini's Daughter.'"
      American Literature, 32 (March, 1960), 39-46.

2136 _____. "James' Use of Hawthorne in 'The Liar.'"
      Modern Language Notes, 76 (March, 1961), 234-
      238.

2137 ROSENFELD, William. "The Divided Burden: Com-
      mon Elements in the Search for a Religious Syn-
      thesis in the Works of Theodore Parker, Horace
      Bushnell, Nathaniel Hawthorne, and Herman Mel-
      ville." Ph. D. diss., Minnesota, 1961. DA, 22
      (1962), 4019A.

2138 ROSENTHAL, Bernard. "Nature's Slighting Hand:
      The Idea of Nature in American Writing, 1820-1860."
      Ph. D. diss., Illinois, 1968. DA, 29 (1969), 2226A.

2139 ROSENTHAL, Melvyn. "The American Writer and
      His Society: The Response to Estrangement in the

Works of Nathaniel Hawthorne, Randolph Bourne,
Edmund Wilson, Norman Mailer, Saul Bellow."
Ph.D. diss., Connecticut, 1968. <u>DA</u>, 29 (1969),
3108A.

2140 ROSES, Jonathan L. "The Family in the Works of
Nathaniel Hawthorne." Ph.D. diss., Massachusetts,
1972. <u>DA</u>, 34 (1973), 1932A.

2141 ROSS, Danforth. <u>The American Short Story</u>. Minneapolis: University of Minnesota Press, 1961.
Hawthorne, pp. 11-14.

2142 ROSS, Donald, Jr. "Hawthorne and Thoreau on
'Cottage' Architecture." <u>American Transcendental
Quarterly</u>, 1 (1969), 100-101.

2143 _____. "Dreams and Sexual Repression in <u>The
Blithedale Romance</u>." <u>PMLA</u>, 86 (1971), 1014-
1017. Compare article by Claire Sprague, 1969.

2144 ROSS, E.C. "A Note on <u>The Scarlet Letter</u>."
<u>Modern Language Notes</u>, 37 (January, 1922), 58-59.

2145 ROSS, Jacqueline Renee. "The Magnetic Chain:
Preternatural Allusions in the Writings of Nathaniel
Hawthorne." Ph.D. diss., Wisconsin, 1976. <u>DA</u>,
37 (1976), 2840A-2841A.

2146 ROSS, Maude Cardwell. "Moral Values of the American Woman as Presented in Three Major American
Authors." Ph.D. diss., Texas (Austin), 1964. <u>DA</u>,
25 (1965), 5262-5263. Studies Hawthorne, James,
and Faulkner.

2147 ROSS, Morton L. "Hawthorne's Bosom Serpent and
Mather's <u>Magnalia</u>." <u>Emerson Society Quarterly</u>,
47 (1967), 13.

2148 _____. "What Happens in 'Rappaccini's Daughter'?"
<u>American Literature</u>, 43 (1971), 336-345.

2149 ROSSKY, William. "Rappaccini's Garden: or the
Murder of Innocence." <u>Emerson Society Quarterly</u>,
19 (1960), 98-100.

2150 ROULSTON, C. Robert. "Hawthorne's Use of Bunyan's

Symbols in 'The Celestial Railroad.'" Kentucky Philological Association Bulletin, 1 (1975), 17-24.

2151 _____. "Hawthorne's Attitude Toward Jews." American Transcendental Quarterly, 29 (1976), 3-8.

2152 ROUNTREE, Thomas J., ed. with Introduction. Critics on Hawthorne. Coral Gables, Fla.: University of Miami Press, 1972. Reprinted criticism.

2153 ROURKE, Constance. American Humor: A Study of the National Character. New York: Harcourt, Brace, 1931. Hawthorne, pp. 186-191. Reprinted New York: Doubleday/Anchor, 1953. Hawthorne, pp. 150.154.

2154 ROUSE, Blair. "Hawthorne and the American Revolution: An Exploration." Nathaniel Hawthorne Journal, 6 (1976), 17-61.

2155 ROVIT, Earl H. "Ambiguity in Hawthorne's The Scarlet Letter." Archiv für das Studium der neueren Sprachen und Literaturen (Heidelberg, West Germany), 198 (June, 1961), 76-88

2156 _____. "James and Emerson: The Lesson of the Master." American Scholar, 33 (Summer, 1964), 434-440. Hawthorne, passim.

2157 ROWSE, Alfred Leslie. "The Americans on England," in Rowse, English Spirit. London: Macmillan, 1944. Pp. 266-272. Reprinted in revised edition New York: Funk and Wagnalls, 1967, pp. 246-269.

2158 ROZENCWAJG-STOCKBRIDGE, Iris Selma. "Nathaniel Hawthorne: The Romances." Ph.D. diss., City University of New York, 1978. DA, 39 (1978), 1575A.

2159 RUBIN, Joseph J. "Hawthorne's Theology: The Wide Plank." Emerson Society Quarterly, 25 (1961), 20-24.

2160 RULAND, Richard. The Rediscovery of American Literature. Cambridge: Harvard University Press, 1967. Hawthorne, pp. 36-52, 238-248, et passim.

2161 RUPP, Richard H., ed. with Introduction and Annotation. The Marble Faun; or The Romance of Monte

Beni. Indianapolis: Bobbs-Merrill, 1971. Merrill
Edition.

2162 RUSK, Ralph L. "Emerson in Salem, 1849." Essex
Institute Historical Collections, 94 (July, 1958), 194-
195. Hawthorne, passim.

2163 RUSSELL, A. Jason. "Hawthorne and the Romantic
Indian." Education, 48 (February, 1928), 381-386.

2164 RUSSELL, Frank Alden (Ted Malone, pseudonym).
"Nathaniel Hawthorne," in American Pilgrimage.
New York: Dodd, Mead, 1942, pp. 51-64.

2165 RUSSELL, James Tunney, Jr. "Hawthorne's Martyrs:
The Sacrificial Theme in His Tales and Novels."
Ph.D. diss., Alabama, 1972. DA, 33 (1973), 5747A.

2166 RUSSELL, John. "Allegory and 'My Kinsman, Major
Molineux.'" New England Quarterly, 40 (September,
1967), 432-440.

2167 RUST, James D. "George Eliot on The Blithedale
Romance." Boston Public Library Quarterly, 7
(October, 1955), 207-215. Based on unsigned notice
in the Westminster Review, October, 1852.

2168 RUST, Richard Dilworth. "Character Change and
Development in the Major Novels of Nathaniel Hawthorne." Ph.D. diss., Wisconsin, 1966. DA, 28
(1967), 641A-642A.

2169 _____. "Coverdale's Confession: A Key to Meaning in The Blithedale Romance," in Falk, Robert,
ed., Literature and Ideas in America. Athens:
Ohio University Press, 1975, pp. 96-110.

2170 RUTLEDGE, Lyman V. The Isle of Shoals in Lore
and Legend. Barre, Mass.: Barre, 1965. Hawthorne notebooks, and other references to the island,
passim.

2171 RYAN, Pat M., Jr. "Young Hawthorne at the Salem
Theatre." Essex Institute Historical Collections, 94
(July, 1958), 243-255.

2172 RYAN, Thomas Joseph. "'Scenes Well Worth Gazing

At': The Effects of Hawthorne's Touristic Vision in The Marble Faun." Ph. D. diss., York University (Canada), 1976. DA, 37 (1977), 7753A-7754A.

2173 RYSKAMP, Charles. "The New England Sources of The Scarlet Letter." American Literature, 31 (November, 1959), 257-272.

2174 SACHS, Viola. "The Myth of America in Hawthorne's The Scarlet Letter." Kwartalnik Neofilogiczny (Warsaw), 14 (1967), 245-267.

2175 _____. "The Myth of America in Hawthorne's The House of the Seven Gables and The Blithedale Romance." Kwartalnik Neofilogiczny, 15 (1968), 267-283.

2176 _____. The Myth of America: Essays in the Structures of Literary Imagination. Preface by Daniel Aaron. The Hague: Mouton, 1974. Studies Hawthorne, Melville, and Faulkner.

2177 SADER, Marion, ed. Comprehensive Index to Little Magazines: 1890-1970, 8 vols. Millwood, N. Y.: Kraus Thompson, 1976. Hawthorne, Vol. 4, pp. 1926-1930. Lists reviews and articles; especially good for listings of reviews.

2178 SAFRANEK, William Paul. "Hawthorne's Use of Setting in His Short Stories." Ph. D. diss., Wisconsin, 1960. DA, 21 (1961), 3462.

2179 ST. ARMAND, Barton Levi. "Hawthorne's 'Haunted Mind': A Subterranean Drama of the Self." Criticism, 13 (1971), 1-25.

2180 _____. "The Golden Stain of Time: Ruskinian Aesthetics and the Ending of The House of the Seven Gables." Nathaniel Hawthorne Journal, 3 (1973), 143-153.

2181 _____. "'Young Goodman Brown' as Historical Allegory." Nathaniel Hawthorne Journal, 3 (1973), 183-197.

2182 ST. JOHN-STEVAS, Norman. "The Author's Struggles

with the Law." Catholic World, March 1962, pp.
345-350. Includes comments on The Scarlet Letter.

2183 SAITO, Tadatoshi. "Notes on Romances: The Study
of Nathaniel Hawthorne." Jimbun-Shizen Kagaku
Kenkya, 4 (March, 1962), 111-133. Japanese publication; article in English.

2184 SAKAMOTO, Masayuki. "Hawthorne on Romance," in
American Literature in the 1840's: Annual Report,
1975. Tokyo: Tokyo Chapter of the American Literary Society of Japan, 1976, pp. 25-32.

2185 SAKAMOTO, Shigetake. "A Study of The Scarlet
Letter." Studies in English Language and Literature,
3 (March, 1963), 1-18; 4 (July, 1963), 1-19. In
Japanese; abstract in English.

2186 SALOMON, Louis B. "Hawthorne and His Father: A
Conjecture." Literature and Psychology, 13 (Winter,
1963), 12-17.

2187 SAMPSON, Edward Coolidge. "A Note on William B.
Stein's Hawthorne's Faust." Notes and Queries,
2 (March, 1955), 137-138.

2188 _____. "The Structure of The Scarlet Letter and
The House of the Seven Gables." Ph.D. diss.,
Cornell, 1957. DA, 27 (1957), 2015.

2189 _____. "Motivation in The Scarlet Letter." American Literature, 28 (January, 1957), 511-513.

2190 _____. "The 'W' in Hawthorne's Name." Essex
Institute Historical Collections, 100 (October, 1964),
297-299.

2191 _____. "Sound Imagery in The House of the Seven
Gables." English Review, 22 (1971), 26-29.

2192 _____, ed. with Afterword. The House of the
Seven Gables. New York: New American Library,
1961.

2193 _____, ed. with Introduction. "Three Unpublished
Letters by Nathaniel Hawthorne to Epes Sargent."
American Literature, 34 (March, 1962), 102-105.

2194 SAMPSON, M. W. "Nathaniel Hawthorne." Reader,
      5 (April, 1905), 775-778.

2195 SAMSON, Joan Phillips. "The Use of Legends in
      The Marble Faun and Hawthorne's Other Works."
      Ph. D. diss., North Carolina (Chapel Hill), 1974.
      DA, 35 (1975), 5362A-5363A.

2196 SANBORN, Frank B., ed. Hawthorne and His Friends:
      Reminiscence and Tribute. Cedar Rapids, Iowa:
      Torch, 1908. Pamphlet. Reprinted in American
      Transcendental Quarterly, 9 Supplement (1971), 5-
      24.

2197 SANDEEN, Ernest. "The Scarlet Letter as a Love
      Story." PMLA, 77 (September, 1962), 425-435.

2198 SANDERLIN, R. Reed. "Hawthorne's Scarlet Letter:
      A Study of the Meaning of Meaning." Southern
      Humanities Review, 9 (1975), 145-157.

2199 SANDERS, Charles. "A Note on Metamorphosis in
      Hawthorne's 'The Artist of the Beautiful.'" Studies
      in Short Fiction, 4 (Fall, 1966), 82-83.

2200 SANFORD, Charles L. "Classics of American Re-
      form Literature." American Quarterly, 10 (Fall,
      1958), 295-311.

2201 SANFORD, John. View from This Wilderness.
      Foreword by Paul Mariani. Santa Barbara, Calif.:
      Capra, 1977. Hawthorne, pp. 46-47.

2202 SANTANGELO, G. A. "The Absurdity of 'The Minis-
      ter's Black Veil.'" Pacific Coast Philology, 5
      (1970), 61-66.

2203 SASTRY, L. S. R. Krishna. "The Dark Is Light
      Enough: Hawthorne's The Scarlet Letter," in Naik,
      M. K.; S. K. Desai; and Mokashi Punekar; eds.,
      Indian Studies in American Fiction. Dharwar:
      Karnatak University; New Delhi: Macmillan, 1974,
      pp. 1-15.

2204 SATO, Takami. "The Revival of Twice-Told Tales:
      Hawthorne's Historical Tales." Sylvan, 7 (May,
      1962), 58-57. In Japanese; abstract in English.

2205 SATTELMEYER, Robert. "The Aesthetic Background
      of Hawthorne's Fanshawe." Nathaniel Hawthorne
      Journal, 5 (1975), 200-209.

2206 SAVARESE, John Edmund. "Some Theories of Short
      Fiction in America in the Nineteenth-Century: Poe,
      Hawthorne, and James." Ph.D. diss., Princeton,
      1975. DA, 37 (1976), 1555A-1556A.

2207 SCANLON, Lawrence E. "The Heart of The Scarlet
      Letter." Texas Studies in Literature and Language,
      4 (Summer, 1962), 198-213.

2208 _____. "That Very Singular Man, Dr. Heidegger."
      Nineteenth-Century Fiction, 17 (December, 1962),
      253-263.

2209 SCHECHTER, Harold George. "Death and Resurrection
      of the King: Elements of Primitive Mythology and
      Ritual in 'Roger Malvin's Burial.'" English Lan-
      guage Notes, 8 (1971), 201-205.

2210 _____. "The Unpardonable Sin in Washington
      Square." Studies in Short Fiction, 10 (1963), 137-
      141. Refers to novella by Henry James; Hawthorne,
      passim.

2211 _____. "The Mysterious Way: Individuation in
      American Literature." Ph.D. diss., State University
      of New York (Buffalo), 1975. DA, 36 (1976), 6691A.

2212 SCHEER, Steven Csaba. "Fiction as the Theme of
      Fiction: Aspects of Self-Reference in Hawthorne,
      Melville, and Twain." Ph.D. diss., Johns Hopkins,
      1974. DA, 38 (1977), 791A.

2213 SCHEER, Thomas F. "Aylmer's Divine Roles in
      'The Birthmark.'" American Transcendental
      Quarterly, 22 (1974), 108.

2214 SCHEICK, William J. "The Hieroglyphic Rock in
      Hawthorne's 'Roger Malvin's Burial.'" Emerson
      Society Quarterly, 24 (1978), 72-76.

2215 SCHERTING, Jack. "The Upas Tree in Dr. Rap-
      paccini's Garden: New Light on Hawthorne's Tale."
      Studies in American Fiction, 1 (1973), 203-207.

2216 SCHEUERMANN, Mona. "Outside the Human Circle:
Views from Hawthorne and Godwin." Nathaniel
Hawthorne Journal, 5 (1975), 182-191.

2217 SCHILLER, Andrew. "The Moment and the Endless
Voyage: A Study of Hawthorne's 'Wakefield.'"
Diameter, 1 (March, 1951), 7-12.

2218 SCHLABACH, Anne V. "A Critical Study of Some
Problems Derived from Nathaniel Hawthorne's Novels
and Emerson's Representative Men." Ph.D. diss.,
Wisconsin, 1947.

2219 SCHNEIDER, Daniel J. "The Allegory and Symbolism
of Hawthorne's The Marble Faun." Studies in the
Novel, 1 (1969), 38-50.

2220 SCHNEIDER, Herbert Wallace. The Puritan Mind.
New York: Holt, 1930, 1939. Reprinted Ann Arbor:
University of Michigan Press, 1958. Hawthorne,
pp. 256-264.

2221 _____. History of American Philosophy. New
York: Columbia University Press, 1946. "Young
America," pp. 133-144.

2222 _____. "The Democracy of Hawthorne." Emory
University Quarterly, 22 (Summer, 1966), 123-132.

2223 SCHNEIDERMAN, Lee. "Hawthorne and the Refuge
of the Heart." Connecticut Review, 3 (1970), 83-101.

2224 SCHNITTKIND, Henry Thomas. "Nathaniel Hawthorne,
the Conscience of America," in The Story of the
United States. Garden City, N.Y.: Doubleday,
1938, pp. 119-128.

2225 _____, and D. A. Schnittkind (Henry Thomas and
Dana Lee Thomas, pseudonyms). "Nathaniel Haw-
thorne," in Living Biographies of Famous Novelists.
Garden City, N.Y.: Doubleday, 1943, pp. 165-177.

2226 SCHOEN, Carol B. "The Pattern of Meaning: Theme
and Structure in the Fiction of Nathaniel Hawthorne."
Ph.D. diss., Columbia, 1968. DA, 29 (1968), 1879A.

2227 _____. "The House of the Seven Deadly Sins."

Emerson Society Quarterly, 19 (1973), 26-33.

2228 SCHOLES, James B. Nathaniel Hawthorne's The
Scarlet Letter: A Study Guide. Bound Brook, N. J.:
Shelley, 1962.

2229 SCHOLES, Robert. The Fabulators. New York:
Oxford University Press, 1967. Hawthorne, passim.

2230 _____, and Robert Kellog. The Nature of Narrative.
New York: Oxford University Press, 1966. Hawthorne, passim.

2231 SCHORER, Calvin E. "The Juvenile Literature of
Nathaniel Hawthorne." Ph.D. diss., Chicago, 1949.

2232 _____. "Hamlin Garland's First Published Story."
American Literature, 25 (March, 1953), 89-92. Re-
fers to "Ten Years Dead," which shows influence of
Hawthorne.

2233 _____. "Hawthorne and Hypnosis." Nathaniel
Hawthorne Journal, 2 (1972), 239-244.

2234 SCHRIBER, Mary Sue. "Emerson, Hawthorne, and
'The Artist of the Beautiful.'" Studies in Short
Fiction, 8 (1971), 607-616.

2235 SCHUBERT, Leland. Hawthorne the Artist: Fine-
Art Devices in Fiction. Chapel Hill: University of
North Carolina Press, 1944. Reprinted New York:
Russell and Russell, 1963.

2236 _____. "Hawthorne Used the Melodic Rhythm of
Repetition." Christian Science Monitor, 37 (March
15, 1945), 6.

2237 _____. "Hawthorne and George W. Childs and the
Death of W.D. Ticknor." Essex Institute Historical
Collections, 84 (April, 1948), 164-168.

2238 _____. "A Boy's Journal of a Trip into New England in 1838." Essex Institute Historical Collections,
86 (April, 1950), 97-105.

2239 SCHULZ, Dieter. "Imagination and Self-Imprisonment:
The Ending of 'Roger Malvin's Burial.'" Studies

in Short Fiction, 10 (1973), 183-186.

2240 _____. "'Ethan Brand' and the Structure of the American Quest Romance." Genre, 7 (1974), 233-249.

2241 SCHUYLER, Eugene. "The Italy of Hawthorne," in Schuyler, Italian Influences. New York: Scribner, 1901, pp. 308-332. Reprinted in Cameron, ed., Hawthorne Among His Contemporaries (1968), pp. 438-443.

2242 SCHWARTZ, Arthur Marvin. "The Heart in Hawthorne's Moral Vision." Ph.D. diss., Wisconsin, 1960. DA, 22 (1961), 2006.

2243 _____. "The American Romantics: An Analysis." Emerson Society Quarterly, 35 (1964), 39-44.

2244 SCHWARTZ, Joseph M. "Nathaniel Hawthorne and Freedom of the Will." Ph.D. diss., Wisconsin, 1952.

2245 _____. "A Note on Hawthorne's Fatalism." Modern Language Notes, 70 (January, 1955), 33-36.

2246 _____. "God and Man in New England," in Gardiner, H.C., ed., American Classics Reconsidered: A Christian Appraisal. New York: Scribner, 1958, pp. 121-145.

2247 _____. "Myth and Ritual in The Marble Faun." Emerson Society Quarterly, 25 (1961), 26-29.

2248 _____. "Three Aspects of Hawthorne's Puritanism." New England Quarterly, 36 (June, 1963), 192-208.

2249 _____. "'Ethan Brand' and the Natural Goodness of Man: A Phenomenological Inquiry." Emerson Society Quarterly, 39 (1965), 78-81.

2250 _____. "Nathaniel Hawthorne and the Natural Desire for God." Nathaniel Hawthorne Journal, 2 (1972), 159-171.

2251 SCOTT, Arthur L. "The Case of the Fatal Antidote." Arizona Quarterly, 11 (Spring, 1955), 38-43.

2252 SCOTT, Nathan A., Jr., ed. The Tragic Vision and the Christian Faith. New York: Association, 1957. "The Vision of Evil in Hawthorne and Melville," by Randall Stewart, pp. 238-263.

2253 SCOVILLE, Samuel, III. "The Domestic Motif in Hawthorne: A Study of the House, the Family, and the Home in His Works." Ph.D. diss., Duke, 1970. DA, 31 (1970), 2889A-2890A.

2254 _____. "Hawthorne's Houses and Hidden Treasures." Emerson Society Quarterly, 19 (1973), 61-73.

2255 SCRIMGEOUR, Gary J. "The Marble Faun: Hawthorne's Faery Land." American Literature, 36 (November, 1964), 271-287.

2256 SCUDDER, H.E., ed. The Complete Writings of Nathaniel Hawthorne, 22 vols. Boston: Houghton Mifflin, 1900. The Old Manse Autograph Edition; see also Lathrop, George P. (1883).

2257 SCUDDER, Harold H. "Hawthorne's Use of Typee." Notes and Queries, 187 (October 21, 1944), 184-186.

2258 SEALTS, Merton M., Jr. "Approaching Melville Through 'Hawthorne and His Mosses.'" Emerson Society Quarterly, 28 (1962), 12-15.

2259 SECOR, Robert. "Hawthorne's 'The Canterbury Pilgrims.'" Explicator, 22 (September, 1963) item 8.

2260 SEELYE, John Douglas. "Ungraspable Phantom: Reflections of Hawthorne in Pierre and The Confidence Man." Studies in the Novel, 1 (Winter, 1969), 436-443.

2261 SEIB, Kenneth "A Note on Hawthorne's Pearl." Emerson Society Quarterly, 39 (1965), 20-21.

2262 SEITZ, D.C. "Fanshawe at the American Top." Publishers' Weekly, 119 (May 16, 1931), 244.

2263 SELBY, Thomas G. "Hawthorne," a lecture delivered in Liverpool, 1896, printed in The Theology of Modern Fiction. London: C.H. Kelly, 1897, pp. 66-87.

2264 SEWALL, Richard B. "The Scarlet Letter," in Se-
      wall, The Vision of Tragedy. New Haven: Yale
      University Press, 1959, pp. 86-91.

2265 SHAFER, Robert E. "Teaching Sequence in Hawthorne
      and Melville," in Leary, Lewis, ed., The Teacher
      and American Literature. Champaign, Ill.:   National
      Coucil of Teachers of English, 1965, pp. 110-114.

2266 SHARF, Frederick Alan. "'A More Bracing Morning
      Atmosphere': Artistic Life in Salem, 1850-1859."
      Essex Institute Historical Collections, 95 (April,
      1959), 149-164.

2267 _____. "Charles Osgood: The Life and Times of
      a Salem Portrait Painter." Essex Institute Historical
      Collections, 102 (July, 1966), 203-212.   Hawthorne
      portrait of 1840 referred to.

2268 SHARMA, T. R. S. "Diabolic World and Naive Hero
      in 'My Kinsman, Major Molineux.'" Indian Journal
      of American Studies (Hyderabad), 1 (1969), 35-43.

2269 SHAW, Peter. "Fathers, Sons, and the Ambiguities
      of Revolution in 'My Kinsman, Major Molineux.'"
      New England Quarterly, 49 (1976), 559-576.

2270 _____. "Their Kinsman, Thomas Hutchinson;
      Hawthorne, the Boston Patriots, and His Majesty's
      Royal Governor." Early American Literature, 11
      (1976), 183-190.

2271 _____. "Hawthorne's Ritual Typology of the Ameri-
      can Revolution," in Salzman, Jack, ed., Prospects,
      Volume III: An Annual Journal of American Cultural
      Studies. New York: Burt Franklin, 1977, pp. 483-
      498.

2272 SHEA, John A. "The Use of Consequence in Haw-
      thorne's Fiction." Ph. D. diss., Indiana, 1972.
      DA, 33 (1973), 4363A.

2273 SHEAR, Walter. "Characterization in The Scarlet
      Letter." Midwest Quarterly, 12 (1971), 437-454.

2274 SHELL, Lois Rugh. "The Laughter Motif in the Work
      of Hawthorne." Ph. D. diss., South Carolina, 1975.

DA, 36 (1976), 7427A-7428A.

2275 SHELTON, Austin J. "Transfer of Socio-Historical
      Symbols in the Interpretation of American Literature
      by West Africans." Phylon, 26 (1965), 372-379.
      Discusses "The Maypole of Merry Mount."

2276 SHERBO, Arthur. "Albert Brisbane and Hawthorne's
      Holgrave and Hollingsworth." New England Quarterly,
      27 (December, 1954), 531-534. Refers to characters
      in The House of the Seven Gables (Holgrave) and
      The Blithedale Romance (Hollingsworth).

2277 SHERMAN, Stuart Pratt. "Hawthorne: A Puritan
      Critic of Puritanism," in Sherman, Americans.
      New York: Scribner, 1922, pp. 122-152.

2278 SHERMAN, William. "Henry Bright in New England:
      His First Meeting with Hawthorne." New England
      Quarterly, 46 (March, 1973), 124-126.

2279 SHIGEHISA, Tokutaro. "Appendix to the Bibliography
      of Japanese Interpretations of The Scarlet Letter."
      Shuryu (Doshisha University), 24 (1962), 68. In
      Japanese; abstract in English.

2280 SHIMADA, Taro. "A Wilderness of Mirrors: A
      Study of Nathaniel Hawthorne." Hiroshima Journal
      of American Studies, 11 (1970), 24-49.

2281 SHIMURA, Masao. "John Barth, The End of the
      Road, and the Tradition of American Fiction."
      Studies in English Literature, 52, English number
      (1971), 73-87. Hawthorne, passim.

2282 SHORT, Raymond Wright, ed. with Introduction.
      Four Great American Novels. New York: Holt,
      1946. Includes The Scarlet Letter.

2283 SHRIVER, M.M. "Young Goody Brown." Etudes
      Anglaises, 30 (1977), 407-419.

2284 SHROEDER, John W. "'That Inward Sphere': Notes
      on Hawthorne's Heart Imagery and Symbolism."
      PMLA, 65 (March, 1950), 106-119.

2285 _____. "Sources and Symbols for Melville's The

Confidence Man." <u>PMLA,</u> 66 (June, 1951), 363-380.

2286 _____. "Hawthorne's 'Egotism; or, The Bosom
Serpent' and Its Source." <u>American Literature,</u> 31
(May, 1959), 150-162.

2287 _____. "Hawthorne's 'The Man of Adamant': A
Spenserian Source Study." <u>Philological Quarterly,</u>
41 (October, 1962), 744-756. Also in <u>Four Quarters</u>
(La Salle College), 1 (1962), 1-28.

2288 _____. "Miles Coverdale as Actaeon, as Faunus,
and as October: With Some Consequences." <u>Papers</u>
<u>on English Language and Literature,</u> 2 (Spring, 1966),
126-139.

2289 _____. "Miles Coverdale's Calendar: or, a Major
Literary Source for <u>The Blithedale Romance.</u>" <u>Essex</u>
<u>Institute Historical Collections,</u> 103 (1967), 353-364.
Refers to Spenser's "The Shepheard's Calendar."

2290 _____. "Alice Doane's Story: An Essay on Hawthorne and Spenser." <u>Nathaniel Hawthorne Journal,</u>
4 (1974), 129-134.

2291 SHULMAN, Robert. "Hawthorne's Quiet Conflict."
<u>Philological Quarterly,</u> 47 (1968), 216-236.

2292 SHUMAN, Edwin L. "Benjamin Frederick Brown
Was Hawthorne's Yankee Privateer." <u>New York</u>
<u>Times Book Review,</u> March 20, 1927, pp. 1, 27.

2293 SIEGEL, Sally D. "Hawthorne's Seven Veiled Ladies."
<u>The Gypsy Scholar</u> (East Lansing, Michigan), 1
(1973), 48-53.

2294 SIMPSON, Claude. "Historical Introduction," in
Charvat, William, et al., eds., <u>The Marble Faun.</u>
Columbus: Ohio State University Press, 1968.
Volume IV, Centenary Edition of Hawthorne.

2295 _____. "Corrections or Corruptions? Nathaniel
Hawthorne and Two Friendly Improvers." <u>Huntington</u>
<u>Library Quarterly,</u> 36 (1973), 367-386.

2296 _____. "A Manuscript Mystery: Hawthorne's 1839
Scrap Book." <u>Nathaniel Hawthorne Journal,</u> 5 (1975),

28-33.

2297 _____. "The Centenary Edition." Hawthorne Society Newsletter, 1 (1975), 2-3.

2298 _____. "Serendipity--Perhaps!" Nathaniel Hawthorne Journal, 6 (1976), 129-132.

2299 _____, ed. with Notes and Commentary. The
American Notebooks. Columbus: Ohio State Uni-
versity Press, 1972. Volume VIII, Centenary
Edition of Hawthorne.

2300 _____; E. H. Davidson; and L. Neal Smith; eds.
The American Claimant Manuscripts: The Ancestral
Footstep, Etherege, and Grimshawe. Columbus:
Ohio State University Press, 1977. Volume XII,
Centenary Edition of Hawthorne.

2301 _____; E. H. Davidson; and L. Neal Smith; eds.
The Elixir of Life Manuscripts: Septimius Felton,
Septimius Norton, The Dolliver Romance. Colum-
bus: Ohio State University Press, 1977. Volume
XIII, Centenary Edition of Hawthorne.

2302 SIMPSON, Lewis P. The Man of Letters in New
England and the South. Baton Rouge: Louisiana
State University Press, 1973. Hawthorne, passim

2303 _____. "John Adams and Hawthorne: The Fiction
of the Real American Revolution." Studies in the
Literary Imagination, 9 (1976), 1-18.

2304 SIMS, Diane Mac. "Chillingworth's Clue in The Scarlet Letter." Nathaniel Hawthorne Journal, 6 (1976),
292-293.

2305 SINGER, David. "Hawthorne and the 'Wild Irish':
A Note." New England Quarterly, 42 (September,
1969), 425-432.

2306/7 SINGER, Jerome L. Daydreaming: An Introduction
to the Experimental Study of Inner Experience.
Foreword by Sylvan Tompkins. New York: Random
House, 1966. Hawthorne, passim.

2308/9 _____. "Fantasy," in Sills, David L., ed.

International Encyclopedia of the Social Sciences.
New York: Macmillan, 1968. Hawthorne, passim.

SISTER, M. Evelyn Joseph see JOSEPH, Sister M.
Evelyn

SISTER, M. Hilda Bonham see BONHAM, Sister
M. Hilda

2310 SITTER, Deborah Ayer. "The Case Against Miles
Coverdale." Massachusetts Studies in English, 3
(1977), 6-12.

2311 SKEY, Miriam. "The Letter A." Kyushu American
Literature (Fukuoka, Japan), 11 (1968), 1-10.

2312 SLETHANG, Gordon E. "Felix Culpa in Hawthorne's
'Custom House.'" English Review, 23 (1972), 32-41.

2313 SMALL, Michael Franklin. "The Tale the Critic Tells:
D.H. Lawrence on Nathaniel Hawthorne." Paunch,
40 (1975), 40-58.

2314 _____. "Between Sympathy and Judgment: Versions of the Obsessional Style in The Scarlet Letter."
Ph.D. diss., State University of New York (Buffalo),
1976. DA, 37 (1976), 974A.

2315 SMITH, Allan Gardner. "Nineteenth-Century Psy-
chology in the Fiction of Charles Brockden Brown,
Poe, and Nathaniel Hawthorne." Ph.D. diss.,
Indiana, 1974. DA, 35 (1975), 7880A-7881A.

2316 SMITH, Charles R. Jr. "The Structural Principle
of The Marble Faun." Thoth, 3 (Winter, 1962),
32-38.

2317 SMITH, David E. "John Bunyan in America: A
Critical Inquiry." Ph.D. diss., Minnesota, 1962.
DA, 23 (1963), 4690-4691.

2318 _____. "Bunyan and Hawthorne," in Smith, John
Bunyan in America. Bloomington: Indiana University Press, 1966, pp. 45-89.

2319 SMITH, Henry Nash. "The Morals of Power: Busi-
ness Enterprise as a Theme in Mid-Nineteenth

Century American Fiction, " in Gohdes, Clarence, ed.,
Essays on American Literature in Honor of Jay B.
Hubbell. Durham, N.C.: Duke University Press,
1967, pp. 90-107.

2320 _____. "Hawthorne: The Politics of Romance, "
in Smith, Democracy and the Novel. New York:
Oxford University Press, 1978, pp. 16-34.

2321 SMITH, Julian. "Coming of Age in America: Young
Ben Franklin and Robin Molineux. " American Quarterly, 17 (Fall, 1965), 550-558.

2322 _____. "Keats and Hawthorne: A Romantic Bloom
in Rappaccini's Garden. " Emerson Society Quarterly,
42 (1966), 8-12.

2323 _____. "Hawthorne and a Salem Enemy. " Essex
Institute Historical Collections, 102 (1966), 299-302.
Refers to Richard L. Rogers.

2324 _____. "The Blithedale Romance--Hawthorne's New
Testament of Failure. " Personalist, 50 (1968), 540-
548.

2325 _____. "Why Does Zenobia Kill Herself?" English
Language Notes, 6 (1968), 37-39.

2326 _____. "A Hawthorne Source for The House of the
Seven Gables. " American Transcendental Quarterly,
1 (1969), 18-19.

2327 _____. "Hawthorne's 'Legends of the Province
House.'" Nineteenth-Century Fiction, 24 (1969),
31-44.

2328 _____. "Historical Ambiguity in 'My Kinsman,
Major Molineux.'" English Language Notes, 8
(1970), 115-120.

2329 _____. "Hester, Sweet Hester Prynne--The
Scarlet Letter in the Movie Market Place. " Liter-
ature/Film Quarterly, 2 (1974), 100-109.

2330 SMITH, L.N. "Manuscript of Our Old Home. "
Certified Editions of American Authors Newsletter,
1 (1968), 2.

2331 SMITH, Laura. "Charactonyms in the Fiction of
      Nathaniel Hawthorne," in Tarpley, Fred, and Ann
      Moseley, eds., Of Edsels and Marauders. Commerce,
      Tex.: Names Institute Press, 1971, pp. 75-81.
      Available from the editors, English Department,
      East Texas State University, Commerce, Texas.

2332 SMITH, Nolan E. "The Image of Puritanism in
      Nathaniel Hawthorne's Fiction." Ph.D. diss.,
      Yale, c. 1970.

2333 _____. "Another Story Falsely Attributed to Haw-
      thorne: 'The First and Last Dinner.'" Papers of
      the Bibliographical Society of America, 65 (1971),
      172-173.

2334 SMYTH, A. H. "Hawthorne's The Marble Faun."
      Chautauquan, 30 (February, 1900), 522-526.

2335 _____. "Hawthorne's 'Great Stone Face.'"
      Chautauquan, 31 (April, 1900), 75-79.

2336 SNELL, George P. Shapers of American Fiction:
      1798-1947. New York: Dutton, 1947. "Nathaniel
      Hawthorne: Bystander," pp. 117-129.

2337 SNYDER, Cecil K., Jr. "Mandala: A Proposed
      Schema for Literary Criticism." Ph.D. diss.,
      Penn State, 1968. DA, 29 (1969), 3588A.

2338 SOKOLOFF, B. "Ethan Brand's Twin." Modern
      Language Notes, 73 (June, 1958), 413-414.

2339 SOLENSTEN, John M. "Hawthorne's Ribald Classic:
      'Mrs. Bullfrog' and the Folktale." Journal of Popu-
      lar Culture, 7 (1973), 582-588.

2340 SOMMAVILLA, Guido. "Nathaniel Hawthorne: Man-
      zoni Americano." Letture, 15 (1960), 403-416. In
      Italian.

2341 SPARLING, Russell P. "A Study of Nathaniel Haw-
      thorne's Skeptical Meliorism." Ph.D. diss., Duke,
      1972. DA, 33 (1973), 5144A.

2342 SPENCER, Benjamin T. "Criticism: Centrifugal and

Centripetal." Criticism, 8 (1966), 139-154. Refers
to Emily Dickinson and "Ethan Brand."

2343 SPENGEMAN, William C. "Nathaniel Hawthorne," in
      Spengeman, The Adventurous Muse: The Poetics of
      American Fiction, 1789-1900. New Haven: Yale
      University Press, 1977, pp. 151-177.

2344 SPICER, Harold. "Hawthorne's Credo of 'The Beauti-
      ful.'" Yearbook of English Studies, 4 (1974), 190-
      196.

2345 SPIGEL, Helen T. "The Sacred Image and the New
      Truth: A Study in Hawthorne's Women." Ph. D.
      diss., Washington University, 1969. DA, 30 (1970),
      2981A.

2346 SPILLER, Robert E. "The Mind and Art of Nathaniel
      Hawthorne." Outlook, 149 (August 22, 1928), 50-52.

2347 _____. "Critical Re-valuations." Saturday Review
      of Literature, 10 (January 13, 1934), 406.

2348 _____. "Closed Room and Haunted Chamber."
      Saturday Review of Literature, 31 (November 6, 1948),
      14.

2349 _____. The Cycle of American Literature. New
      York: Macmillan, 1955. Reprinted New York: New
      American Library of World Literature, 1957. "The
      Artist in America: Poe, Hawthorne, pp. 61-76.

2350 _____, et al., eds. Literary History of the
      United States, 3 vols. New York: Macmillan,
      1948. "Nathaniel Hawthorne," by Stanley Williams,
      Volume I, pp. 416-440; Hawthorne Bibliography, by
      Thomas Johnson, Volume III, pp. 544-553.

2351 SPITZER, Michael. "Hawthorne's Women: Female
      Influences on the Life and Fiction of Nathaniel
      Hawthorne." Ph.D. diss., New York University,
      1974. DA, 35 (1975), 4561A.

2352 SPRAGUE, Claire. "Dream and Disguise in The
      Blithedale Romance." PMLA, 84 (1969), 596-597.

2353 STAAL, Arie. "The Role of Foreshadowing in the

Fiction of Nathaniel Hawthorne." Ph.D. diss.,
Michigan, 1970. DA, 31 (1970), 2356A.

2354 _____. Hawthorne's Narrative Art. New York:
Revisionist, 1976.

2355 STAFFORD, Arnold John. "Hawthorne and Society."
Kyushu American Literature (Fukuoka, Japan), 6
(1963), 3-7.

2356 STAFFORD, John. The Literary Criticism of "Young
America": A Study in the Relationship of Politics
and Literature, 1837-1850. Berkeley: University of
California Press, 1952. Hawthorne, passim.

2357 STAGGS, Kenneth W. "The Structure of Nathaniel
Hawthorne's 'Hollow of the Three Hills.'" Linguistics in Literature, 2 (1977), 1-18.

2358 STALLMAN, Robert W., and R.E. Watters, eds.
The Creative Reader. New York: Ronald, 1954.
"Source Material for 'Ethan Brand,'" pp.207-212 et
passim.

2359 STANBOROUGH, Beverly Jane. "Hawthorne and the
Question of Romance." Ph.D. diss., Denver, 1971.
DA, 32 (1972), 4635A.

2360 STANFIELD, Elizabeth. "Nathaniel Hawthorne's Use
of Folklore in His Tales." Ph.D. diss., Illinois,
c.1966.

2361 STANTON, R.J. "Secondary Studies in Hawthorne's
'Young Goodman Brown,' 1845-1975." Bulletin of
Bibliography, 83 (1976), 32-44, 52.

2362 STANTON, Robert Bruce. "The Significance of Women
in Nathaniel Hawthorne's American Romances." Ph.D.
diss., Indiana, 1953. DA, 13 (1953), 1188-1189.

2363 _____. "Hawthorne, Bunyan, and the American
Romances." PMLA, 71 (March, 1956), 155-156.

2364 _____. "Dramatic Irony in Hawthorne's Romances."
Modern Language Notes, 71 (June, 1956), 420-426.

2365 _____. "The Trial of Nature: An Analysis of The

Blithedale Romance." PMLA, 76 (December, 1961), 528-538.

2366 _____. "The Scarlet Letter as Dialectic of Temperament and Idea." Studies in the Novel, 2 (1970), 474-486.

2367 STAVROU, C. N. "Hawthorne's Quarrel with Man." Personalist, 42 (July, 1961), 352-360.

2368 _____. "Hawthorne on Don Juan." Georgia Review, 16 (Summer, 1962), 210-221.

2369 STEARNS, Frank Preston. "Hawthorne Centennial: Hawthorne as Art Critic," in Stearns, Cambridge Sketches. Philadelphia: Lippincott, 1905, pp. 365-374.

2370 _____. The Life and Genius of Nathaniel Hawthorne. Philadelphia: Lippincott, 1906.

2371 STEELE, Oliver L. "On the Imposition of the First Edition of Hawthorne's The Scarlet Letter." Library, 17 (September, 1962), 250-255.

2372 STEGNER, Wallace, ed. The American Novel: From James Fenimore Cooper to William Faulkner. New York: Basic Books, 1965. "Nathaniel Hawthorne: The Scarlet Letter," by David Levin, pp. 13-24.

2373 STEIN, Allen F. "Hawthorne's Zenobia and Melville's Urania." American Transcendental Quarterly, 26 (1975), 11-14.

2374 STEIN, William Bysshe. "The Faust Myth and Nathaniel Hawthorne." Ph. D. diss., Florida, 1951.

2375 _____. "A Possible Source of Hawthorne's 'English Romance.'" Modern Language Notes, 67 (January, 1952), 52-55.

2376 _____. Hawthorne's Faust: A Study of the Devil Archetype. Gainesville: University of Florida Press, 1953.

2377 _____. "The Parable of the Anti-Christ in 'The Minister's Black Veil.'" American Literature, 27

(November, 1955), 386-392.

2378 _____. "Teaching Hawthorne's 'My Kinsman, Major
Molineux.'" College English, 20 (November, 1958),
83-86.

2379 _____. "'The Artist of the Beautiful': Narcissus
and the Thimble." American Imago, 18 (Spring, 1961),
35-44.

2380 STEINBRINK, Jeffrey. "Attitudes Toward History:
Uses of the Past in Cooper, Hawthorne, Mark Twain,
and Fitzgerald." Ph.D. diss., North Carolina
(Chapel Hill), 1974. DA, 36 (1975), 288A-289A.

2381 _____. "Hawthorne's Holgravian Temper: The
Case Against the Past." American Transcendental
Quarterly, 31 (1976), 21-23.

2382 STEINKE, Russell. "The Scarlet Letters of Puritanism." University of Kansas City Review, 31 (June,
1965), 289-291.

2383 STEPHEN, Leslie. Studies of a Biographer, 4 vols.
London: Duckworth, 1902. Hawthorne, passim.

2384 _____. "Nathaniel Hawthorne," in Stephen, Hours
in a Library, 2 vols. New York: Putnam, 1904.
Vol. I, pp.204-237.

2385 STEPHENS, Robert O. "The Odyssey of Sarah Kemble
Knight." College Language Association Journal, 7
(March, 1964), 247-255. Relates Knight's Journal
(1825), to Hawthorne.

2386 STEPHENS, Rosemary. "'A' is for 'Art' in The
Scarlet Letter." American Transcendental Quarterly,
1 (1969), 23-27.

2387 STEPHENSON, Edward R. "'The Wives of the Dead.'"
Explicator, 25 (1967), item 63.

2388 STERNE, Richard Clark. "A Mexican Flower in
Rappaccini's Garden: Madame Calderon de la Bar-
ca's Life in Mexico Revisited." Nathaniel Hawthorne
Journal, 4 (1974), 277-279.

2389   _____. "Hawthorne's Politics in The House of the
        Seven Gables." Canadian Review of American Stu-
        dies, 6 (1975), 74-83.

2390   _____. "Hawthorne Transformed: Octavio Paz's
        La hija de Rappaccini." Comparative Literature
        Studies, 13 (1976), 230-239.

2391   STEVENSON, Lionel. "The Hawthorne and Browning
        Acquaintance: An Addendum." Victorian Newsletter,
        21 (Spring, 1962), 16.

2392   STEWART, Randall. "Ethan Brand." Saturday Re-
        view of Literature, 5 (April 27, 1929), 967.

2393   _____. "A Critical Edition of Nathaniel Hawthorne's
        American Notebooks." Ph. D. diss., Yale, 1930.

2394   _____. "The Adaptation of Materials from the
        American Notebooks in Hawthorne's Tales and Novels,"
        in The American Notebooks (1932), pp. xxii-xliii.

2395   _____. "The Development of Character Types in
        Hawthorne's Fiction," in The American Notebooks
        (1932), pp. xliv-lxvii.

2396   _____. "Recurrent Themes in Hawthorne's Fiction,"
        in The American Notebooks (1932), pp. lxviii-lxxxix.

2397   _____. "Hawthorne and Politics: Unpublished Let-
        ters to William B. Pike." New England Quarterly,
        5 (April, 1932), 237-263.

2398   _____. "Hawthorne and The Faerie Queene."
        Philological Quarterly, 12 (April, 1933), 196-206.

2399   _____. "Hawthorne's Contribution to The Salem
        Advertiser." American Literature, 5 (January, 1934),
        327-341. Review of Melville's Typee, etc.

2400   _____. "Hawthorne in England: The Patriotic
        Motive in the Notebooks." New England Quarterly,
        8 (March, 1935), 3-13.

2401   _____. "Hawthorne's Speeches at Civil Banquets."
        American Literature, 7 (January, 1936), 415-423.

2402 _____. "Two Uncollected Reviews by Hawthorne."
New England Quarterly, 9 (September, 1936), 504-
509. Reviews of Whittier's The Supernaturalism of
New England and C. W. Webber's The Hunter Naturalist (1851).

2403 _____. "The Concord Group." Sewanee Review,
44 (October-December, 1936), 434-446.

2404 _____. "Hawthorne and the Civil War." Studies
in Philology, 34 (January, 1937), 91-106.

2405 _____. "Letters to Sophia." Huntington Library
Quarterly, 7 (August, 1944), 387-395.

2406 _____. "'Pestiferous Gail Hamilton': James T.
Fields and the Hawthornes." New England Quarterly,
17 (September, 1944), 418-423.

2407 _____. "The Hawthornes at the Wayside, 1860-
1864." More Books, 19 (September, 1944), 263-
279.

2408 _____. "Hawthorne's Last Illness and Death."
More Books, 19 (October, 1944), 303-313. Continuation of September article.

2409 _____. "Recollections of Hawthorne by His Sister
Elizabeth." American Literature, 16 (January,
1945), 316-331.

2410 _____. "Editing Hawthorne's Notebooks: Selections
from Mrs. Hawthorne's Letters to Mr. and Mrs.
Fields, 1864-1868." More Books, 20 (September,
1945), 299-315.

2411 _____. "Mrs. Hawthorne's Financial Difficulties:
Selections from Her Letters to James T. Fields,
1865-1868." More Books, 21 (February, 1946), 43-
53.

2412 _____. "Mrs. Hawthorne's Quarrel with James T.
Fields." More Books, 21 (September, 1946), 254-
263.

2413 _____. Nathaniel Hawthorne: A Bibliography.
New Haven: Yale University Press, 1948.

2414   _____. "Melville and Hawthorne." South Atlantic
Quarterly, 51 (July, 1952), 436-446.

2415   _____. "The Golden Age of Hawthorne Criticism."
University of Kansas City Review, 22 (August, 1955),
44-46.

2416   _____. "The Outlook for Southern Writing: Diag-
nosis." Virginia Quarterly Review, 31 (Spring, 1955),
252-263.

2417   _____. "Hawthorne and Faulkner." College English,
17 (February, 1956), 258-262.

2418   _____. "The Vision of Evil in Hawthorne and
Melville," in Scott, Nathan A., Jr., ed., The Tragic
Vision (1957), pp. 238-263.

2419   _____. American Literature and Christian Doctrine. Baton Rouge: Louisiana State University
Press, 1958. Hawthorne, pp. 73-89. Similar to
article in Scott, The Tragic Vision (1957).

2420   _____. "Editing The American Notebooks." Essex
Institute Historical Collections, 94 (July, 1958), 277-
281.

2421   _____. "Moral Crisis as Structural Principle in
Fiction: A Few American Examples." Christian
Scholar, 42 (December, 1959), 284-289.

2422   _____. "Editing Hawthorne." Mississippi Quarterly, 15 (Summer, 1962), 98-104.

2423   _____. Regionalism and Beyond: Essays of
Randall Stewart. Edited by George Core. Nash-
ville, Tenn.: Vanderbilt University Press, 1968.
Hawthorne, pp. 3-140.

2424   _____, ed. The American Notebooks of Nathaniel
Hawthorne. New Haven: Yale University Press,
1932. Edited from manuscript sources.

2425   _____, ed. The English Notebooks of Nathaniel
Hawthorne. New York: Modern Language Association; London: Oxford University Press, 1941. Reprinted New York: Russell and Russell, 1962.

Based on manuscript in Pierpont Morgan Library, 300,000 word record.

2426 STIBITZ, E. Earl. "Ironic Unity in Hawthorne's 'The Minister's Black Veil.'" American Literature, 34 (May, 1962), 182-190.

2427 STINEBACK, D. C. "'The Fluctuating Waves of Our Social Life': Nathaniel Hawthorne's The House of the Seven Gables," in Stineback, Shffting World. Lewisburg, Pa.: Bucknell University Press, 1976, pp. 19-36.

2428 STOCK, Ely. "History and the Bible in Hawthorne's 'Roger Malvin's Burial.'" Essex Institute Historical Collections, 100 (October, 1964), 279-296.

2429 _____. "The Biblical Context of 'Ethan Brand.'" American Literature, 37 (May, 1965), 115-134.

2430 _____. "Studies in Hawthorne's Use of the Bible." Ph.D. diss., Brown, 1966. DA, 28 (1968), 645A-646A.

2431 _____. "Some Recent Books on Hawthorne." Nineteenth-Century Fiction, 25 (1971), 482-493. Review article.

2432 _____. "The Search for a Usable Hawthorne." CEA Critic, 34 (1972), 35-36. Review article.

2433 _____. "Witchcraft in 'The Hollow of the Three Hills.'" American Transcendental Quarterly, 14 (1972), 31-33.

2434 STOCK, Irvin. "Hawthorne's Portrait of the Artist: A Defense of The Blithedale Romance." Novel: A Forum on Fiction, 11 (1978), 144-156.

2435 STOCKING, D. M. "An Embroidery on Dimmesdale's Scarlet Letter." College English, 13 (March, 1952), 336-337.

2436 STODDARD, Richard H. "Reminiscences of Hawthorne and Poe." Independent, 54 (November 20, 1902), 2756-2758.

2437 _____. "My Acquaintance with Hawthorne," in
Recollections: Personal and Literary. New York:
Barnes, 1903, pp. 116-133.

2438 STOEHR, Taylor. "Hawthorne and Mesmerism."
Huntington Library Quarterly, 33 (1969), 33-60.

2439 _____. "'Young Goodman Brown' and Hawthorne's
Theory of Mimesis." Nineteenth-Century Fiction,
23 (1969), 393-412.

2440 _____. "Physiognomy and Phrenology in Hawthorne." Huntingtington Library Quarterly, 37
(1974), 355-400.

2441 _____. "Art vs Utopia: The Case of Nathaniel
Hawthorne and Brook Farm." Antioch Review,
36 (1978), 89-102.

2442 _____. Hawthorne's Mad Scientists: Pseudoscience
and Social Science in Nineteenth-Century Life and
Letters. Hamden, Conn.: Shoe String, 1978.

2443 STOKES, E. "Bleak House and The Scarlet Letter."
Journal of Australasian Universities Language and
Literature Association, 32 (1969), 42-47.

2444 STOLLER, Leo. "American Radicals and Literary
Works of the Mid-Nineteenth-Century: An Analogy,"
in Browne, Ray B., et al., eds., New Voices in
American Studies. Lafayette, ind.: Purdue University Press, 1966, pp. 13-20. Papers collected
from Mid-America Conference of Literature, History,
Popular Culture, and Folklore.

2445 STONE, Albert Edward. "The Antique Gentility of
Hester Prynne." Philological Quarterly, 36 (January,
1957), 90-96.

2446 _____. "The Devil Is White," in Krause, ed.,
Essays on Determinism (1964), pp. 55-66.

2447 _____. "Two More Glimpses of Hawthorne."
English Language Notes, 3 (September, 1965), 52-
55.

2448 _____. A Certain Morbidness: A View of American Literature. Preface by Harry T. Moore. Carbondale: Southern Illinois University Press, 1969.
Hawthorne, passim.

2449 _____. "The Two Faces of America." Ohio Review, 13 (1972), 5-11. Refers to "The Maypole of
Merry Mount."

2450 _____. "Hawthorne's Other Drowning." Nathaniel
Hawthorne Journal 2 (1972), 231-237. Refers to The
House of the Seven Gables.

2451 _____. "Other 'Desert Places': Frost and Hawthorne," in Tharpe, Jac, ed., Frost: Centennial
Essays. Jackson: University Press of Mississippi,
1974, pp. 275-287.

2452 _____. "More on Hawthorne and Melville."
Nathaniel Hawthorne Journal, 5 (1975), 59-70.

2453 _____. "Hawthorne's House of Pyncheon: A
Theory of American Drama," in DeMott, Robert J.,
and Sanford E. Marovitz, eds., Artful Thunder:
Versions of the Romantic Tradition in American
Literature in Honor of Howard P. Vincent. Kent,
Ohio: Kent State University Press, 1975, pp. 69-84.

2454 _____. "Chillingworth and His Dark Necessity."
College Literature, 4 (1977), 136-143.

2455 _____. "Of Lambence and Hawthorne: Hell Fire."
Nathaniel Hawthorne Journal, 6 (1976), 196-204.

2456 _____. "The Spirit World of The Blithedale Romance." Colby Library Quarterly, 14 (1978), 172-
176.

2457 STOTT, Jon Copeland. "Hawthorne's 'My Kinsman,
Major Molineux' and the Agrarian Ideal." Michigan
Academician, 4 (1971), 197-203.

2458 _____. "Hawthorne's Gardens: A Study of Sources,
Techniques, and Meaning." Ph.D. diss., Toronto,
1971. DA, 33 (1972), 7670A.

2459 STOUCK, David. "The Surveyor of the Custom-House:

A Narrator for The Scarlet Letter." Centennial
Review, 15 (1971), 309-329.

2460 STOVALL, Floyd. "Contemporaries of Emerson,"
in American Idealism. Norman: University of
Oklahoma Press, 1943, pp. 55-78.

2461 _____, ed. Eight American Authors. New York:
Modern Language Association, 1956. Reprinted New
York: Norton, 1963. "Hawthorne," by Walter Blair,
pp. 100-152. Revised edition, edited by James Wood-
ress, New York: Norton, 1971. "Hawthorne" by
Walter Blair, pp. 85-128.

2462 STRANDBERG, Victor. "The Artist's Black Veil:
Hawthorne." New England Quarterly, 41 (December,
1968), 567-574.

2463 STRAUCH, Carl F. "The Problem of Time and the
Romantic Mode in Hawthorne, Melville, and Emerson."
Emerson Society Quarterly, 35 (1964), 50-60. Also
published in Strauch, et al., eds., A Critical Sym-
posium on American Romanticism. Hartford, Conn.:
Transcendental, 1964, pp. 50-60.

2464 _____, ed. "Symposium on Nathaniel Hawthorne."
Emerson Society Quarterly, 25 (1961), 2-36. Articles by the following: Davidson, pp. 2-3; Doubleday,
pp. 4-6; Garlitz, pp. 6-7; Gerber, pp. 8-11; Gross,
pp. 11-13; Lane, pp. 13-16; Male, pp. 16-18; Pochmann,
pp. 18-20; Rubin, pp. 20-24; Ringe, pp. 24-26; Schwartz,
pp. 26-29; Walsh, pp. 29-35; Cameron, pp. 35-36.

2465 STREETER, Robert E. "Hawthorne's Misfit Politician
and Edward Everett." American Literature, 16
(March, 1944), 26-28.

2466 STROUT, Cushing. The American Images of the Old
World. New York: Harper and Row, 1963. Hawthorne, pp. 100-106.

2467 _____. "Hawthorne's International Novel." Nineteenth-Century Fiction, 24 (1969), 169-181.

2468 _____, ed. Hawthorne in England: Selections from
"Our Old Home" and The English Notebooks. Ithaca,
N.Y.: Cornell University Press, 1965.

2469 STROZIER, Robert M. "Dynamic Patterns: A Psycho-
      Analytic Theory of Plot." Southern Review (Adelaide,
      Australia), 7 (1974), 254-263.

2470 STUBBS, John Caldwell. "The Theory of the Prose
      Romance: A Study in the Background of Hawthorne's
      Literary Theory." Ph.D. diss., Princeton, 1964.
      DA, 25 (1965), 4709.

2471 _____. "Hawthorne's The Scarlet Letter: The
      Theory of the Romance and the Use of New England
      Situation." PMLA, 83 (1968), 1439-1447.

2472 _____. "A Note on the Source of Hawthorne's
      Heraldic Device in The Scarlet Letter." Notes and
      Queries, 15 (1968), 175-176.

2473 _____. "The Ideal in the Literature and Art of the
      American Renaissance." Emerson Society Quarterly,
      55 (1969), 55-63. Hawthorne, passim.

2474 _____. The Pursuit of Form: A Study of Haw-
      thorne and the Romance. Urbana-Champaign: Uni-
      versity of Illinois Press, 1970.

2475 STUDIES IN THE NOVEL, 2 (1970), 395-587. Special
      Hawthorne Issue.

2476 STUDIES IN THE NOVEL, 7 (1975). Special issue,
      "Textual Studies in the Novel." Hawthorne included.

2477 SUDDARTH, L.C. "The Houses that Hawthorne Built:
      The Study of an Image." Ph.D. diss., Wisconsin,
      1976. DA, 37 (1977), 5834A.

2478 SUH, In-Jae. "Hawthorne's Attitude Toward New
      England Religious Doctrine." English Language and
      Literature (Korea), 14 (1963), 78-105.

2479 SULLIVAN, Barbara W. "A Gallery of Grotesques:
      The Alienation Theme in the Works of Hawthorne,
      Twain, Anderson, Faulkner, and Wolfe." Ph.D.
      diss., Georgia, 1968. DA, 30 (1969), 698A-699A.

2480 SULLIVAN, Elizabeth Quay. "1. Lawrence Among
      the Aztecs: Travels, Readings, and Poems. 2.
      Functions of Disguise in Ben Jonson's Comedies. 3.

The Language of the Theater in Hawthorne's <u>Tales</u>
and <u>The Scarlet Letter.</u>" Ph. D. diss., Rutgers,
1975. <u>DA</u>, 36 (1976), 6665A.

2481   SUMMERHAYES, Donald C. "The Relation of Illusion
and Reality to Formal Structure in Selected Works
of Fiction by Nathaniel Hawthorne, Melville, and
James." Ph. D. diss., Yale, c. 1958.

2482   SUMNER, D. Nathan. "The Function of Historical
Sources in Hawthorne, Melville, and Robert Penn
Warren." <u>Research Studies,</u> 40 (1972), 103-114.

2483   SUNDQUIST, Eric John. "Home as Found: Authority
and Genealogy in Cooper, Thoreau, Hawthorne, and
Melville." Ph. D. diss., Johns Hopkins, 1978. <u>DA,</u>
39 (1978), 2279A-2280A.

2484   SUTHERLAND, Judith Cleveland. "At the Edge:
Problematic Fictions of Poe, James, and Hawthorne."
Ph. D. diss., Iowa, 1977. <u>DA,</u> 39 (1978), 289A-
290A.

2485   SUZUKI, Jukichi. "Hawthorne as a Symbolic Romancer." <u>Hiroshima Studies in English Language
and Literature,</u> 9 (June, 1963), 2-10. In Japanese;
abstract in English.

2486   SWANN, Charles. "Hawthorne: History Versus Romance." <u>Journal of American Studies</u> (Manchester,
England), 7 (1973), 153-170.

2487   _____. "A Note on <u>The Blithedale Romance,</u> or
'Call Him Fauntleroy.'" <u>Journal of American
Studies,</u> 10 (1976), 103-104.

2488   _____. "The Practice and Theory of Storytelling:
Nathaniel Hawthorne and Walter Benjamin." <u>Journal
of American Studies,</u> 12 (1978), 185-202.

2489   SWANSON, Donald R. "On Building <u>The House of the
Seven Gables.</u>" <u>Ball State University Forum,</u> 10
(1969), 43-50.

2490   SWEENEY, Gerard M. "Melville's Hawthornian Bell-
Tower: A Fairy Tale Source." <u>American Literature,</u>
45 (1973), 279-285. Reference to the Minotaur story.

2491 SWEENEY, Mark Francis. "An Annotated Edition of
      Nathaniel Hawthorne's Official Dispatches to the State
      Department, 1853-1857." Ph.D. diss., Bowling
      Green, 1974. DA, 36 (1975), 2209A.

2492 _____. "An Annotated Edition of Nathaniel Haw-
      thorne's Official Dispatches to the State Department,
      1853-1857," Part I, in Myerson, ed., Studies: 1977
      (1978), pp. 331-388.

2493 _____. "An Annotated Edition of Nathaniel Haw-
      thorne's Official Dispatches to the State Department,
      1853-1857," Part II, in Myerson, ed., Studies: 1979
      (1979), pp. 355-398.

2494 SYMONS, Arthur. "Hawthorne." The Lamp, 28
      (March, 1904), 102-107.

2595 TAKIGAWA, Motoo. "The Relationship Between God
      and Human Beings in American Literature." Studies
      in English Literature, 53 (1976), 59-73. In Japanese;
      abstract in English.

2596 TAKUWA, Shinji. "Hawthorne, James and Soseki: The
      Sense of Sin." Studies in English Language and Liter-
      ature, 12 (January, 1962), 13-28.

2597 _____. "Theme in The Scarlet Letter." Kyushu
      American Literature (Fukuoka, Japan), 6 (1963), 35-
      40.

2598 TANNER, Bernard R. "Tone as an Approach to The
      Scarlet Letter." English Journal 53 (October, 1964),
      528-530.

2499 TANNER, Tony. "Problems and Roles of the American
      Artist as Portrayed by the American Novelist." Pro-
      ceedings of the British Academy, 57 (1971), 159-179.

2500 TANSELLE, G. Thomas. "A Note on the Structure of
      The Scarlet Letter." Nineteenth-Century Fiction,
      17 (December, 1962), 283-285.

2501 _____. "BAL Addenda: Some Hawthorne Printings,
      1884-1921." Papers of the Bibliographical Society of
      America, 67 (1973), 65-66. Refers to Joseph Blanck,

Bibliography of American Literature (1955).

2502 _____. "The New Editions of Hawthorne and
Crane." Book Collector, 23 (1974), 214-229.

2503 _____. "Problems and Accomplishments in Editing
the Novel." Studies in the Novel, 7 (1975), 323-360.

2504 TAPLEY, H. S. "Hawthorne's 'Pot-8-0 Club' at Bowdoin College." Essex Institute Historical Collections,
67 (July, 1931), 225-232.

2505 TASHJIAN, Nouvart, and Dwight Eckerman. Nathaniel
Hawthorne: An Annotated Bibliography. New York:
William-Frederick, 1948.

2506 TASSI, Nina Carey. "The Force of Irony and Humor
in Nathaniel Hawthorne's Fiction." Ph.D. diss.,
Fordham, 1977. DA, 38 (1977), 2131A.

2507 TATAR, M. M. "Masters and Slaves: The Creative
Process in Hawthorne's Fiction," in Tatar, Spell-
bound. Princeton: Princeton University Press,
1978, pp. 189-229.

2508 TAYLOR, John Golden. "Hawthorne's Transmutations
of Puritanism." Ph.D. diss., Utah, 1958. DA,
19 (1959), 2605.

2509 _____. Hawthorne's Ambivalence Toward Puritanism. Logan: Utah State University Press, 1965.
Monograph Series.

2510 TAYLOR, Walter Fuller. A History of American
Letters. New York: American Book, 1936. Hawthorne, pp. 167-180. Revised and expanded to The
Story of American Letters. Chicago: Regnery,
1956. "Hawthorne Bibliography," by Harry Hartwick,
pp. 515-519.

2511 TEN BROEKE, Patricia Anne Mullins. "The Shadow
of Satan: A Study of the Devil Archetype in Selected
American Novels from Hawthorne to the Present Day."
Ph.D. diss., Texas (Austin), 1971. DA, 32 (1972),
6457A.

2512 TEPA, Barbara J. "Breakfast in 'Young Goodman

Brown.'" American Notes and Queries, 16 (1978),
120-121.

2513 TERRELL, Horace C. "The Nathaniel Hawthorne
Problem: Another View." Ph.D. diss., University
of Washington, 1939.

2514 THARP, Louise H. The Peabody Sisters of Salem.
Boston: Little, Brown, 1950. Hawthorne, passim.

2515 THARPE, Coleman W. "The Disappearing Path: A
Study in Hawthorne's Imaginative Re-Creation of the
Myth of the Quest." Ph.D. diss., Florida State,
1974. DA, 35 (1975), 4565A.

2516 THARPE, Jac L. "Sibyl and Sphinx: Themes of
Identity and Knowledge in Nathaniel Hawthorne."
Ph. D. diss., Harvard, 1965.

2517 _____. Nathaniel Hawthorne: Identity and Knowl-
edge. Carbondale: Southern Illinois University
Press, 1967. Cross Currents Modern Critique
Series.

2518 _____. "Hawthorne and Hindu Literature."
Southern Quarterly, 10 (1972), 107-115.

2519 _____, ed. Frost: Centennial Essays. Jackson:
University Press of Mississippi, 1974. "Other "
'Desert Places': Frost and Hawthorne," by Edward
Stone, pp. 275-287.

2520 THOMAS, Lloyd Spencer. "Scarlet Sundays: Updike
vs Hawthorne." CEA Critic, 39 (1977), 16-17.

2521 _____. "'Rappaccini's Daughter': Hawthorne's
Distillation of His Sources." American Transcendental Quarterly, 38 (1978), 177-191.

2522 THOMAS, Stanley Mack. "Portraits: Portraitists in
Hawthorne and James." Ph.D. diss., Lehigh, 1976.
DA, 37 (1977), 7131A.

2523 THOMAS, Wright, and Stuart Gerry Brown, eds.
Reading Prose: An Introduction to Critical Study.
New York: Oxford University Press, 1952. "Ethan
Brand," pp. 680-681.

2524 THOMPSON, David J. S. "Societal Definitions of
Individualism and the Critique of Egotism as a Major
Theme in American Fiction." Ph.D. diss., Brown,
1972. DA, 33 (1973), 4435A.

2525 THOMPSON, William R. "Aminadab in Hawthorne's
'The Birthmark.'" Modern Language Notes, 70
(June, 1955), 413-415.

2526 _____. "Theme and Method in Hawthorne's 'The
Great Carbuncle.'" South-Central Bulletin, 21
(Winter, 1961), 3-10.

2527 _____. "The Biblical Sources of Hawthorne's
'Roger Malvin's Burial.'" PMLA, 77 (March,
1962), 92-96.

2528 _____. "Patterns of Biblical Allusions in Hawthorne's 'The Gentle Boy.'" South-Central Bulletin,
22 (Winter, 1962), 3-10.

2529 THORNER, Horace E. "Hawthorne, Poe, and Literary Ghost." New England Quarterly, 7 (March,
1934), 146-154. "Howe's Masquerade," based on
legend of Luis Enius.

2530 THORP, Willard. "Did Melville Review The Scarlet
Letter?" American Literature, 14 (November, 1942),
302-305. Refers to review in Literary World, March
30, 1850.

2531 THORPE, Dwayne. "'My Kinsman, Major Molineux':
The Identity of the Kinsman." Topic, 18 (1969), 53-
63.

2532 THORPE, James, and Claude M. Simpson, Jr. The
Task of an Editor: Papers Read at a Clark Library
Seminar, February 3, 1969. Los Angeles: William
Andrews Clark Memorial Library at the University
of California, 1970.

2533 THORSLEV, Peter L., Jr. "Hawthorne's Determinism:
An Analysis." Nineteenth-Century Fiction, 19 (September, 1964), 141-157.

2534 THURSTON, Jarvis, et al., eds. Short Fiction
Criticism: A Checklist. Denver: Alan Swallow,

1960. Hawthorne, pp. 70-81.

2535 TICKNOR, Caroline. Hawthorne and His Publisher.
Boston: Osgood, 1913. Reprinted Port Washington,
N. Y.: Kennikat, 1969. Similar to Ticknor, William
D. ed., Letters of Hawthorne.

2536 _____. "Hawthorne and His Publisher." Dial, 56
(January 1, 1914), 13-16.

2537 _____. "Hawthorne and His Friend," in Ticknor,
Glimpses of Authors. Boston: Houghton Mifflin,
1922, pp. 31-42.

2538 TICKNOR, H. M. "Hawthorne as Seen by His Publisher." Critic, 45 (July, 1904), 23-26.

2539 TICKNOR, William D., ed. Letters of Hawthorne
to William D. Ticknor, 1851-1864, 2 vols. Newark,
N. J.: Cateret Book Club, 1910.

2540 TIMMS, David. "Hawthorne Studies in Britain."
Nathaniel Hawthorne Journal, 5 (1975), 259-263.

2541 TIMPE, E. F. "Hawthorne in Germany." Symposium,
19 (Summer, 1965), 171-179.

2542 TINTNER, Adeline R. "'The Impressions of a Cous-
in': Henry James' Transformation of The Marble
Faun." Nathaniel Hawthorne Journal, 6 (1976), 205-
213.

2543 TIPPETTS, Robert Houston. "A Comparative Study
of Human Relations in Three Moral States in Selected
Writings of Nathaniel Hawthorne, Jean-Jacques Rous-
seau, and George Sand." Ph. D. diss., Hawaii, 1976.
DA, 37 (1976), 2990A.

2544 TODD, Robert E. "The Magna Mater Archetype in
The Scarlet Letter." New England Quarterly, 45
(1972), 421-429.

2545 TOMMASINI, Margaret C. "The Marble Faun: Eden
Revisited and Re-examined." Ph. D. diss., Brown,
1971. DA, 32 (1972), 5809A.

2546 TOWNSEND, H. G. Philosophical Ideas in the United

States. New York: American Book, 1934. Hawthorne, p. 86 et passim.

2547 TRAVIS, Mildred K. "Past vs Present in The House
of the Seven Gables." Emerson Society Quarterly,
58 (1970), 109-111.

2548 _____. "Hawthorne's 'Egotism' and 'The Jolly
Corner.'" Emerson Society Quarterly, 63 (1971),
13-18.

2549 _____. "Hawthorne and Melville's Enceladas."
American Transcendental Quarterly, 14 (1972), 5-6.

2550 _____. "Echoes of Emerson in Plinlimmon."
American Transcendental Quarterly, 14 (1972), 47-
48.

2551 _____. "A Note on 'Wakefield' and 'Old Mr.
Marblehall.'" Notes on Contemporary Literature,
4 (1974), 9-10.

2552 _____. "Of Hawthorne's 'The Artist of the Beauti-
ful' and Spenser's 'Muiopotmos.'" Philological
Quarterly, 54 (1975), 537. Replies to article by
Zivley, 1969.

2553 TREMBLAY, William A. "A Reading of Nathaniel
Hawthorne's 'The Gentle Boy.'" Massachusetts
Studies in English, 2 (1970), 80-87.

2554 TRENSKY, Ann Tropp. "The Bad Boy in Nineteenth-
Century American Fiction." Georgia Review, 27
(Winter, 1973), 503-517.

2555 _____. "The Saintly Child in Nineteenth-Century
American Fiction," in Salzman, Jack, ed., Pros-
pects: An Annual Journal of American Cultural
Studies, Vol. I. New York: Burt Franklin, 1975,
pp. 389-414.

2556 TRENT, William P., and John Erskine. Great
American Writers. New York: Holt, 1912.
"Nathaniel Hawthorne," pp. 57-84.

2557 _____, et al., eds. Cambridge History of American Literature, 4 vols. New York: Macmillan,

1917-1921. Reprinted in one-volume edition, 1944.
"Nathaniel Hawthorne," by John Erskine, Vol. II,
pp. 16-31.

2558 TRILLING, Lionel. The Liberal Imagination. New
York: Macmillan, 1948. Reprinted New York:
Doubleday/Anchor, 1957. "Reality in America,"
pp. 1-119. Hawthorne, passim.

2559 _____. "Our Hawthorne." Partisan Review, 21
(Summer, 1964), 329-351. Reprinted in Pearce,
Roy Harvey, ed., Centenary Essays (1964), pp. 429-
458.

2560 _____. "Hawthorne in Our Time," in Trilling,
Beyond Culture: Essays on Literature and Learning.
New York: Viking, 1965. Pp. 179-208.

2561 _____, ed. The Experience of Literature: A
Reader with Commentary. New York: Holt, Rine-
hart, and Winston, 1967. "My Kinsman, Major
Molineux," pp. 438-440.

2562 TRIPATHY, Biyot K. "Hawthorne, Art and the
Artist: A Study of 'Drowne's Wooden Image' and
'The Artist of the Beautiful.'" Indian Journal of
American Studies, 1 (1971), 63-71.

2563 TROLLOPE, Anthony. "The Genius of Nathaniel
Hawthorne." North American Review, 129 (September, 1879), 203-222. Excerpt later reprinted
in North American Review, 201 (February, 1915),
313-314.

2564 TROUGHTON, Marion. "Americans in Britain."
Contemporary Review, No. 1104 (December, 1957),
338-342.

2565 TRYON, Warren S., and William Charvat, eds.
The Cost Books of Ticknor and Fields and Their
Predecessors, 1832-1858. New York: Bibliographical
Society of America, 1949.

2566 TUERK, Richard. "'An Exceedingly Pleasant Men-
tion': The Scarlet Letter and Holden's Dollar
Magazine." Nathaniel Hawthorne Journal, 4 (1974),
209-230.

2567 TURNER, Arlin. "A Study of Nathaniel Hawthorne's
      Origins." Ph.D. diss., Texas, 1934.

2568 _____. "Autobiographical Elements in Hawthorne's
      The Blithedale Romance." University of Texas
      Studies in English, 15 (1935), 39-62.

2569 _____. "Hawthorne's Literary Borrowings."
      PMLA, 51 (June, 1936), 543-562.

2570 _____. "A Note on Hawthorne's Revisions."
      Modern Language Notes, 51 (November, 1936), 426-
      429.

2571 _____. "Hawthorne as Self-Critic." South Atlantic
      Quarterly, 37 (April, 1938), 132-138.

2572 _____. "Hawthorne at Martha's Vineyard." New
      England Quarterly, 11 (June, 1938), 394-400. Re-
      prints 1836 article.

2573 _____. "Hawthorne's Methods of Using His Source
      Materials," in Caffee, N.M., and T. A. Kirby, eds.,
      Studies for William A. Read. Baton Rouge: Loui-
      siana State University Press, 1940, pp.301-312.

2574 _____. "Hawthorne and Reform." New England
      Quarterly, 15 (December, 1942), 700-714.

2575 _____. Nathaniel Hawthorne: An Introduction and
      an Interpretation. New York: Barnes and Noble,
      1961.

2576 _____. "Nathaniel Hawthorne in American Studies."
      College English, 26 (November, 1964), 133-139.

2577 _____. "Recent Scholarship on Hawthorne and
      Melville," in Leary, Lewis, ed., The Teacher and
      American Literature. Champaign, Ill.: National
      Council of Teachers of English, 1965, pp.95-109.

2578 _____. "Needs in Hawthorne Biography." Nathaniel
      Hawthorne Journal, 2 (1972), 43-45.

2579 _____. "Hawthorne's Final Illness and Death:
      Additional Reports." Emerson Society Quarterly, 19
      (1973), 124-127. Reprint of letters, miscellaneous
      items.

2580 _____. "Consistency in the Mind and Work of
Hawthorne," in Bruccoli, Matthew J., ed., The
Chief Glory of Every People: Essays on Classic
American Writers. Carbondale: Southern Illinois
University Press, 1973, pp. 97-116.

2581 _____. "Elizabeth Peabody Reviews Twice-
Told Tales." Nathaniel Hawthorne Journal, 4 (1974)
75-84.

2582 _____. "Park Benjamin on the Author and Illus-
trator of 'The Gentle Boy.'" Nathaniel Hawthorne
Journal, 4 (1974), 85-91.

2583 _____, ed. Hawthorne as Editor: Selections
from His Writings in "The American Magazine for
Useful and Entertaining Knowledge." Baton Rouge:
Louisiana State University Press, 1972.

2584 _____, ed. with Notes. The Blithedale Romance.
New York: Norton, 1958.

2585 _____, ed. Studies in The Scarlet Letter. Columbus, Ohio: Merrill, 1970. Merrill Studies
Series.

2586 TURNER, Frederick W., III. "Hawthorne and the
Myth of Paradise." Serif, 3 (September, 1966),
9-12.

2587 _____. "Hawthorne's Black Veil." Studies in
Short Fiction, 5 (1968), 186-187.

2588 TUTTIETT, M.G. "Hawthorne the Mystic." Nineteenth-Century Fiction, 87 (January, 1920), 118-
125.

2589 UROFF, M. "The Doctors in 'Rappaccini's Daughter.'"
Nineteenth-Century Fiction, 27 (June, 1972), 61-70.

2590 VAHANIAN, Gabriel. "Nathaniel Hawthorne: The
Obsolescence of God," in Vahanian, Wait Without
Idols. New York: Braziller, 1964, pp. 49-71.

2591 VALENTI, Patricia Dunlavy. "Hawthorne's Use of
Visual Elements." Ph.D. diss., North Carolina

(Chapel Hill), 1977. DA, 39 (1978), 290A.

2592 VANCE, William L. "The Comic in the Works of
Nathaniel Hawthorne." Ph.D. diss., Michigan, 1962.
DA, 23 (1963), 3389.

2593 _____. "The Comic Element in Hawthorne's Sketches."
Studies in Romanticism, 3 (Spring, 1964), 144-160.

2594 _____. "Tragedy and 'The Tragic Power of Laughter': The Scarlet Letter and The House of the Seven
Gables." Nathaniel Hawthorne Journal, 1 (1971),
232-254.

2595 VAN CROMPHOUT, Gustaaf. "Emerson, Hawthorne,
and The Blithedale Romance." Georgia Review,
25 (1971), 471-480.

2596 _____. "Blithedale and the Androgyne Myth:
Another Look at Zenobia." Emerson Society Quarterly, 18 (1972), 141-145. Refers to a botanical term
that designates male and female principle in the same
plant.

2597 VAN DEN BERG, Jan Hendrik. The Phenomenological
Approach to Psychiatry. Springfield, Ill.: Thomas,
1955. Hawthorne, passim; useful for psychological
background study.

2598 VAN DER BEETS, Richard, and Paul Witherington.
"My Kinsman, Brockden Brown: Robin Molineux
and Arthur Mervyn." American Transcendental
Quarterly, 1 (1969), 13-15. Refers to a novel,
Arthur Mervyn, by Brown, 1799-1800.

2599 VANDERBILT, Kermit. "The Unity of Hawthorne's
'Ethan Brand.'" College English, 24 (March, 1963),
453-456.

2600 _____. "From Passion to Impasse: The Structure
of a Dark Romantic Theme in Hawthorne, Howells,
and Barth." Studies in the Novel, 8 (1976), 419-
429.

2601 VAN DER KROLF, J.M. "Zen and the American
Experience." Visva-Bharati Quarterly, 25 (August,
1959), 122-132.

2602 VAN DEUSEN, Marshall. "Narrative Tone in 'The Custom House' and The Scarlet Letter." Nineteenth-Century Fiction, 21 (June, 1966), 61-71.

2603 VAN DOREN, Carl. "Flower of Puritanism: Hawthorne's Scarlet Letter." Nation, 111 (December 8, 1920), 649-650.

2604 _____. What Is American Literature? New York: Morrow; London: Routledge, 1935. Hawthorne, pp. 56-60 et passim.

2605 _____. The American Novel: 1789-1939. New York: Macmillan, 1940. Revised edition of 1921 publication. Hawthorne, pp. 58-83.

2606 _____, ed. Tales by Hawthorne. London: World's Classics, 1928.

2607 VAN DOREN, Mark. Nathaniel Hawthorne. New York: William Sloane, 1949. Reprinted New York: Viking/ Compass, 1957; also reprinted Westport, Conn.: Greenwood, 1975.

2608 _____. "The Scarlet Letter," excerpt from Nathaniel Hawthorne (1949), pp. 143-166, in Kaul, ed., Hawthorne (1966), pp. 129-140.

2609 _____, ed. with Introduction and Notes. The Best of Hawthorne. New York: Ronald, 1951.

2610 VAN LEER, David Mark. "Aylmer's Library: Transcendental Alchemy in Hawthorne's 'The Birthmark.'" Emerson Society Quarterly, 22 (1976), 211-220.

2611 _____. "The Apocalypse of the Mind: Idealism and Annihilation in the American Renaissance." Ph.D. diss., Cornell, 1978. DA, 39 (1978), 2280A-2281A.

2612 VAN PELT, Rachel Elizabeth Stanfield. "Folklore in the Tales of Nathaniel Hawthorne." Ph.D. diss., Illinois, 1961. DA, 23 (1963), 627.

2613 VAN WINKLE, Edmund S. "Aminadab, the Unwitting 'Bad Anima.'" American Notes and Queries, 8 (1970), 131-133.

237   Vernon

2614 VERNON, Magdalen Dorothea. The Psychology of
      Perception. Baltimore: Penguin, 1962. Hawthorne,
      passim.

2615 VICKERY, John B. "The Golden Bough at Merry
      Mount." Nineteenth-Century Fiction, 12 (December,
      1957), 203-214.

2616 VINCENT, Howard P., ed. Melville and Hawthorne
      in the Berkshires. Kent, Ohio: Kent State University
      Press, 1968.

2617 VINCENT, L. H. "Nathaniel Hawthorne, " in Vincent,
      American Literary Masters. Freeport, N. Y.:
      Books for Libraries Press, 1969.

2618 VOGEL, Dan. "Roger Chillingworth: The Satanic
      Paradox in The Scarlet Letter." Criticism, 5
      (Summer, 1963), 272 280.

2619 _____. "Hawthorne's Concept of Tragedy in The
      Scarlet Letter." Nathaniel Hawthorne Journal, 2
      (1972), 183-193.

2620 _____. The Three Masks of American Tragedy.
      Baton Rouge: Louisiana State University Press, 1974.
      Hawthorne and Melville, pp. 151-159 et passim.

2621 VOGEL, Stanley M. German Literary Influence on the
      American Transcendentalists. New Haven: Yale
      University Press, 1955. Hawthorne, passim.

2622 VOIGHT, Gilbert P. "Nathaniel Hawthorne: Author
      for Preachers." Lutheran Church Quarterly, 21
      (January, 1943), 82-86.

2623 _____. "Hawthorne and the Roman Catholic Church."
      New England Quarterly, 19 (September, 1946), 394-
      398.

2624 _____. "The Meaning of 'The Minister's Black
      Veil.'" College English, 13 (March, 1952), 337-
      338.

2625 VOLPE, Edmund L. "The Reception of Daisy Miller."
      Boston Public Library Quarterly, 10 (January, 1958),

55-59. Comments on James's <u>Hawthorne</u>.

2626 VON ABELE, Rudolph. "<u>The Scarlet Letter</u>: A
      Reading." <u>Accent</u>, 11 (August, 1951), 211-227.

2627 _____. "Baby and Butterfly." <u>Kenyon Review</u>,
      15 (Spring, 1953), 280-292. Refers to "The Artist
      of the Beautiful."

2628 _____. <u>The Death of the Artist: A Study of Haw-
      thorne's Disintegration</u>. The Hague: Martinus
      Nijhoff, 1955. International Scholars Forum, Vol.
      II.

2629 VON HIBLER, Leo. "Hawthorne in England." <u>Die
      neueren Sprachen</u>, 4 (1955), 145-153.

2630 VOSS, Arthur. "Romance, Allegory, and Morality:
      Nathaniel Hawthorne and Herman Melville," in Voss,
      <u>The American Short Story</u>. Norman: University of
      Oklahoma Press, 1973, pp. 15-46.

2631 WAGENKNECHT, Edward C. "Soul's Romance: Haw-
      thorne," in <u>Cavalcade of the American Novel</u>. New
      York: Holt, Rinehart, and Winston, 1952, pp. 38-57.

2632 _____. "Mrs. Hawthorne on Dickens." <u>Boston
      Public Library Quarterly</u>, 12 (April, 1960), 120-121.

2633 _____. <u>Nathaniel Hawthorne: Man and Writer</u>.
      New York: Oxford University Press, 1961.

2634 WAGES, Jack Douglas. <u>Hawthorne's Minister</u>.
      Austin: University of Texas Press, 1963.

2635 WAGGONER, Hyatt Howe. "Nathaniel Hawthorne: The
      Cemetery, the Prison, and the Rose." <u>University
      of Kansas City Review</u>, 14 (Spring, 1948), 175-190.

2636 _____. "Hawthorne's 'Canterbury Pilgrims':
      Theme and Structure." <u>New England Quarterly</u>,
      22 (September, 1949), 373-387.

2637 _____. <u>Hawthorne: A Critical Study</u>. Cambridge:
      Harvard University Press, 1955. Reprinted in re-
      vised edition 1963.

2638 _____. "The Scarlet Letter," excerpt from Hawthorne (1955), in Feidelson, Charles, Jr., and Paul
Brodtkorb, Jr., eds., Interpretations of American
Literature. New York: Oxford University Press,
1959, pp. 3-29.

2639 _____. "Hawthorne's Beginning: 'Alice Doane's
Appeal.'" University of Kansas City Review, 16
(Summer, 1960), 254-260.

2640 _____. Nathaniel Hawthorne. Minneapolis: Uni-
versity of Minnesota Press, 1962. University of
Minnesota Pamphlets on American Writers Series,
No. 23. Reprinted in Foster, Richard, ed., Six
American Novelists of the Nineteenth-Century (1968),
pp. 45-81.

2641 _____. "Hawthorne." Review of Current Scholarship in American Literary Scholarship. 1963, 1964,
1966, 1967, pp. 17-28, 16-31, 12-24, 17-28.

2642 _____. "Art and Belief," in Pearce, Roy Harvey
ed., Centenary Essays (1964), pp. 167-195.

2643 _____. "The Marble Faun," excerpt from Hawthorne (1955), in Kaul, ed., Hawthorne (1966), pp.
164-176.

2644 _____. "'Grace' in the Thought of Emerson,
Thoreau, and Hawthorne." Emerson Society Quarterly, 54 (1969), 68-72.

2645 _____. "Hawthorne and Melville Acquaint the
Reader with Their Abodes." Studies in the Novel,
2 (1970), 420-424.

2646 _____. "A Hawthorne Discovery: The Lost Notebook, 1835-1841." New England Quarterly, 49
(1976), 618-626.

2647 _____. "Hawthorne Explained." Sewanee Review,
86 (1978), 130-138. Review article of Nina Baym,
The Shape of Hawthorne's Career (1976); Kenneth
Dauber, Re-discovering Hawthorne (1977); and Edgar
A. Dryden, Nathaniel Hawthorne: The Poetics of
Enchantment (1977).

2648 _____. "The New Hawthorne Notebook: Further
Reflections on the Life and Work." Novel, 11
(1978), 218-226.

2649 _____, ed. The House of the Seven Gables. Boston:
Houghton Mifflin, 1964. Riverside Series.

2650 _____, ed. with Introduction. Selected Tales and
Sketches. New York: Holt, Rinehart, and Winston,
1970. Rinehart Series.

2651 _____, and George Monteiro, eds. with Introduction,
Bibliography, and Annotation. The Scarlet Letter:
A Romance. San Francisco: Chandler, 1968.
Facsimile reprint of first edition.

2652 WAGNER, Linda Welshimer. "Embryonic Characterization in 'The Custom House.'" English Record, 16
(February, 1966), 32-35.

2653 WAGNER, Vern. "Hawthorne's Smile." Texas Quarterly, 16 (1973), 6-31.

2654 WALCUTT, Charles Child. "The Scarlet Letter and Its
Modern Critics." Nineteenth-Century Fiction, 7
(March, 1953), 251-264.

2655 _____. Man's Changing Mask: Modes and Methods
of Characterization in Fiction. Minneapolis: University of Minnesota Press, 1966. "The Idle Inquiry,"
pp. 124-130. Studies "Young Goodman Brown."

2656 WALKER, Warren S., ed. Twentieth-Century Short
Story Explications: Interpretations 1900-1966 of
Short Fiction Since 1800. Hamden, Conn.: Shoe
String, 1967. Hawthorne, pp. 226-258, plus Sup-
plements for 1970 and 1973.

2657 WALLACE, A. "Religious Faith of Great Authors,"
in Wallace, Religious Faith of Great Men. Man-
hasset, N.Y.: Round Table, 1934, pp. 30-55, Hawthorne, passim.

2658 WALLACE, Robert K. "A Probable Source for
Dorothea and Casaubon: Hester and Chillingworth."
English Studies, 58 (1976), 23-25. Refers to novel
by George Eliot, Middlemarch (1872).

241 Wallins

2659 WALLINS, Roger P. "Robin and the Narrator in 'My Kinsman, Major Molineux.'" Studies in Short Fiction, 12 (1975), 173-179.

2660 WALSH, Thomas Francis, Jr. "Nathaniel Hawthorne's Handling of Point of View in His Tales and Sketches." Ph.D. diss., Wisconsin, 1956. DA, 17 (1957), 623.

2661 _____. "The Bedeviling of Young Goodman Brown." Modern Language Quarterly, 19 (December, 1958), 331-336.

2662 _____. "Hawthorne: Mr. Hooper's 'Affable Weakness.'" Modern Language Notes, 74 (May, 1959), 404-406.

2663 _____. "Rappaccini's Literary Gardens." Emerson Society Quarterly, 19 (1960), 9-13.

2664 _____. "Hawthorne's Satire in 'Old Esther Dudley.'" Emerson Society Quarterly, 22 (1961), 31-33.

2665 _____. "Character Complexity in Hawthorne's 'The Birthmark.'" Emerson Society Quarterly, 23 (1961), 12-15.

2666 _____. "'Wakefield' and Hawthorne's Illustrated Ideas: A Study in Form." Emerson Society Quarterly, 25 (1961), 29-35.

2667 _____. "Dimmesdale's Election Sermon." Emerson Society Quarterly, 44 (1966), 64-66.

2668 _____. "The Devils of Hawthorne and Flannery O'Connor." Xavier University Studies, 5 (June, 1966), 117-122. Also in Thought, 41 (1966), 545-560.

2669 WALTER, James Frank. "Hawthorne's Romance Subject: 'Real Life' and the Dream." Ph.D. diss., Dallas, 1974. DA, 36 (1975), 895A.

2670 _____. "The Metaphysical Vision of History in Hawthorne's Fiction." Nathaniel Hawthorne Journal, 6 (1976), 276-285.

2671 _____. "A Farewell to Blithedale: Coverdale's

Aborted Pastoral." South Atlantic Quarterly, 76
(1977), 73-92.

2672 WALTERS, Charles Thomas. "Hawthorne in Relation
to Art: The Marble Faun and the Sculptural Aesthetic." Indian Journal of American Studies, 8
(1978), 36-45.

2673 WAPLES, Dorothy. "Suggestions for Interpreting
The Marble Faun." American Literature, 13 (November, 1941), 224-239.

2674 WARD, Alfred C. Aspects of the Modern Short Story:
English and American. New York: Dial, 1925.
Hawthorne, pp. 22-25.

2675 WARD, J. A. "Self-Revelation in The Scarlet Letter."
Rice University Studies, 61 (1975), 141-150.

2676 WARD, W. S. "Nathaniel Hawthorne and Brook Farm."
Letters, 4 (August, 1931), 6-14.

2677 WARFEL, Harry R. "Metaphysical Ideas in The
Scarlet Letter." College English, 24 (March, 1963),
421-425.

2678 WARNER, Lee H. "With Pierce, and Hawthorne, in
Mexico." Essex Institute Historical Collections,
111 (1975), 213-220. Hawthorne's Life of Franklin
Pierce (1852).

2679 WARREN, Austin. "Hawthorne's Reading." New
England Quarterly, 9 (December, 1935), 480-497.

2680 _____. "Hawthorne, Margaret Fuller, and 'Nemesis.'" PMLA, 54 (June, 1939), 613-615.

2681 _____. "Nathaniel Hawthorne," in Warren, A
Rage for Order. Chicago: University of Chicago
Press, 1948, pp. 84-103.

2682 _____. "The Scarlet Letter: A Literary Exercise
in Moral Theology." Southern Review, 1 (Winter,
1965), 22-45. Reprinted in Warren, Connections.
Ann Arbor: University of Michigan Press, 1970,
pp. 45-69.

2683 _____. "Nathaniel Hawthorne," in Warren, The New England Conscience. Ann Arbor: University of Michigan Press, 1966, pp. 132-142.

2684 _____, ed. with Introduction, Bibliography, and Notes. Nathaniel Hawthorne: Representative Selections. New York: American Book, 1934. American Writers Series.

2685 _____, ed. with Introduction. The Scarlet Letter. New York: Holt, Rinehart, and Winston, 1947. Rinehart Edition.

2686 WARREN, Robert Penn. "Hawthorne, Anderson, and Frost." New Republic, 54 (May 16, 1928), 399-401.

2687 _____. "Hawthorne Was Relevant." Nathaniel Hawthorne Journal, 2 (1972), 85-89. Based on speech when Warren received the National Medal for Literature at the Library of Congress.

2688 _____. "Hawthorne Revisited: Some Remarks on Hellfiredness." Sewanee Review, 81 (1973), 75-111.

2689 WASSERSTROM, William. "The Spirit of Myrrha." American Imago, 13 (Winter, 1956), 455-472.

2690 _____. Heiress of All the Ages: Sex and Sentiment in the Genteel Tradition. Minneapolis: University of Minnesota Press, 1959. Hawthorne, pp. 77-78, et passim.

2691 WATERFALL, Gaillard Fitzsimons. "The Manipulation Theme in the Works of Nathaniel Hawthorne and Henry James." Ph.D. diss., South Carolina, 1972. DA, 34 (1973), 1874A.

2692 WATERMAN, Arthur E. "Dramatic Structure in The House of the Seven Gables." Studies in the Literary Imagination, 2 (1969), 13-19.

2693 WATSON, Charles N., Jr. "The Estrangement of Hawthorne and Melville." New England Quarterly, 46 (1973), 380-402.

2694 WEBB, Jane Carter. "The Implications of Control

for the Human Personality: Hawthorne's Point of View. " <u>Tulane Studies in English,</u> 21 (1974), 57-66.

2695 WEBBER, Everett. <u>Escape to Utopia: The Communal Movement in America.</u> New York: Hastings House, 1959. Hawthorne, passim.

2696 WEBER, C. J. "A Hawthorne Centenary. " <u>Colby Mercury,</u> 7 (May, 1942), 97-102.

2697 WEBER, J. Sherwood, et al. <u>From Homer to Joyce: A Study Guide to Thirty-Six Great Works.</u> New York: Holt, 1959. "Hawthorne: <u>The Scarlet Letter,</u> " pp. 200-209.

2698 WEBNER, Helene L. "Hawthorne, Melville, and Lowell: The Old Glory. " <u>Re: Artes Liberales,</u> 4 (1970), 1-17.

2699 WEDDLE, Mary Francis Ray. "The Garden and the Wilderness: Traditional Moral Landscape in Hawthorne's Fiction. " Ph. D. diss., California (Davis), 1971. <u>DA,</u> 32 (1972), 7014A-7015A.

2700 WEGELIN, Christof. "Europe in Hawthorne's Fiction. " <u>Journal of English Literary History,</u> 14 (September, 1947), 219-245.

2701 _____. "The Rise of the International Novel. " <u>PMLA,</u> 77 (June, 1962), 305-310.

2702 WEIFFENBACH, Rose E. "A Technical Analysis of Nathaniel Hawthorne's Style. " Ph. D. diss., Boston, 1939.

2703 WELDON, Roberta F. "Wakefield's Second Journey. " <u>Studies in Short Fiction,</u> 14 (1977), 69-74.

2704 _____. "From 'The Old Manse' to 'The Custom-House': The Growth of the Artist's Mind. " <u>Texas Studies in Literature and Language,</u> 20 (1978), 36-47.

2705 WELLAND, Dennis. "The Artist and the Fly: Some Notes on Puritanism and Romanticism in Hawthorne. " <u>Yearbook of English Studies,</u> 8 (1978), 54-66. Compares Hawthorne with Edward Taylor and Walpole.

2706 WELLBORN, Grace Pleasant. "The Mystic Seven in
The Scarlet Letter." South Central Bulletin, 21
(Winter, 1961), 23-31.

2707 _____. "Plant Lore and The Scarlet Letter."
Southern Folklore Quarterly, 27 (June, 1963), 160-
167.

2708 _____. "The Symbolic Three in The Scarlet
Letter." South Central Bulletin, 23 (Winter, 1963),
10-17.

2709 _____. "The Golden Thread in The Scarlet Letter."
Southern Folklore Quarterly, 29 (June, 1965), 169-
178.

2710 WENDELL, Barrett. A Literary History of America.
New York: Scribner, 1900.

2711 _____, and Chester Noyes Greenough. A History
of Literature in America. New York: Scribner,
1904.

2712 WERGE, Thomas. "Thomas Shepard and Crèvecoeur:
Two Uses of the Image of the Bosom Serpent Before
Hawthorne." Nathaniel Hawthorne Journal, 4 (1974),
236-239.

2713 WERNER, William L. "The First Edition of Hawthorne's The Scarlet Letter." American Literature,
5 (January, 1934), 359.

2714 WEST, Harry Carter. "The Atmospherical Medium
of Hawthorne's Fiction." Ph.D. diss., Duke, 1970.
DA, 31 (1971), 5433A.

2715 _____. "Hawthorne's Editorial Pose." American
Literature, 44 (1972), 208-221.

2716 _____. "Hawthorne's Magic Circle: 'The Artist
as Magician.'" Criticism, 16 (1974), 311-325.

2717 _____. "The Sources for Hawthorne's 'The Artist
of the Beautiful.'" Nineteenth-Century Fiction, 30
(1975), 105-111.

2718 _____. "The Evolution of Hawthorne's 'The Birthmark.'" Nathaniel Hawthorne Journal, 6 (1976),
240-256.

.2719 WEST, Ray B., Jr., and Robert W. Stallman, eds.
The Art of Modern Fiction. New York: Holt,
Rinehart, and Winston, 1949. "Rappaccini's Daugh-
ter," an analysis, pp. 28-33.

2720 WESTERSDORF, Karl P. "The Genesis of Hawthorne's
'The Birthmark.'" Jahrbuch für Amerikastudien, 8
(1963), 171-186.

2721 _____. "The Element of Witchcraft in The Scarlet
Letter." Folklore (London), 83 (1972), 132-153.

2722 WHEELER, Otis B. "Hawthorne and the Fiction of
Sensibility." Nineteenth-Century Fiction, 19 (September, 1964), 159-170.

2723 _____. "Love Among the Ruins: Hawthorne's
Surrogate Religion." Southern Review, 10 (1974),
535-565.

2724 WHEELOCK, Alan Sterling. "Architecture's Moral
Dimension: The House Image in Hawthorne's Fiction."
Ph.D. diss., State University of New York (Albany),
1972. DA, 34 (1973), 1874A.

2725 _____. "The Burden of the Past." Essex Institute
Historical Collections, 110 (1974), 86-110.

2726 _____. "The House of Pride." Essex Institute
Historical Collections, 112 (1976), 306-332. Hawthorne's mansions, illustrated.

2727 WHELAN, Robert Emmet, Jr. "The Invisible World
of The Scarlet Letter." Ph.D. diss., Michigan,
1960. DA, 21 (1961), 3793-3794.

2728 _____. "Hester Prynne's Little Pearl: Sacred
and Profane Love." American Literature, 39 (1968),
488-505.

2729 _____. "'Roger Malvin's Burial': The Burial of
Reuben Bourne's Cowardice." Research Studies, 37
(1969), 112-121.

247 Whelan

2730 _____. "'Rappaccini's Daughter' and Zenobia's
Legend." Research Studies, 39 (1971), 47-52.

2731 _____. "Hawthorne Interprets 'Young Goodman
Brown.'" Emerson Society Quarterly, 62 (1971),
2-4.

2732 _____. "The Blithedale Romance: The Holy War
in Hawthorne's Mansoul." Texas Studies in Literature and Language, 13 (1971), 91-110.

2733 _____. "The Marble Faun: Rome as Hawthorne's
Mansoul." Research Studies, 40 (1972), 163-175.

2734 WHIBLEY, Charles. "Two Centenaries." Blackwood's
Magazine, 176 (August, 1904), 255-262.

2735 WHICHER, Stephen. "Review of Randall Stewart's
Biography, Nathaniel Hawthorne (1948)." American
Literature, 21 (November, 1949), 354-357.

2736 WHIPPLE, Edwin Perry. Character and Characteristic
Men. Boston: Houghton Mifflin, 1866. Hawthorne,
pp. 218-242.

2737 WHITE, John. "'Romance' in The Blithedale Romance."
American Notes and Queries, 9 (1979), 72-73.

2738 WHITE, Morton Gabriel, and L. White. "Bad Dreams
of the City: Melville, Hawthorne, and Poe," in White
and White, The Intellectual Versus the City. Cambridge: Harvard University Press, 1962, pp. 36-53.

2739 WHITE, Paula Kopacz. "Hawthorne's Use of the Puritan Theory of History." Ph.D. diss., Columbia,
1975. DA, 38 (1978), 4144A.

2740 _____. "Puritan Theories of History in Hawthorne's
Fiction." Canadian Review of American Studies, 9
(1978), 135-153.

2741 WHITE, Peter. "The Monstrous Birth and 'The Gentle Boy': Hawthorne's Use of the Past." Nathaniel
Hawthorne Journal, 6 (1976), 172-188.

2742 WHITE, Robert L. "Washington Allston: Banditti in
Arcadia." American Quarterly, 13 (Fall, 1961), 387-
401.

2743   _____. "'Rappaccini's Daughter': The Cenci and
          the Cenci Legend." Studi Americani, 14 (1968), 63-
          86.

2744   WHITE, William M., Jr. "The Personal Philosophy
          of Nathaniel Hawthorne." Ph.D. diss., Florida,
          1953.

2745   _____. "Hawthorne's Eighteen-Year Cycle: Ethan
          Brand and Reuben Bourne." Studies in Short Fiction,
          6 (1969), 215-218.

2746   WHITFORD, Kathryn. "'On a Field, Sable, the Letter
          "A" Gules.'" Lock Haven Review, 10 (1968), 33-38.

2747   _____. "The Blithedale Romance: Hawthorne's
          Reveries of a Bachelor." Thoth, 15 (1974-1975),
          19-28. Refers to Donald Grant Mitchell's book of
          essays (1850), as a source for Hawthorne's work.

2748   WILLAUER, George Jacob, Jr. "Incongruity in Se-
          lected Works of Nathaniel Hawthorne." Ph.D. diss.,
          Penn State, 1965. DA, 26 (1966), 3931.

2749   WILLETT, Maurita. "'The Letter A, Gules,' and
          the Black Bubble," in Vincent, Howard P., ed.,
          Melville and Hawthorne in the Berkshires (1968),
          pp. 70-78.

2750   WILLIAMS, J. Gary. "History in Hawthorne's 'The
          Maypole of Merry Mount.'" Essex Institute His-
          torical Collections, 108 (1972), 173-189.

2751   WILLIAMS, Joan. "The Reality of the Fair Maidens
          in Nathaniel Hawthorne's Completed Romances."
          Ph.D. diss., Auburn, 1976. DA, 37 (1977), 4359A-
          4360A.

2752   WILLIAMS, Melvin G. "Hawthorne's Ministers of
          Spiritual Torment." Christianity and Literature,
          20 (1971), 18-23.

2753   WILLIAMS, Philip Eugene. "The Biblical View of
          History: Nathaniel Hawthorne, Mark Twain, Faulk-
          ner, and Eliot." Ph.D. diss., Pennsylvania, 1964.
          DA, 25 (1965), 4159A-4160A.

2754 _____. "The Scarlet Letter and Hope for History."
Essays and Studies in English Language and Litera-
ture (Tohoku Gakuin University Review, Sendai,
Japan), 47 (Winter, 1965), 31-64.

2755 WILLIAMS, Stanley. "Nathaniel Hawthorne," in Spiller,
et al., eds., Literary History (1948), Vol. I, pp.
416-440. Revised and updated 1963.

2756 WILLOUGHBY, John C. "'The Old Manse' Revisited:
Some Analogues for Art." New England Quarterly,
46 (1973), 45-61.

2757 WILSON, Edmund, ed. The Shock of Recognition.
Garden City, N.Y.: Doubleday, Doran, 1943.
"Hawthorne and His Mosses," by Melville, pp. 187-
204, with editorial comment.

2758 WILSON, James Grant, and John Fisk, eds. Appleton's Cyclopaedia of American Biography, 7 vols.
New York: Appleton, 1887-1901. Enlarged edition,
issued 1915; supplementary volumes, 1931.

2759 WILSON, Rod. "Further Spenserian Parallels in
Hawthorne." Nathaniel Hawthorne Journal, 2 (1972),
195-201.

2760 WILSON, William D. "The Contemporaneous Critical
Response to Hawthorne's Use of Allegory," Parts I
and II. Ph.D. diss., Columbia, 1966. DA, 27
(1967), 4232A-4233A.

2761 WINKLEMAN, Donald A. "Goodman Brown, Tom
Sawyer, and Oral Tradition." Keystone Folk Quarterly, 10 (Spring, 1965), 43-48.

2762 WINNER, Anthony. "Adjustment, Tragic Humanism,
and Italy." Studi Americani, 7 (1961), 311-361.

2763 WINNER, Viola Hopkins. "The American Pictorial
Vision: Objects and Ideas in Hawthorne, James,
and Hemingway." Studies in American Fiction, 5
(1977), 143-159.

2764 WINSLOW, David J. "Hawthorne's Folklore and the
Folklorist's Hawthorne: A Re-examination." Southern
Folklore Quarterly, 34 (1970), 34-52.

2765 WINSLOW, Joan D.   "New Light on Hawthorne's Miles
      Coverdale." Journal of Narrative Technique, 7
      (1977), 189-199.

2766 WINTERICH, John T.   "Nathaniel Hawthorne and 'The
      Scarlet Letter,'" in Winterich, Books and the Man.
      New York: Greenberg, 1929, pp. 212-229.

2767 _____.   "Good Second Hand Condition." Publishers'
      Weekly, 121 (June 18, 1932), 2423-2424.

2768 WINTERS, Yvor.   "Maule's Curse: Hawthorne and the
      Problem of Allegory." American Review, 9 (Sep-
      tember, 1937), 339-361.   Also in Winters, Maule's
      Curse: Seven Studies in the History of American
      Obscurantism.   Norfolk, Conn.:   New Directions,
      1938, pp. 3-22.   Later in Winters, In Defense of
      Reason.   New York: Swallow, 1947, pp. 157-175.
      Reprinted frequently, as in the following: Howe,
      Irving, ed., Modern Literary Criticism.   Boston:
      Beacon, 1958, pp. 152-167; Beaver, Harold L., ed.,
      American Critical Essays: Twentieth Century.   New
      York and London: Oxford University Press, 1959.
      pp. 143-165; Kaul, ed., Hawthorne (1966), pp. 11-24.

2769 _____.   "Henry James and the Relation of Morals
      to Manners." American Review, 9 (November,
      1937), 482-503.   Relates to Hawthorne's allegory.

2770 WITTEVELD, Peter Jan.   "A Light in the Dark Place:
      The Hawthorne-Robert Penn Warren Relationship."
      Ph.D. diss., Brown, 1976.   DA, 38 (1977), 270A-
      271A.

2771 WOOD, Clifford A.   "Teaching Hawthorne's 'The
      Celestial Railroad.'" English Journal, 54 (October,
      1965), 601-605.

2772 WOODBERRY, George Edward.   "Hawthorne and
      Everett." Nation, 75 (October 9, 1902), 283.

2773 _____.   Nathaniel Hawthorne.   Boston: Houghton
      Mifflin, 1902.   American Men of Letters Series.
      Detroit: Gale, 1967.

2774/5 _____.   "The Literary Age of Boston." Har-
      per's, 106 (February, 1903), 424-430.

2776 _____. Nathaniel Hawthorne: How To Know Him.
Indianapolis: Bobbs-Merrill, 1918.

2777 _____. "Hawthorne," in Literary Memoirs of the
Nineteenth-Century. New York: Harcourt, Brace,
1921. Reprinted Port Washington, N. Y.: Kennikat,
1969.

2778 WOODRESS, James, ed. American Literary Scholarship: An Annual Survey, 1963--to date. Durham,
N. C.: Duke University Press. See "Hawthorne,"
by different authors in each volume.

2779 _____, ed. Ph. D. Dissertations in American
Literature, 1891-1966. Durham, N. C.: Duke University Press, 1968.

2780 _____, ed. Eight American Authors. New York:
Norton, 1971 edition. "Hawthorne," by Walter Blair,
pp. 85-128. See also Stovall, Floyd, ed., Eight
American Authors, original 1956 edition.

2781 WOODSON, Thomas. "Robert Lowell's 'Hawthorne,' "
Yvor Winters, and the American Tradition." American Quarterly, 19 (1967), 575-582.

2782 WOODWARD, Robert H. "Automata in Hawthorne's
'Artist of the Beautiful' and Taylor's 'Meditation 56.' "
Emerson Society Quarterly, 31 (1963), 63-66.

2783 WRIGHT, John W. "Borges and Hawthorne." Tri-
Quarterly, 25 (1972), 334-355.

2784 WRIGHT, Nathalia. "Hawthorne and the Praslin
Murder." New England Quarterly, 15 (March, 1942),
5-14. Refers to a French crime, 1847, and its
relation to The Marble Faun.

2785 _____. "Mosses from an Old Manse and Moby-Dick:
The Shock of Discovery." Modern Language Notes,
67 (June, 1952), 387-392.

2786 _____. "The Influence of Italy on The Marble
Faun." Tennessee Studies in Literature, Special
Number, (1961), 141-149. Published as Davis,
Richard Beale, and John Lievsay, eds., Studies in
Honor of John C. Hodges and Alvin Thaler. Knox-
ville: University of Tennessee Press, 1961.

2787 _____. "The Language of Art: Hawthorne," in Wright, American Novelists in Italy. Philadelphia: University of Pennsylvania Press, 1965, pp. 138-167.

2788 WYCHERLY, H. Alan. "Hawthorne's 'The Minister's Black Veil.'" Explicator, 23 (October, 1964), item 11.

2789 WYSS, Hal H. "Involuntary Evil in the Fiction of Brown, Cooper, Poe, Hawthorne, and Melville." Ph.D. diss., Ohio State, 1971. DA, 32 (1971), 1489A.

2790 YAGI, Toshio. "The Scarlet Letter Through 'The Custom-House.'" Studies in English Literature (Japan), English Number (1974), 237-239.

2791 YAGYU, Nozomu. "Hawthorne's Concept of Original Sin as Seen in 'The Birthmark.'" Eibungaku Tenbo (Japan), 1 (February, 1962), 1-6.

2792 YAHNKE, Robert Eugene. "Conscience and Love in Hawthorne's Fiction." Ph.D. diss., Wisconsin, 1975. DA, 36 (1976), 6075A.

2793 YAMAMOTO, Masashi. "On the Significance of 'Nature' in Hawthorne's Works." Hiroshima Studies in English Language and Literature, 18 (1971), 47-68. In Japanese; English summary.

2794 YAMAYA, Saburo. "Poe, Hawthorne, and Melville's 'Benito Cereno.'" Studies in English Literature (Hosei University), 4 (March, 1961), 21-32.

2795 YATES, Norris. "Ritual and Reality: Mask and Dance Motifs in Hawthorne's Fiction." Philological Quarterly, 34 (October, 1955), 56-70.

2796 _____. "An Instance of Parallel Imagery in Hawthorne, Melville, and Frost." Philological Quarterly, 36 (April, 1957), 276-280.

2797 YODER, Ralph A. "Hawthorne and His Artist." Studies in Romanticism, 7 (1968), 193-206.

2798 _____. "Transcendental Conservatism, and The House of the Seven Gables." Georgia Review, 28 (1974), 33-51.

2799 YOKOZAWA, Shiro. "Hawthorne's Use of Pearl in The Scarlet Letter." Liberal Arts Review (Japan), 5 (March, 1960), 16-26.

2800 YOSHIKAWA, June G. "Hawthorne's Greek Myths," 3 parts. Asphodel (Kyoto), 2 (1969); 3 (1970); and 4 (1970). Reprinted in Annual Report of Studies, Vol. 23, 1972, pp. 58-89.

2801 YOUNG, Philip. "Hawthorne and 100 Years: A Report from the Academy." Kenyon Review, 27 (Spring, 1965), 215-234. Review-essay of Pearce, Roy Harvey, ed., Centenary Essays (1964).

2802 _____. Three Bags Full. New York: Harcourt Brace Jovanovich, 1973. "Centennial, or The Hawthorne Caper," pp. 79-98; and "Hawthorne's Gables Ungarbled," pp. 113-135.

2803 _____, ed. with Introduction. The House of the Seven Gables. New York: Holt, Rinehart, and Winston, 1957.

2804 ZAITCHIK, Joseph Abraham. "Nathaniel Hawthorne as Truth-Teller: An Analysis of Moralistic Techniques in the Tales and Sketches." Ph.D. diss., Boston, 1964. DA, 26 (1965), 2734-2735.

2805 ZANGWILL, O. L. "A Case of Paramnesia in Nathaniel Hawthorne." Character and Personality, 13 (March-June, 1945), 246-260. Refers to an illusion of remembrance.

2806 ZAULI NALDI, Camilla. "La Fortuna di Hawthorne in Italia: Nota bibliografiea." Studi Americani, 6 (1960), 183-201. In Italian.

2807 ZIFF, Larzer. "The Ethical Dimension of 'The Custom-House.'" Modern Language Notes, 73 (May, 1958), 338-344. Reprinted in Kaul, ed., Hawthorne (1966), pp. 123-128.

2808 _____. "The Artist and Puritanism," in Pearce, Roy Harvey, ed., Centenary Essays (1964), pp. 245-269.

2809 _____, ed. with Introduction. The Scarlet Letter. Indianapolis: Bobbs-Merrill, 1963.

2810 ZIMMERMAN, Melvin. "Baudelaire, Poe, and Hawthorne." Revue de Littérature Comparée, 39 (July-September, 1965), 448-450.

2811 ZIPES, Jack David. "Studies of the Romantic Hero in German and American Literature." Ph.D. diss., Columbia, 1965. DA, 27 (1965), 191A.

2812 ZIVKOVIC, Peter D. "The Evil of the Isolated Intellect: Hilda in The Marble Faun." Personalist, 43 (Spring, 1962), 202-213.

2813 ZIVLEY, Sherry. "Hawthorne's 'The Artist of the Beautiful' and Spenser's 'Muiopotmos.'" Philological Quarterly, 48 (1969), 134-137.

2814 ZLOTNICK, Joan. "The Damnation of Theron Ware, with a Backward Glance at Hawthorne." Markham Review, 5 (1971), 90-92.

2815 ZUCKERMAN, Michael. "Pilgrims in the Wilderness: Community, Modernity, and the Maypole at Merry Mount." New England Quarterly, 50 (1977), 255-277.

2816 ZUNDER, T.A. "Walt Whitman and Hawthorne." Modern Language Notes, 47 (May, 1932), 314-316.

SUBJECT INDEX

Aesthetic Papers 1309
Alcott, Amos B. 64
Alcott, Louisa May 443
"Alice Doane's Appeal" 186, 321, 528, 775, 900, 1031,
    1159, 1701, 2290, 2639
Allegory 158, 194, 195, 222, 357, 861, 870, 1049, 1061,
    1173, 1202, 1203, 1294, 1303, 1554, 1871, 1892,
    2081, 2219, 2630, 2760, 2768, 2769
Ambiguity 87, 641, 869, 871, 1080, 1243, 1293, 1328,
    1437, 1546, 1689, 2155
"The Ambitious Guest" 397, 534, 542, 659, 702, 763,
    1048, 1832
American Literature (includes histories, studies that have
    sections on Hawthorne) 104, 159, 232, 247, 252,
    280, 295, 297, 298, 313, 323, 332, 335, 344, 365, 372,
    376, 386, 387, 389, 393, 396, 422, 427, 446, 506,
    519, 550, 551, 561, 581, 624, 634, 677, 711, 768,
    793, 867, 875, 903, 910, 912, 931, 962, 964, 1003,
    1062, 1083, 1084, 1168, 1189, 1196, 1216, 1220,
    1221, 1222, 1307, 1308, 1346, 1361, 1419, 1473,
    1503, 1539, 1543, 1565, 1577, 1618, 1656, 1657,
    1658, 1775, 1776, 1784, 1840, 1843, 1888, 1935,
    1941, 1942, 1944, 1945, 1957, 2027, 2044, 2056,
    2057, 2160, 2335, 2349, 2350, 2419, 2448, 2510,
    2556, 2557, 2558, 2604, 2605, 2631, 2710, 2711
The American Notebooks 521, 2393, 2394, 2420
"The Ancestral Footstep" 395
Anderson, Sherwood 849, 1399, 1495, 1498, 2686
Artist, The (includes Art, Artistic, etc.) 110, 180, 197,
    455, 459, 809, 854, 1053, 1155, 1362, 1412, 1489,
    1640, 1662, 1663, 1765, 1839, 1858, 1893, 1904,
    2142, 2235, 2462, 2499, 2522, 2562, 2628, 2642,
    2704, 2716, 2787, 2795, 2797, 2808
"The Artist of the Beautiful" 164, 180, 239, 314, 629, 680,
    692, 699, 872, 886, 947, 1537, 1556, 1623, 1810,

259

2199, 2234, 2344, 2379, 2552, 2562, 2627, 2717, 2782, 2813
Austin, William   1170

Bacon, Delia   1204, 1393
Barth, John   2281
Bayle, Pierre   204
Benjamin, Park   969
Berkshire   240, 241
Bible   518, 2428, 2429, 2430, 2527, 2528, 2753
Bibliography (studies of primary and secondary sources)
    65, 198, 251, 254, 340, 341, 354, 396, 403, 404,
    405, 407, 453, 484, 490, 497, 501, 591, 618, 619, 701,
    876, 904, 905, 917, 964, 1047, 1095, 1238, 1299,
    1300, 1304, 1319, 1322, 1472, 1475, 1476, 1674,
    1883, 2014, 2015, 2104, 2177, 2279, 2413, 2431,
    2461, 2501, 2505, 2534, 2576, 2577, 2641, 2656,
    2778, 2779, 2780, 2806
Biographical Studies of Hawthorne
    Short essays, sketches, memories, appreciations, etc.
    33, 244, 245, 275, 276, 331, 343, 344, 352, 366, 376,
    377, 450, 569, 570, 582, 583, 586, 587, 607, 623,
    636, 705, 742, 781, 794, 806, 847, 893, 920, 950,
    954, 987, 1046, 1059, 1092, 1117, 1119, 1120, 1122,
    1124, 1129, 1130, 1135, 1136, 1137, 1140, 1169,
    1185, 1228, 1232, 1258, 1259, 1270, 1278, 1317,
    1363, 1410, 1433, 1434, 1535, 1536, 1581, 1602,
    1605, 1606, 1614, 1625, 1703, 1723, 1787, 1814,
    1826, 1860, 1958, 1959, 1960, 1978, 1979, 2164,
    2190, 2194, 2225, 2263, 2383, 1384, 2406, 2407,
    2436, 2437, 2447, 2494, 2559, 2563, 2572, 2578,
    2586, 2587, 2617, 2653, 2681, 2755, 2758, 2777
    Book-length biographical studies   103, 311, 423, 437,
    513, 568, 611, 792, 846, 848, 851, 995, 1023, 1105,
    1109, 1114, 1115, 1146, 1186, 1264, 1447, 1453,
    1565a, 1566, 1682, 1708, 1820, 2196, 2370, 2567,
    2575, 2607, 2628, 2633, 2637, 2640, 2773, 2776
"The Birthmark"   94, 176, 324, 462, 559, 838, 1154, 1206,
    1376, 1865, 2019, 2091, 2213, 2525, 2610, 2613,
    2665, 2718, 2720, 2791
Blake, William   1255
The Blithedale Romance   26, 118, 140, 141, 145, 178, 189,
    197, 229, 414, 415, 421, 487, 526, 594, 595, 598,
    626, 674, 696, 777, 778, 864, 882, 980, 1005, 1020,
    1151, 1178, 1179, 1216, 1223, 1298, 1331, 1334,
    1354, 1359, 1366, 1439, 1487, 1493, 1527, 1571, 1574,

2446, 2455, 2511, 2596, 2668, 2789, 2791, 2812

Family, Hawthorne family (see also individual names) 1132,
    1182, 1241, 2186
"Fancy's Show Box" 723
Fanshawe 186, 264, 370, 436, 481, 978, 1027, 1028, 1276,
    1530, 1561, 1915, 2205, 2262
Faulkner, William 53, 149, 160, 312, 558, 559, 687, 735,
    843, 967, 1333, 1413, 1436, 1901, 2037, 2122, 2146,
    2417, 2753
Faust (see also Goethe) 2374, 2376
"Feathertop" 749, 800, 1193, 1379, 1380
Fields, James T. 123, 1408, 2406, 2412, 2565
Film (includes T. V., Movies, Visual Arts) 72, 131, 360,
    361, 798, 799, 1345, 1987, 2329
Fitzgerald, F. Scott 687
Folklore (includes Legends; see also Mythology) 44, 148,
    150, 255, 342, 531, 681, 688, 721, 859, 1811, 2195,
    2360, 2612, 2764
Fowles, John 1341
Franklin, Benjamin 785, 788
Frederic, Harold 520, 653, 2814
French (includes France) 137, 597, 703, 720, 1367, 1570,
    1744, 1882, 2101, 2120, 2810
Frost, Robert 614, 779, 1560, 2451, 2519, 2686, 2796
Fuller, Margaret 426, 526, 690, 757, 758, 928, 1167,
    1365, 2069, 2680

Gardens 45, 86, 318, 2458, 2699
Garland, Hamlin 2232
Gaskell, Elizabeth 765
General Notes and Commentary (see also Short Biographical
    Sketches) 9, 391, 392, 410, 592, 638, 776, 1007,
    1078, 1240, 1311, 1312, 1430, 1488, 2223, 2224
"The Gentle Boy" 656, 716, 740, 921, 1030, 1917, 2528,
    2553, 2582
German (includes Germany) 1559, 1569, 1886, 2025, 2541,
    2621, 2811
Goethe, Johann Wolfgang von 647, 1425
Goldsmith, Oliver 748
Goodrich, S. G. 969, 1318, 1323
Gothic 186, 227, 395, 466, 474, 630, 631, 632, 729, 907,
    1074, 1236, 1333, 1335, 1442, 1583, 1597, 1701, 1759,
    1880, 2070
"Graves and Goblins" 234

Laughter (see also Humor)   70, 207, 1358
Lawrence, D.H.   96, 97, 98, 1458-1466, 1683, 1700, 1790,
     2313
Lecture   413
"Legends of the Province House" (includes "Howe's Masquer-
     ade," "Edward Randolph's Portrait," "Lady Eleanore's
     Mantle," and "Old Esther Dudley")   51, 67, 69, 84,
     473, 516, 760, 899, 1032, 1546, 2076, 2085, 2327,
     2529, 2664
Le Sage, Alain René   28
Letters (includes single publications and collected letters)
     11, 12, 13, 14, 18, 58, 353, 486, 493, 495, 496,
     498, 502, 504, 505, 755, 845, 1109, 1116, 1228,
     1321, 1393, 1408, 1795, 1797, 1799, 1859, 1909,
     1985, 2193, 2405, 2410, 2411, 2539
"The Lily's Quest"   1524
The Literary Artist, Hawthorne as   8, 10, 21, 34, 49, 52,
     66, 70, 109, 139, 175, 180, 190, 206, 226, 256, 258,
     355, 364, 431, 449, 454, 507, 508, 522, 527, 556,
     574, 654, 655, 661, 662, 714, 733, 738, 746, 771,
     820, 874, 877, 879, 894, 895, 902, 922, 966, 984,
     985, 1051, 1057, 1060, 1091, 1112, 1261, 1347, 1394,
     1407, 1454, 1457, 1704, 1707, 1806, 1910, 2041, 2140,
     2176, 2236, 2346, 2507, 2569, 2570, 2571, 2573, 2580,
     2591, 2691, 2700, 2701, 2702, 2704, 2722, 2723, 2748
Longfellow, Henry W.   502, 649, 1024, 1095, 1131, 1181,
     1578, 1579, 1953
Lowell, James Russell   1411, 1573
Lowell, Robert   1588, 1610, 2698, 2781

Magazines and Journals (includes special Hawthorne issues
     and publications devoted to Hawthorne)   783, 795, 796,
     797, 821, 1761, 1869, 1885, 2464, 2475, 2476
"The Man of Adamant"   939, 953, 1301, 1928, 2287
Manuscripts   991, 1044, 1310, 1320, 1431, 1446, 1449,
     2109, 2296, 2330
The Marble Faun   28, 100, 147, 155, 156, 183, 200, 216,
     217, 219, 220, 227, 229, 237, 249, 260, 263, 301,
     319, 332, 338, 339, 476, 639, 643, 652, 737, 741,
     774, 858, 873, 885, 933, 935, 976, 981, 999, 1027,
     1050, 1068, 1217, 1247, 1313, 1337, 1386, 1389,
     1422, 1511, 1529, 1544, 1586, 1615, 1665, 1691,
     1702, 1755, 1765, 1780, 1830, 1833, 1930, 1947,
     1999, 2004, 2009, 2011, 2172, 2195, 2219, 2247,
     2255, 2294, 2316, 2334, 2467, 2542, 2545, 2643,
     2672, 2673, 2733, 2784, 2786, 2812

Saintine, Joseph Xavier   447
Salem   327, 385, 390, 913, 989, 990, 1107, 1244, 1509,
    1630, 1872, 1873, 1912, 2064, 2162, 2266, 2267,
    2323
Scandinavia   214
The Scarlet Letter
    Centenary of publication   7
    Character studies   43, 1352, 1355, 1432, 2273
    Chillingworth   29, 127, 1256, 1486, 1660, 2304, 2454,
        2618, 2658
    "Custom House Sketch"   185, 358, 402, 700, 756,
        844, 913, 945, 1234, 1281, 1428, 1478, 1611, 1653,
        1789, 1827, 2059, 2203, 2312, 2459, 2602, 2652,
        2704, 2790, 2807
    Dimmesdale   33, 91, 418, 665, 709, 1001, 1272,
        1494, 1706, 1710, 1890, 1905, 2435, 2634, 2667
    General commentary on The Scarlet Letter (includes
        studies of themes, symbolism, philosophy, structure,
        background, possible sources, influences, etc.)   25,
        39, 99, 101, 119, 120, 136, 152, 163, 174, 179,
        202, 209, 212, 213, 225, 246, 280, 305, 325, 382,
        389, 417, 419, 420, 440, 447, 458, 479, 482, 523,
        554a, 584, 585, 590, 601, 664, 700, 762, 787, 801,
        830, 842, 957, 958, 966, 971, 972, 998, 1009, 1014,
        1038, 1042, 1060, 1073, 1075, 1080, 1089, 1093,
        1101, 1110, 1123, 1148, 1183, 1191, 1257, 1260,
        1262, 1268, 1275, 1311, 1352, 1370, 1429, 1480,
        1481, 1500, 1503, 1528, 1580, 1609, 1644, 1680,
        1681, 1788, 1847, 1878, 1908, 1923, 1929, 1989,
        2022, 2068, 2086, 2087, 2088, 2092, 2128, 2174,
        2185, 2189, 2197, 2198, 2207, 2264, 2314, 2366,
        2372, 2386, 2443, 2471, 2472, 2480, 2497, 2498,
        2500, 2594, 2603, 2608, 2619, 2635, 2675, 2677,
        2682, 2706, 2707, 2708, 2709, 2727
    Hester   24, 121, 269, 272, 345, 441, 724, 747, 1198,
        1213, 1231, 1280, 1341, 1593, 1607, 1766, 1920,
        2311, 2445, 2544, 2658, 2746, 2749
    Pearl   22, 83, 770, 948, 1647, 1747, 2261, 2728,
        2799
Science (includes Science Fiction)   908, 910, 1209, 1390,
    1420, 1828, 2440, 2442
Scott, Sir Walter   968, 1002, 1414, 1415, 1915
Self   753, 1245, 1491, 1557
Septimius Felton   31, 395
Setting-Atmosphere, Use of   153, 155, 250, 431, 435, 1415,
    2084, 2178, 2716
"The Seven Vagabonds"   1273

Travelogues 1953
Twain, Mark 1194, 1336, 1420, 2753
Twice-Told Tales 342, 608, 609, 612, 853, 1578, 1642,
  2028, 2029, 2204, 2480

Updike, John 2520
Utopian (includes Brook Farm) 189, 270, 326, 478, 635,
  637, 778, 868, 994, 996, 1134, 2048, 2441, 2676,
  2695

Vanzetti, Bartolomeo (of Sacco-Vanzetti fame) 1048
Very, Jones 92
"The Village Uncle" 112, 1054, 1520
"Vision of the Fountain" 1033

"Wakefield" 259, 946, 951, 1648, 1823, 2003, 2217, 2251,
  2666, 2703
Warren, Robert Penn 1484, 2482, 2770
"The Wedding Knell" 805, 1201
Welty, Eudora 16, 1399
Wharton, Edith 850, 1560
"The White Old Maid" 149
Whitman, Walt 524, 621, 753, 1420, 1590, 2816
Whittier, John Greenleaf 1024
Wilderness 368
"Wives of the Dead" 433, 2387
Women (includes Feminine, Wives, Marriage, Love, etc.)
  182, 242, 439, 517, 557, 605, 626, 724, 757, 758,
  790, 865, 916, 925, 926, 932, 1076, 1085, 1152,
  1212, 1341, 1549, 1599, 1730, 1779, 1805, 2004,
  2064, 2146, 2293, 2345, 2351, 2690, 2751
The Wonder-Book for Boys and Girls 184, 557

"Young Goodman Brown" 20, 279, 336, 416, 425, 445,
  472, 509, 512, 525, 541, 543, 555, 563, 564, 565,
  572, 675, 682, 707, 786, 787, 789, 835, 869, 941,
  992, 1086, 1243, 1246, 1284, 1385, 1425, 1502, 1533,
  1555, 1620, 1641, 1661, 1731, 1774, 1825, 1835,
  1952, 2098, 2115, 2181, 2266, 2283, 2361, 2439,
  2512, 2655, 2661, 2731, 2761

Zola, Emil 1882